"The most significant conflicts we face today trigger neurological fight or flight reflexes that lead to escalation and impasse. To understand and successfully resolve these issues, we need to understand how the brain perceives, models, and responds to conflict. Over several decades, cutting-edge scientific research has brought hope that neurophysiology can help mediators reduce the chemical and biological sources of aggression. If you would like to know more about how to do so in conflicts on all scales, Jeremy Pollack has written an excellent review for nonscientists, showing how the brain works and how mediators can turn this information into practical techniques that expand our skills and make us more successful in resolving our disputes. It is packed with life- and game-changing information we can all learn from."

—Kenneth Cloke,
Author of *The Dance of Opposites*
and *The Magic in Mediation*

"In *Wired for Peace*, Jeremy has offered up a true gift that explains the complex and evolving understanding of neuroscience and practical guideposts for how we can mobilize this cutting-edge research to more constructively respond to both divisive and escalating conflict. I can think of nothing more useful in the current state of toxic polarization that seems to grip many of our social, identity, and political divides. A must-read for us all!"

—John Paul Lederach,
Professor Emeritus, University of
Notre Dame; Author of *The Moral Imagination:
The Art and Soul of Building Peace*

"This is an excellent read for those seeking tools to improve their ability to navigate conflict in their lives. It is full of practical tools to help readers understand their own and others' conflict behaviors. Dr. Pollack offers a theoretically rich approach to working with conflict that will deepen understanding for scholars, leaders, and practitioners in local to global contexts. This book is well researched, easy to read, and at the cutting edge of interdisciplinary conflict resolution."

—Katy Collin,
Director of Graduate Studies in
Conflict Resolution, Georgetown University

"In *Wired for Peace*, Jeremy connects neuroscience with real-life conflict in a way that feels accessible and immediately practical. He challenges us to look inward first—to understand our own nervous systems—before trying to change anyone else. The result is a deeply human, science-informed guide to resolving conflict and building lasting collaboration."

—Parag Shah,
CEO of Miles Mediation and Arbitration

WIRED *for* PEACE

WIRED

for

PEACE

USING **7** NEUROSCIENCE-BASED PRINCIPLES TO RESOLVE CONFLICTS

JEREMY POLLACK, PH.D.

WILEY

To Mabel. May you always find a path to peace.

Contents

Preface

It was June 2022, just a month after my 43rd birthday. I was in the process of purchasing my first home, which—as many homebuyers will tell you—can be one of the more stressful life experiences. I was navigating increasingly tedious demands from the bank to settle the mortgage within the dwindling timeline of the purchase contract, having to come up with more and more up-front money to make the purchase happen, having to negotiate the purchase timeline with the seller's attorney, worrying whether this would go through and if my wife and I would be able to live in the place we really loved, not sure what we would do if this didn't work, all while working 12-hour days running a growing conflict resolution consulting business and managing a team of peacebuilders, trainers, and consultants. All of it was piling up emotionally and psychologically.

I went to bed on June 23, feeling the most stress I had felt in a long time, perhaps ever. I remember thinking to myself that night: *If I don't relax, I'm going to have a nervous breakdown.* The pressure felt suffocating. I went to bed feeling hot and shaky but somehow managed to fall asleep. Not two hours later, in the middle of the night, I woke up with the room spinning.

I never experienced vertigo before. I didn't know anything about it, so my brain and nervous system went into a tailspin. I tried to sit up, the walls and ceiling spinning in all directions, my eyes unable to focus, and I had a massive panic attack. The panic would last for about 24 hours. It was hell. Even writing about it now twists my stomach and makes my heart beat faster. I would not wish this experience on anyone.

Fortunately, I was able to see a physical therapist the next day, who educated me on what I was experiencing. I learned that benign paroxysmal position dizziness or BPPD was an acute symptom of tiny crystals in the ear canal becoming dislodged, that it was the most common cause of vertigo, that it was ultimately not dangerous, and that it would resolve with a few minor head adjustments that he could perform. I felt optimistic but skeptical. He performed the techniques. The dizziness did not go away.

Over the next few days, the dizziness did get less intense, but what persisted was a feeling of swaying, as though I was on a ship, feeling lightheaded, like I couldn't quite focus, a feeling of being out of my body, and constant nausea. I was also having daily anxiety attacks. My nervous system had never experienced such an intense and long panic, and so it was in hyperdrive. Weeks later, I was still somewhat dizzy, nauseous, and generally just feeling off. I was pretty sure the ear crystals were back in their right place, so what was going on? I went to various doctors and specialists, who performed multiple tests and exams, and no one could point to anything structurally wrong with my ear or brain. I was increasingly frustrated and worried. What if I had a brain tumor? What if I had to live with this for the rest of my life? What if it didn't go away? With each of these thoughts, my anxiety levels rose.

Of course, I was diving into Google the entire time, trying to discover anything I could about persistent dizziness. Through online forums, I discovered so many other people dealing with chronic dizziness and symptoms related to it—very similar to my experience. In my Googling, I eventually came across the YouTube channel of Dr. Yonit Arthur, aka. "The Steady Coach"—an audiologist specializing in something she called *neural circuit dizziness*. I hadn't come across this term on any of the medical websites, but she was speaking directly to me and my symptoms: unexplainable, chronic dizziness and related symptoms, starting with a stressful, triggering event, feeling anxious all the time, and so on. I watched virtually every video on her channel and read everything I could find on the subject.

Her content led me down a rigorous path of study in the world of chronic pain management, which is centered on how the nervous system produces all varieties of chronic symptoms in the human experience. I found a group of psychologists and psychiatrists doing medical research in this area and took their certification course in a modality called *pain reprocessing therapy.* I began reading and researching everything I could about neural circuit loops—how the brain responds to signals of danger by, unfortunately, amplifying those very signals, which, as a consequence, become our symptoms. And how fear, anxiety, and chronic symptoms, such as pain and dizziness, are all produced solely by the nervous system. It was fascinating. Not only did the learning excite me intellectually but it also began to help relieve my symptoms. And this relief was by design. I came to learn that psychoeducation—specifically about how the brain, mind, and body work together—was actually a key component of symptom relief.

The more I understood about the nervous system and about regulating it with regard to particular anxiety-producing stimuli, the more I felt grateful for the entire experience that led me along this journey. Yes, it was painful and difficult and frightening. But it propelled my interest in neuroscience—a subject I had always been intrigued by but was never quite motivated enough to dive deeply into. At the time of this writing, it has been almost three years since the catalyzing episode of vertigo, and I'm still on a journey of exploring neuropsychology while navigating the remnants of my own heightened nervous system.

One day along this journey, while mediating a dispute between two coworkers who had an ongoing, perhaps years-long combative relationship, something dawned on me. The mediation was not going well, and I realized: these two individuals will never be able to get along, no matter what I helped them agree to, because they were simply too defensive with one another. Their perceptions of one another's hostility were too intense, and they were constantly emotionally triggered by even the mere presence of the other. My revelation was that this was not just an interpersonal issue. This was a nervous system issue.

They had each become a stimulus for the other's nervous system reaction. Just as I was hypervigilant about sensations of dizziness and my nervous system erupted in stress and anxiety any time I noticed such a sensation, they were hypervigilant of each other (or at least of their own perceptions of the other), and their nervous systems were producing anxiety at the mere presence of one another. It was clear: they were in a neural circuit conflict—a conflict loop that perpetuated itself internally for each person. Any attempt to interpersonally solve this would fail if we did not simultaneously address the internal state of each individual's nervous system when interacting.

I knew then this was the key to my evolution as a conflict resolution practitioner and peace educator. I knew that this was part of the opportunity from my experience with chronic dizziness, which led me to learn about neural circuit dizziness and chronic symptom management. I had to bring this knowledge to the world of peacebuilding and integrate it in a useful way for people looking to transform their conflicts and build peace. I could also immediately see that this concept was relevant not only for small interpersonal disputes but also for more significant group-level conflicts, especially violent conflicts where peacebuilding has historically been applied.

Traditionally, conflict resolution and peacebuilding have been approached via two core dimensions. The first dimension is at the acute conflict level—dealing directly with the interpersonal or intergroup conflict. Methods of resolution within this dimension may include facilitated dialogue or mediation, communication skills training, conflict management skill building, individual or group coaching, and other modalities of helping involved parties directly address, manage, and transform the conflict(s) they're navigating.

The second dimension is at the structural or systemic level. The notion is that in many cases of conflict, we must not only address the acute conflict itself but also the wider system in which the conflict exists, as the system or structure surrounding a conflict may be set up in such a way to encourage, willingly or not, the present and future conflicts to emerge. So, we might resolve the current conflict or at least get parties to learn how to manage it; however, if we don't change something in the larger system within which the parties exist, it's unlikely for peace to be sustainable. Whether we are looking at the system of a family, an organization, a community, or a larger society, methods within this dimension may include reexamining cultural norms, processes, policies, leadership capabilities, alignment of expectations and values, and a variety of other structural elements that may require modification to set up the system's inhabitants for sustainable peace rather than ongoing conflict.

These two dimensions of peacebuilding continue to be important and must continually be examined during peace processes. However, the third dimension I am addressing in this book has been vastly overlooked by the conflict resolution discipline and is only beginning to be seriously explored.

This is the dimension of the individual internal system: the nervous system of each person involved in the conflict.

Even if we impart to people better conflict management skills and communication techniques, help them clarify and better understand each other, and address broader systemic issues that may be influencing the conflict, nothing will ultimately shift if people are still escalated and defensive around each other. Yes, working through the first two dimensions *should* lead to a more relaxed internal state for each person involved. With less friction and more supportive structures, people's nervous systems should theoretically calm down over time. However, once a trauma or fear circuit has been associated with a particular stimulus—be it a sensation of dizziness, another human being, or even an idea or memory—the circuit can be reactivated at any exposure to the stimulus, and that stress can return.

We might get conflicted parties to feel more hopeful, communicate more productively, and even collaborate toward workable solutions, but if we have not addressed the conflict at the internal neural level, we are setting them up for failure. The first bit of trouble that comes about—and there will inevitably be trouble—will reactivate the old neural circuit and set their nervous systems right back to where they were. When this happens, people quickly fall back into old patterns. With new communication tools and a more supportive system surrounding the issue, they might be able to bounce back from the recurring conflict more efficiently. Or they might not. Without an understanding of their neural conditioning and a grasp of nervous system regulation tools, the task of maintaining peace is, in my estimation, unlikely.

This book, therefore, aims to fill the gap in the field of conflict resolution by diving deeply into the internal dimension. We will use seven principles of neuroscience and social neuropsychology in the application of conflict resolution and peacebuilding and will connect several more traditional practices to the underlying neurobiological mechanisms at play. Psychoeducation on how neuroplasticity and conditioning lead to fear-response loops around targeted stimuli and how these concepts are relevant to interpersonal conflict is key to resolving current conflict and setting ourselves and others up for sustainable future peace. Ultimately, we will use a basic understanding of neural systems to devise principles and practical tools to both enhance and add to best practices in day-to-day conflict resolution.

This book is for anyone who is experiencing conflict in their lives, whether it's with another person, a group of people, with oneself, or with a concept. It is also for leaders of families, organizations, and communities as well as conflict resolution practitioners and conflict coaches to add tools to your conflict transformation toolboxes. Each chapter has a "Tools" section, which is designed for anyone experiencing conflict and can be used by leaders, trainers, mediators, and coaches helping to manage conflict as well.

I hope that the tools you learn in this book help you solve conflicts and maintain peace more effectively and, more broadly, help you live a more relaxed, engaged, and peaceful life. Your nervous system is responsible for everything you experience. Learning to regulate and use it effectively will not only help you resolve conflict but also help you understand all aspects of your human experience.

Now, for a caveat. First, regarding science in general: anything based on scientific research is by its nature not necessarily or absolutely true. All scientific findings are based on statistical probabilities. Just because a hypothesis is found to be supported by data presented in a peer-reviewed journal does not mean the hypothesis is true, at least not in all contexts at all times. Rather, when reading scientific material or material that claims to be supported by science, as this book purports, remember that the conclusions drawn are simply what is inferred by the researchers to be most statistically likely compared with other explanations. With that in mind, it doesn't mean that what has been found in research happens all the time or is the only thing that happens. There are exceptions to every finding, and findings are often updated as new experimental techniques, instruments, and perspectives develop. So, when reading any literature based on scientific findings, including this material, keep your skeptical, critical thinking hat on. A critical, thoughtful perspective is fundamental to the spirit of scientific inquiry.

With regard to the nervous system and the brain specifically, our amazing internal systems are still mostly an enigma. Whatever we think we know at this point, it will almost undoubtedly be updated, modified, or completely altered based on future research methods, instruments, and accumulated knowledge, including insights from artificial intelligence. In fact, it serves to reason that there is a lot more we *don't* know about how the nervous system works than what we *do* know (or think we know). With that in mind, if you're interested in the scientific literature used to support the ideas in this book, visit jeremypollack.com/books/wired-for-peace, where you'll find a list of references for each claim or idea organized by chapter.

So, with your critical thinking hat fastened, and recognizing that the brain and nervous system are indeed some of life's greatest mysteries, let's dive into some of what the research purports to tell us and how we can use this knowledge to build more innovative and informed approaches to conflict resolution and peacebuilding in daily life.

Introduction

Our brains are composed of more than 170 billion cells, about half of which are called *neurons*—the information processing cells that communicate via electrical and chemical signals. The other half are called *glial cells*, which provide several supportive cellular functions, including helping to maintain homeostasis. If that sounds like a whole lot of cells, it is! Although the brain is only about 2% of body's mass, it consumes roughly 20% of the body's total energy at rest, reflecting an extraordinary concentration of metabolic investment in this information processing center.

To grasp all that we're about to dive into, it's important to have at least a basic understanding of how our neurons "wire and fire" with one another. When groups of neurons repeatedly activate together, they can strengthen their connections, forming a neural circuit. Multiple interacting neural circuits create broader neural networks, which underlie complex functions like perception, memory, and decision-making. Neurons connect across synapses—specialized junctions where the axon terminal of one neuron meets the dendrite, soma, or axon of another. A synapse includes the presynaptic terminal, the tiny gap called the *synaptic cleft*, and the postsynaptic membrane (see Figure I.1). Signals travel electrically within a neuron and chemically across most synapses via neurotransmitters (though some synapses are purely electrical). The average adult human brain has between 100 and 500 trillion synaptic connections (depending on whom you ask), which produce hundreds of trillions of synaptic events every minute.

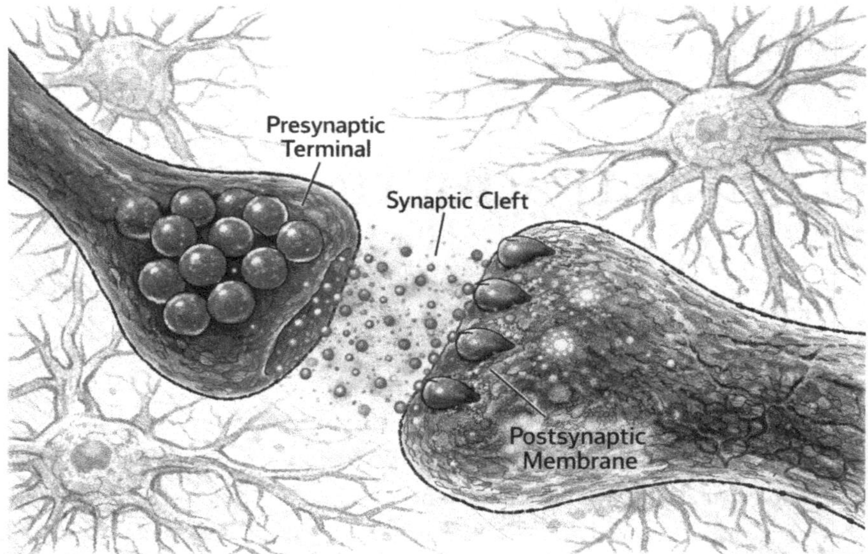

Figure I.1   Synapse.

These magnitudes, and the resulting, interdependent mental, emotional, and physiological outputs, are impossible to conceptualize or to understand even for sophisticated neuroscientists. In fact, the most respected neurobiologists still don't have a full grasp of how this incredible enigma works. In this sense, our internal universe is probably as mysterious and complex as the external universe. It is one of the last frontiers on earth, perhaps as enigmatic as the deep seas, of which only about 5 percent have been explored. In my opinion, the ocean depths, the cosmos, and the brain should all be considered on the same plain when it comes to mystery and, ideally, awe.

There are three main functions of your brain: coordination, regulation, and prediction. To put it succinctly, your brain's core functions are to coordinate your body's organs and biochemical processes in order to regulate their metabolic output to best meet the demands that it predicts the body will need in each situation. I have laid these out in a particular order, beginning with what we might call *bottom-up functionality*, pointing to coordination as the bottom of the funnel: the most unconscious and, thus, most uncontrollable component of your brain's functions. There's nothing much we can or should do to interrupt the brain's ability to coordinate the rest of the body and its processes.

So, let's discuss instead the middle of the funnel: regulation. Neurobiologists and psychologists use the term *regulation* to refer to the activity of the nervous system. This could be conscious, goal-directed activity (e.g., how we can deliberately regulate our system) or nonconscious activity (e.g., how the brain regulates the body). The term *regulation* on its own often refers to a state of homeostatic balance, wherein the brain is attempting to coordinate the body's various elements in a way that brings them back to a manageable baseline. So, when the nervous system is responding to the demands of the immediate environment—whether those demands require little metabolic outlay or a hefty level of metabolic resources—if it responds adequately and appropriately, the system can be said to be regulated.

When particular systems or networks are more active, we call those systems *upregulated*, and when systems are less active or blunted, we call those *downregulated*. The sympathetic nervous system, a branch of the autonomic or unconscious system, is the network of neural circuits that facilitate physiological mobilization, activating energy expenditure and arousal states that prepare the organism for action. Hence, when we are excited, our sympathetic nervous system can be said to be upregulated. When we calm back down, it becomes downregulated. Simultaneously, our parasympathetic system—the network associated with restoration, relaxation, and recovery—become upregulated, sort of like the opposite end of a see-saw.

In cases where there seems to be a mismatch of up- or downregulation of the nervous systems' or its subsystems' components, leading to some disruption of normal or healthy function, we call this *dysregulation*. In other words, if the system is not responding adequately or appropriately to the immediate demands of the situation, likely because of faulty or inapplicable predictions, the system can be said to be dysregulated.

The regulation function of the brain is what I'm calling middle of the funnel, suggesting that we are somewhat aware of and have some, albeit limited, control over its functionality. For example, when we are anxious for no good reason—presumably a state of dysregulation—we can and often do become aware of the feeling of anxiety. Perhaps we notice our heart beating faster, our stomach feeling butterflies, our chest tightening, or any number of sensations indicating an upregulation of the sympathetic nervous system. And if there is no obvious need for such a metabolic output, we label it as anxiety, since it is obviously not responding to the demands of the immediate environment but rather some imagined or predicted future. In dysregulation of this sort, we might take steps to regulate the system by slowing and deepening our breathing and consciously relaxing the body, thereby hoping to upregulate the parasympathetic system and downregulate the sympathetic system. We don't have total control over our regulation at this level, but we do have some, and with practice we can get better at regulating our autonomic system.

Many of us are motivated to learn more about the nervous system because we feel dysregulated. That is, we feel chronically anxious or depressed or nervous about some particular circumstances or, in many cases, about seemingly nothing at all, pointing to the largely nonconscious nature of regulation. If you're reading this book, perhaps you're acutely aware of your own dysregulation as a result of internal, interpersonal, or intergroup conflict you are personally experiencing or witnessing. So, you may be looking for ways to change it. Perhaps interacting with a coworker or a family member, or even the thought of being around them, elevates your heart rate or stirs the butterflies in your stomach (and not in a good way). So, you're looking for ways to alter the dynamic in order to stop feeling so stressed or dysregulated around that person. Well then, let's move into the top of the brain function funnel: prediction.

The model I'm presenting, with regard to the brain's functionality, suggests that the brain predicts the metabolic resources the body will need to meet the demands of the immediate to long-term situations. This model stems from the most widely accepted conception of brain functionality at the time of this writing, which blends a top-down and bottom-up framework, where incoming sensory information (from the bottom) is checked against predictive processing (from the top). These processes then cause up- and/or downregulation of various components of the nervous system, all of which are managed through nonconscious biochemical coordination. Unlike the middle and bottom portions of the funnel, however, we can become more acutely aware of and, thus, have more control over prediction—the top of the funnel.

To be clear, much of what our brains are predicting is either totally nonconscious (i.e., purely physiological) or hidden within the subconscious (i.e., beneath conscious awareness). We might be acutely aware of the stress or anxiety we feel in a situation or we might not be, but we are often unaware of exactly what the brain is predicting might happen or why it's making such a prediction.

With some reflective work, however, we can uncover a great deal of what lies beneath the surface of awareness to learn what exactly our brains are predicting (and even why they're predicting such things, though it's unclear how much the why matters for purposes of changing predictive patterns). Once we become aware of predictions that cause components of the autonomic nervous system to up-, down-, and dysregulate, we can take conscious steps to interrupt the patterns if desired. We might tell ourselves new predictive messages, such as "it's going to be okay" or "I can handle this," which can help calm the nervous system from this top-down approach. However, there is an even more important aspect to this business of interrupting neural patterns and predictions that cause dysregulation: memory.

Inherent in the brain's future-focused prediction function is a past-focused memory function. In fact, it stands to reason that the entire reason the brain remembers and learns from past experiences is to appropriately position resources to meet the demands of the predicted future. In order to accurately predict and carry out its main functions, therefore, the brain pulls from past experience. It's the only way the brain can predict what it thinks the body will need. So, in a sense, we could even think of memory as the true top of the funnel, since prediction relies on it.

To truly interrupt or change neural patterns, we need to consider and work with how the brain functions. We cannot change the function of the brain and nervous system (and trust me, you wouldn't want to). Instead, we have to understand it and use its functionality to our advantage. So, yes, we can self-regulate by taking a physiological approach like breathing and body relaxation. And yes, we can interrupt dysregulating predictions by telling ourselves more empowering or soothing messages about the future. But if we really want to use the brain's functionality to our advantage, we should start at the top. That is, we should alter memory, experience, learning, and conditioning. This will cause the brain to predict differently—ideally in ways that will not produce dysregulation.

To accomplish this, we need to create new experiences that our brains will pull from when making their predictions. And how do we do this? Counterintuitively, we start doing things that our brains and bodies are afraid of or nervous about so that we can create new experiences of those stimuli. And not just everyday, forgettable experiences, but emotionally powerful experiences that override and update memories and conditioning. We need to take a leap of faith and actually *do and think* something different, despite what our brains remember and predict. The true and final top of the funnel, then, is behavior and deliberate thought. Change behavior and thought to change learning and memory to change predictions to change the patterns of dysregulation.

With this said, it's clear that learning to regulate our nervous systems is a core component of conflict resolution. It's the area of neurobiology that's gotten the most attention from conflict researchers and practitioners, which is why Principle 1, dealing with this topic, is the longest principle. But self-regulation is only the beginning of what the brain can teach us about peacebuilding and conflict resolution. There are so many more hidden lessons in our brains that can lead us to peace. Some of the most important of these lessons will be discussed throughout this book, along with practical techniques to implement in your daily life.

This book is meant to be provocative. The tools and techniques are designed to help jolt your nervous system out of its learned or conditioned patterns and to use your brain's capacity for resolving conflicts in new ways. At times, you might feel a bit uncomfortable, which is also why the first principle discusses self-regulation. You can use the calming techniques in Principle 1 with the tools discussed throughout the book and immediately in the laboratory of your life. Have fun with these experiments, testing new and different ways of thinking about your own nervous system, others' systems, and the central currency between your nervous systems: communication, in all its forms.

We can't change the basic functionality of our brains. But we can use how they function to modify neural patterns and change our experiences of ourselves and the world. So, the real question is, how do we get our neurons and neural circuits to fire and wire differently? We use experience, behavior, and directed cognition. Throughout this book, we will look at various ways to create new experiences that will help wire the brain for peace. Each chapter will explain various foundational concepts in neurobiology and psychology, along with cognitive and behavioral tools based on this knowledge, to help us manage and ideally resolve conflicts more effectively.

1 | Solutions and Stress Don't Mix; Always De-escalate First

Think about the last time you were angry, upset, or extremely frustrated. I mean, really think about it. Close your eyes and reflect on the situation. What was going on? With what or whom were you angry or frustrated? What did it feel like? What sensations did you experience?

Some people feel hot and flustered, shaky, dizzy, stomach flutters, chest tightening, heart racing, sweaty, or myriad other physiological states. And how did you behave? Did you shut down and withdraw? Did you get aggressive and blow up? Did you do or say anything that later, when reflecting, seemed out of character for you?

Welcome to the world of escalation. We've all been there. Yes, all of us! Because we're human, and humans have lots of mental stuff interacting with physical stuff, producing and interacting with the ever-so-tricky-for-scientists-to-define *emotional* stuff.

When it comes to conflict, escalation is common. But escalated conflict is different than just your every-day, run-of-the-mill conflict. All of us have obstacles, challenges, and competing interests that we navigate every day, all of which can generally be defined as conflicts. But when most of us think

of the concept *conflict*, what we think of is what I would call *escalated* conflict. *Escalated conflict is the perception of a threat or impediment to one's fundamental needs, goals, or values that subsequently produces a stress response.* While
everyday stressors can also activate this response, escalated conflict regularly involves interpersonal or intergroup dynamics where another person
(or group) is perceived as the source of the threat.

Now, think back to your example, when you felt escalated . . . How
creative and solution-focused were you in that state? Do you think you
were in a reasonable place to think outside the box, find innovative solutions to the conflict, and collaborate and communicate with whomever
necessary to find a workable solution? Likely not. You probably wanted to
avoid the perceived cause of conflict or aggressively defeat it. That's because
escalated states are produced in brain regions that lead to a narrowing or
constraining of one's psychological and behavioral repertoires, rather than
to the widening aperture required for interpersonal connection, information intake, and creative problem-solving.

That's why escalation and solutions don't mix and why de-escalation is
Principle 1 in conflict resolution. None of us can effectively communicate,
solve problems, or get creative when we are escalated.

When *you* are escalated, you'll need to self-regulate—a self-directed de-
escalation. And when someone else is escalated, you'll need to de-escalate
them, if possible. That is, if we hope to resolve the conflict peacefully and
effectively.

So, how do we de-escalate a situation or a person? To answer this, it
would serve us to gain a deeper understanding of exactly what escalation is
at a neurobiological level, how stress or escalated states affect our abilities to
resolve conflict effectively, and why we become escalated during conflict.
Then, we'll be better equipped to create solutions that counteract these
effects and help us and others move from escalated states into regulated states.

The Arousal System

On March 27, 2022, during a live taping of the 94th Academy Awards, actor
Will Smith walked on stage and slapped fellow actor Chris Rock across the
face. This was not a joke and not part of the act. Smith's behavior came in
response to a joke made moments earlier by Rock, who commented on
Smith's wife's bald head—a symptom of her alopecia. There were, of course, a

variety of ways Smith could have responded to the joke. Assaulting his colleague in front of hundreds of other colleagues on live television in front of tens of millions of fans and viewers was presumably not the most constructive response. The next day, Smith apologized to Rock publicly and expressed remorse about his behavior, calling it "inexcusable" and "unacceptable." Certainly, there was a better way to handle that conflict—the seemingly competing interests between the actor on stage looking for a laugh and the actor in the audience attempting to protect his wife. But in that moment, Smith's rage took over. His mind and behavior were dictated by escalation.

What Is Escalation?

The term *escalation*—particularly in psychological and interpersonal contexts—often refers to a combination of behavioral reactivity, emotional intensity, and physiological hyperarousal, all of which are driven by sympathetic nervous system upregulation (i.e., increased activation of neural circuits associated with energy mobilization and vigilance) and reduced parasympathetic regulation (i.e., decreased activation of neural circuits associated with relaxation and social attunement). In the introduction, we discussed how the sympathetic nervous system works and what it means to be upregulated. So, let's talk a little bit more about arousal and what it means to be either hyper- or hypoaroused.

The term *arousal* refers to a general state of physiological and psychological activation, modulated by both the sympathetic and parasympathetic branches of the autonomic nervous system. Arousal is absolutely normal, healthy, and necessary for any living, animate organism. All living animals need varying levels of arousal to pump their hearts, activate their hormones, and move their bodies in ways that help them survive and reproduce in the environments in which they evolved. Most living things—at least those that evolved in environments with natural predators—have the ability to produce states of hyperarousal (i.e., activation of fast, strong movement) and hypoarousal (i.e., states of shutdown or freezing) to enact defensive behavioral responses to threats. When states of hyper- or hypoarousal last for too long or become chronic—no longer in response to present stimuli—this is, again, what we would call *dysregulation*.

If we conceive of arousal as existing on a spectrum, from low to high, we can theoretically conceive of where arousal levels should be in an optimal range for various activities. Generally speaking, we can assume optimal arousal ranges toward the low end of the spectrum for activities such as sleep, nonsleep deep rest, and meditation. We move a bit higher on the spectrum doing activities that we're not very interested in (e.g., boring tasks) and then higher again when we are engaged in interesting work and exciting projects. We move higher still on arousal when we get into deeply engaging work and even higher when involved in fun, vigorous activities such as exercise, sports, or desired sexual activity.

Some of us like to move into peak arousal where we feel some fear or perceive a bit of danger. In this range, we move into what can typically be thought of as high stress. In psychology and neuroscience, *stress* refers both to the force or pressure being placed on an organism and that organism's physiological response to the force. A distinction is often made between what's been called *eustress*, which is a positive stress when someone feels highly engaged and motivated as a result of demands or pressure, and *distress*, which is a state of dysregulation when someone perceives their resources (energetic or otherwise) will be overwhelmed by the demands of the situation.

People who enjoy engaging in somewhat dangerous activities have higher stress thresholds for those particular activities due to their excitement about the activities without the perception that their survival is seriously in danger. This would be considered eustress—a welcomed hyperarousal or high-stress range. In fact, the ability to control stimuli that create hyperarousal seems to have a major impact on whether someone experiences eustress or distress. In other words, if you feel in control of the stressful experience or the experience feels predictable, you likely won't spiral into an anxiety attack. So, our experience of eustress versus distress all depends on the valence, evaluation, or interpretation of the stressor as either a negative/dangerous stimulus or a positive/exciting stimulus. Rock climber Alex Honnold is famous for scaling some of the most difficult mountain faces on earth, often without the use of any safety ropes, and he is thrilled by the danger—an obvious form of eustress. For just about every other human being, this situation would be perceived as overwhelming, thus manifesting as fear and anxiety, and so would be considered a state of distress. Again, each individual's ranges for optimal arousal and tolerating stress are based on their perception of threat at a given moment, which is based on their previous experiences (i.e., memories) of similar situations or lack thereof.

While there are various potential reasons for hyperarousal and high stress (e.g., vigorous activity, exciting work, sexual behavior), during conflict, escalation typically implies a particular form of hyperarousal and distress called the *acute stress response (ASR)*—commonly known as the fight-flight-freeze response. This state involves not just sympathetic arousal but also specific threat detection and behavioral survival circuits in the brain. During an ASR, various hormones are released into the bloodstream, such as adrenaline, noradrenaline, and cortisol, which stimulate several fascinating, adaptive neuropsychological processes that prepare the organism for fighting or escaping danger. This shift toward defensive, reactive states impair communication and problem-solving. This is where de-escalation comes in: it's an attempt to counteract the stress response. After all, we don't talk about de-escalating from fun, engaging activities. We do so from perceived threat.

The ASR is a rapid, automatic surge in physiological arousal triggered by a perceived threat, activating neural and hormonal systems to prepare the body for immediate action. It is a particular form of hyperarousal, driven by heightened autonomic and neuroendocrine activation, including upregulation of the sympathetic system. While the ASR is classically a survival response to perceived threat, high-arousal states that are interpreted as challenging but manageable or under someone's control (e.g., public speaking or skydiving) are better understood as "challenge responses" or eustress, which share some features with the ASR but involve different hormonal and cardiovascular patterns. Though the ASR is typically the result when we're dealing with escalated conflict, individuals can sometimes feel exhilarated, excited, and highly engaged in conflict resolution processes, especially when they feel they have agency in the process and they see the conflict as an opportunity for growth (more on that topic in Principle 2).

An ASR during a conflict can certainly be an appropriate response, indicating an adaptive arousal state, if there is a true threat endangering the individual at that moment. Indeed, it would be suboptimal to *not* react with high stress to a dangerous person charging at you. However, if the ASR is activated when no true threat exists, it would be indicative of maladaptive arousal or dysregulation. In interpersonal and intergroup conflict, danger is often perceived as more threatening than it actually is—at least in the immediate—leading to an inappropriate stress response and ultimately nonconstructive behavior.

When an ASR does not properly resolve, it can lead to a state of chronic stress. Chronic stress is never considered positive or eustress; it is always a form of distress and dysregulation. If you feel anxious, upset, frustrated, or angry at the mere thought of someone, let alone when you are actually around them, you are experiencing chronic conflict escalation, and this is a sure way for the conflict to persist and, in many cases, worsen. Plus, keeping the body and nervous system in a reactionary state for long periods is unhealthy for the individual. Chronic stress is associated with dysregulation of the hypothalamic-pituitary-adrenal (HPA) axis, the body's core neuroendocrine stress-response system. Prolonged activation of the HPA axis has been linked with cardiovascular disease, weakened immunity, metabolic disorders, and mood disorders like depression and anxiety.

In addition to having such negative consequences, chronic stress leads to psychological hypervigilance, during which we interpret danger and threats in places where there likely is none, creating even more distress. In other words, chronic stress compounds itself, creating cycles of fear and distress, which affect the mind and body in significant ways. If you've got a boss or a family member who seems to make your heart race every time they walk in the room, you're experiencing the stress of chronic conflict.

Eventually, chronic hyperarousal may lead to chronic hypoarousal. When an organism is unable to fight or flee in response to perceived or real danger, and the threat persists, most animals have the extraordinary ability to employ a last-ditch effort at survival: the feign or faint response. You'll see this often with prey animals who play dead to escape an impending attack. This is not a conscious, strategic behavior; rather, the animal's hypoaroused nervous system forces it into paralysis. Evolutionary biologists think this adaptive behavior is meant to indicate to the predator that the prey is no longer worth pursuing or that the opponent is no longer a threat.

In human beings who experience intense distress that they are unable to escape or fight their way out of, their nervous systems may shut down the mind and body so that the individual mentally dissociates and physically goes numb. This can happen as a result of acute danger, such as during a violent physical attack, in which case such a response can be adaptive. However, when individuals, especially children, undergo ongoing fear or perceived danger throughout their lives—what psychologists call *complex trauma*—their nervous systems may fall into chronic hypoarousal due to the consistent perception of danger coupled with the real or perceived inability to fight back or escape the danger. These are individuals who are often withdrawn or isolated. Individuals experiencing chronic hypoarousal report feeling numb or emotionally flat like they can no longer experience any feelings whether positive or negative. They also report feeling dissociated from reality, as if existing in a waking dream—not really alive. Hypoarousal can even be a driving force in people who consistently feel bored or disengaged from most activities in life. Those who have lost any zest or excitement for life, in general, are often experiencing a maladaptive, hypoaroused nervous system.

Chronic hypoarousal can become the case when intense conflict lasts for long periods without any perceived end or escape in sight. People feel helpless and hopeless and simply become withdrawn. This depressed state is the downstream consequence of unresolved escalation, when the system collapses into hypoarousal rather than remain escalated. When chronic escalation is perceived as inescapable, sometimes the only thing a person can do to manage the conflict psychologically is to shut down, and this happens with or without the individual's conscious awareness. Indeed, escalation can lead to different behavioral and psychological effects: blow up or shut down.

To summarize, at all times, our nervous systems interpret our bodies as somewhere on the spectrum from "about to die" to "totally safe." And one of our brain's primary functions is to predict potential threats to determine exactly where we are on that spectrum in each moment and give instructions to our autonomic nervous system to respond accordingly. An accurate reading or prediction of the situation and an appropriate response would be optimal. Unfortunately, our brains—due to their complexity—are often inaccurate. And so, we regularly perceive danger where there is little or none at all, and this perception profoundly affects our ability to handle conflicts effectively.

How Escalation Affects Conflict Resolution

When an individual experiences conflict escalation and their acute stress response is activated, their brain and body shift from a mode of social engagement to one of self-preservation. In response to perceived danger, the HPA axis and sympathetic nervous system are activated, releasing cortisol, adrenaline, and other stress hormones. This cascade increases arousal and prepares the individual for rapid defensive responses but simultaneously impairs the prefrontal cortex (PFC)—the region largely responsible for emotion regulation, moral reasoning, and perspective taking. Also during escalation, the amygdala becomes hyperactive. The amygdala is a small, almond-shaped brain structure involved in assessing the emotional salience and valence of stimuli, meaning it helps determine how important something is and whether it's good or bad. We actually have two amygdalae, one in each medial temporal lobe, nestled deep in the brain near the hippocampus, a structure involved in memory. During the stress response, the hippocampus contributes contextual memory that helps the brain interpret potential threats, while the amygdala rapidly signals the salience of stimuli and coordinates fear responses via connections to the hypothalamus and brain stem. Under stress, however, cortisol can impair hippocampal function, which may distort contextual memory and bias perception even further toward threat detection and self-protection.

These neurobiological processes have a profound effect on what I call the *five Cs of conflict resolution: curiosity, communication, care, collaboration, and creativity.* Without the capacity to engage the five Cs effectively, our ability to resolve conflicts peacefully is significantly diminished. We will dive even deeper into each of these capacities throughout this book, exploring how we can use brain science to enhance them. For now, let's look specifically at how they become constrained by escalated states.

Curiosity   In both practice and scientific research, curiosity has proven to be a critical component to effective conflict resolution. If we do not keep an open mind and remain curious about others' experiences and perspectives, then we apparently already know the solution, the truth, or what's right versus wrong. Believing that one's own perspective or experience is the sole source of truth, rightness, or highest moral good and not being open to another perspective, automatically makes the other person wrong, malicious, and/or ignorant. As you can imagine, this closed mindset is never productive for peacebuilding. When we are curious, we are open to different ideas about what happened in the past and new, potentially useful ideas about what to do going forward.

During a stress response, including the activation of the HPA axis and downregulation of the PFC, our capacity for open-mindedness and curiosity become severely impaired. Curiosity, which supports exploration and adaptive social engagement, is supported by dopaminergic systems and prefrontal regions such as the ventromedial PFC and anterior cingulate cortex, and it also draws on the hippocampus and default mode network, which help generate novel connections and possibilities. These areas enable individuals to tolerate ambiguity, stay open to disconfirming information, and consider alternative interpretations—abilities that are crucial for de-escalating conflict. However, under stress, amygdala hyperactivation suppresses these areas, impairing flexible thinking and prosocial motivation.

Stress also narrows attentional focus, a phenomenon known as *cognitive narrowing*, when individuals shift from exploratory to defensive mental states. This makes it difficult to remain curious about another person's perspective, especially when the brain prioritizes survival over social understanding. In this state, people are more likely to narrow their focus to only their own perspective, experiences, and goals rather than remain open to and curious about those of other people.

Communication　We cannot resolve conflict in a way that improves relationships without effective communication. Communication comes in many forms: the content of our words, the tone of our speech, the position of our bodies, our eye movement, the way we gesture, and so on. It also comes through various channels, such as talking, writing, symbolism, and even silence. In all communications, there is a sender, a receiver, and a transmission channel, that is, the behavior of the messenger, the channel through which the message is sent, and the recipient's nervous system, including its perception of the messenger and interpretation of the message. All of these elements must be taken into consideration, especially when attempting to communicate during conflict.

We should frequently ask ourselves these questions: What is the most effective way to communicate? How will my intention most clearly be communicated so as to be accurately interpreted by and have the intended impact on the receiver? This analysis seems quite a bit more complex than what we typically consider during everyday communication. But it's all happening constantly nonetheless. So many conflicts erupt initially and/or worsen because of miscommunications and misinterpretations—messages being inaccurately interpreted and thus having an unintended impact. And, of course, when we are in escalated states, our intentions, let alone the way we communicate them, can become suboptimal.

Effective interpersonal communication depends on multiple components, including emotional regulation, perspective taking, perceptual fluency, and the capacity to interpret nonverbal cues—functions that are significantly compromised when an individual is in an escalated state of distress. The acute stress response directly impairs the neural circuits that support open, thoughtful, and prosocial communication. Activation of the HPA axis and upregulation of the sympathetic nervous system deprioritize neural resources for social cognition and verbal reasoning. The PFC, especially regions involved in language regulation, emotion management, and social inference, is suppressed during acute stress. Meanwhile, the amygdala becomes hyperactive, increasing reactivity and reducing the ability to distinguish between real and perceived interpersonal threats. As a result, individuals under stress become more defensive, less able to listen, and more likely to misinterpret neutral or ambiguous cues as hostile—a phenomenon known as *hostile attribution bias*.

Distress also impairs access to working memory and verbal fluency, reducing an individual's ability to articulate thoughts clearly and engage in reflective dialogue. Nonverbal synchrony, such as facial mirroring, vocal tone regulation, and eye contact, is also disrupted under stress, diminishing the interpersonal rapport necessary for effective communication. Also, oxytocin-mediated systems that support social bonding, empathy, and trust are inhibited in escalated states, making it more difficult to engage in compassionate or cooperative dialogue. This contributes to reduced social attunement and increased likelihood of miscommunication during interpersonal conflict.

In short, escalated states diminish the neurological foundations of interpersonal communication. The acute stress response reroutes brain activity away from reflective and relational circuits toward defensive and reactive systems.

Care   If we're attempting to resolve conflict, we have to make it clear that we actually *care* about the other person's goals, needs, and values. If they sense we do not care—that we're only here for our own defense or agenda—then peaceful and sustainable resolution is much less likely. The ability to care about another person's needs, goals, and values depends on elements such as cognitive empathy, emotional regulation, and social attunement. But these capacities are neurobiologically diminished during escalated emotional states because of our shift toward self-protection and goal-preservation. This attentional shift inward inhibits neural networks such as the default mode network and brain areas like the medial prefrontal cortex, both of which have been shown to play central roles in empathic concern and understanding others' mental state.

Elevated cortisol levels also suppress the oxytocin system. Oxytocin is sometimes referred to as the trust or love hormone. While oxytocin is not the sole basis for caring, it plays a key role in facilitating social bonding and caregiving. When stress suppresses oxytocin activity, it becomes significantly harder to express warmth and concern for others. Instead, we become neurologically predisposed to protect ourselves rather than consider or prioritize the well-being of anyone else, especially those we perceive as opponents.

Collaboration   Conflict resolution also requires collaborating with the other people involved in the conflict, enabling each person to have agency in building solutions that work for them. The only way to build effective and sustainable solutions is to get buy-in from all sides, especially if they will be responsible for meeting expectations and keeping the peace moving forward. The only route to win-win solutions is when everybody can contribute or at least agree to the solutions.

When a person experiences escalation, particularly through activation of the acute stress response, neurobiological changes occur that directly impair the brain systems necessary for collaborative behavior. People are more likely to engage in self-other distancing, which includes reduced trust, diminished empathy, and impaired communication. These effects are compounded by cognitive narrowing, in which attention and decision-making become more rigid and risk averse. As a result, individuals under stress tend to prioritize self-protection over mutual goals, suppressing the motivation to collaborate.

Collaboration also relies on neurochemical systems associated with social bonding, such as oxytocin and dopamine. Again, these systems are inhibited during a stress response, which can shift individuals into adversarial rather than cooperative modes of interaction. When people feel unsafe or threatened, their brains are neurologically biased against co-regulation and joint problem-solving. This is why escalated states undermine collaboration. The acute stress response hijacks the brain's social and executive circuits, making it difficult for individuals to stay engaged and flexible, which are both essential for true collaboration.

Creativity Finally, effective conflict resolution is a creative process; it often requires us to think outside the box for solutions we may not have previously thought about. Solution building is also iterative and multilateral, meaning it should be like a brainstorm session, with all parties involved having a voice to express their goals and needs, offer possible solutions, and riff off each other for new and innovative ideas to complex problems. Sometimes the solution is easy and quick, and we don't need much creative thinking. But in more intense, complex conflicts, such as those that cause escalated states, we often have to get creative.

Creativity depends on cognitive flexibility and associative thinking among other cognitive capacities that employ a range of neural networks. These brain functions are significantly impaired during an ASR, which shifts the brain from a state of exploration and synthesis to one of survival and threat management. In particular, PFC activity (especially in the dorsolateral and medial regions), central to executive functions and novel idea generation, is reduced, while amygdala activity increases. This shift biases the brain toward vigilance and habit-based behaviors, limiting the cognitive flexibility required for creative problem-solving.

Creativity also involves dynamic interaction between the default mode network and the executive control network, enabling individuals to draw on memories and imagine new possibilities. Distress disrupts this balance by reducing connectivity between these networks, leading to a narrowed focus and inhibition of divergent thinking.

Distress additionally impairs access to dopaminergic pathways in the mesolimbic system, which are linked to intrinsic motivation and reward-based exploration—both critical drivers of creative engagement. Finally, elevated cortisol levels negatively affect the hippocampus, impairing memory recall and associative thinking, which further undermines the integration of new and old ideas.

At the end of the day, escalated states inhibit creativity by deprioritizing the brain's exploratory and integrative functions. The acute stress response biologically reallocates resources away from open-ended thinking and toward immediate problem detection and defense, thus closing the cognitive space needed for imagination and idea synthesis.

Reflecting on the five Cs, it's clear that critical elements for resolving conflicts peacefully are significantly weakened by escalated states during a stress response. Now that we understand what happens to our capacities for effective conflict resolution during escalated states, we have one more central question to address: Why do we become escalated in the first place? Perhaps someone was inconsiderate, rude, or verbally aggressive, but why should that necessarily cause an escalated state?

Why We Become Escalated

A foundational model of human motivation is a set of theories generally referred to as human needs theories. These models suggest that human beings have a suite of fundamental, irreducible needs—primary needs unto themselves that must be satisfied for proper functionality of the organism, and which do not satisfy any deeper, underlying psychological or physiological components. These needs are universal, cross-cultural, and central to the human animal. Human beings, like all animals, are in a constantly fluctuating state between satisfaction and depletion of these needs. When a basic need is depleted, we feel a painful or otherwise uncomfortable sensation that drives us to satisfy the need in order to reduce the discomfort. In other words, we are almost always being driven to seek out things (i.e., satisfiers) that will meet or fulfill our basic needs, or to avoid things (i.e., threats) that might deplete those needs. These drives underly just about all our motivated behaviors, whether or not we're aware of this primary source of motivation.

So, what are human beings' basic needs? We, of course, have a set of fundamental physical needs to survive, such as energy, hydration, oxygenation, internal system regulation, and bodily safety. Each of these has a fairly straightforward satisfier: nutritious food, clean water, clean air, clothing/shelter, and a safe environment, respectively. We are constantly in a state of real or perceived satisfaction or depletion of these needs, and thus consistently seeking satisfiers to meet these needs while scanning our environments for impediments or threats. When any of these needs become depleted, we feel increasing pain or discomfort specific to that need (e.g., hunger, thirst, cold, etc.) that drives us to remove the impediments and seek out satisfiers that will meet the need and reduce the discomfort. If a person or group perceives another person or group to be standing in the way of their needs, this obviously presents a conflict. And you can imagine, as has often been the case throughout history, how escalation and violence can erupt when these conflicts are not solved effectively or swiftly. If a person or group of people appears to be impeding another from attaining food, water, or warmth, it's only natural that the impeded party take extreme measures to survive.

Human needs theories have been a foundational concept in theories of conflict and peace psychology. When we perceive a threat or impediment to our basic needs, we are driven to eliminate it by avoiding, influencing, or eliminating the perceived cause of that threat or impediment. Often, the actual or perceived threat is another person or group of people. This can lead to violent conflict, which is always a form of escalated conflict. Realistic conflict theory, developed by social psychologists in the mid-20th century, suggests that intergroup conflict arises from competition of scarce resources. These resources can be thought of as the satisfiers of basic needs.

When we are motivated to satisfy a need or diminish a perceived impediment or threat, our sympathetic nervous system—the excitatory system— becomes upregulated. This gets us to take action. Unfortunately, not everyone believes they can actually change their circumstances and get a need satisfied. So, while the discomfort and the motivation to relieve the discomfort exist, many people feel they have no way out and so tend to move from hyperarousal into hypoarousal. This belief or prediction, generated from memory and experience, instead downregulates their sympathetic system and upregulates their parasympathetic system to dysfunctional levels, causing them to shut down and withdraw into feeling hopeless and helpless. While not action-oriented, this hypoarousal is still a survival mechanism. Remember, this is one of the two basic behaviors during escalated conflict: blow up or shut down.

Now, the fascinating thing about human beings is, we also have a suite of psychological needs that are just as fundamental to our neural architecture and thus cause just as much conflict when threatened. While nonhuman animals, especially social animals, also have psychological needs, human beings are special—maybe especially *needy*. We presumably have more psychological needs than any other animal. When these needs are depleted, threatened, or impeded, we similarly feel extreme pain, discomfort, or distress and are highly motivated to reduce that discomfort and get these needs satisfied. This is because these needs were fundamental to our survival and reproduction throughout human evolution. Interestingly, psychological pain, due to the depletion of or perceived threat to our psychological needs, is processed in many of the same brain regions that process physical pain and threats. And the behavioral outputs of this phenomenon are just as evident. Human beings throughout history and still today become escalated and violent in reaction to perceived threats to their psychological needs, even when all of their physical needs are satisfied. And they will shut down and withdraw if they feel helpless and hopeless about not being able to satisfy those needs.

So, what are our psychological needs? There have been dozens of basic psychological needs theories espoused over recorded history, most prominently since the early 20th century. From humanist psychologist Abraham Maslow and his hierarchy of needs to economist Manfred Max-Neef's human scale development model; from social psychologists Richard Ryan and Edward Deci's widely supported basic psychological needs theory to motivational coach Tony Robbins's six psychological needs and many more. I have read and researched these theories for several years, finding as many different approaches and models as I could find, and have come to the conclusion that all of these theories have identified six basic psychological needs, each of which has been labeled in various ways by the different theorists. I use the acronym SAPIEN to identify these needs: safety, affiliation, positive self-concept, independence, engaging activities, and noble pursuits (see Figure 1.1). Let's briefly review each need, which will help illuminate exactly why we become escalated during conflict.

NOTE: *For a deeper, more academic discussion on the SAPIEN model and how various researchers have discussed these needs, please see jeremypollack.com/needs.*

Safety   The psychological need for safety has also been labeled security, stability, certainty, predictability, and protection. This is essentially

Figure 1.1   The universal basic psychological needs.

a two-dimensional construct, illuminating the need for both future security/ stability and for what has often been termed in the organizational literature as *psychological safety*. On the stability dimension, people need to feel that their world is somewhat predictable. They need to have a belief that they and their loved ones will be generally safe in their environments, which means having predictable environmental patterns that they can count on, such as a stable source of income, stable housing, stable relationships, and nonviolence. When one or several domains of their lives feel chaotic or unpredictable, their need for safety becomes diminished. You can see how this need coincides with the most basic function of the brain: prediction. Indeed, this need is essentially a psychological manifestation of our most basic neurobiological operation. The brain's predictive functioning sets a neurobiological foundation that drives the psychological need for safety and certainty.

The second dimension of safety is the need to feel psychologically safe, which refers to the ability to take risks and make mistakes without the fear of retaliation or humiliation. In our personal lives, starting in childhood and running throughout our adult relationships, we're always taking risks with how we behave, how we communicate, and what we say. We test boundaries, sometimes making errors and course correcting based on feedback, which helps us learn, grow, and thrive as individuals. This is absolutely essential for healthy development. The same is true at work: to be innovative and growth oriented, we need to think outside the box and sometimes challenge the status quo. However, when people feel they must never make a mistake and must walk on eggshells to avoid being humiliated, attacked, rejected, or abandoned, all of these opportunities for growth are stunted, and the need for psychological safety will become depleted.

Affiliation   The psychological need for affiliation has also been called the need for relatedness, belonging, love, attachment, affection, unity, and connection. It identifies the deep requirement to be cared for and paid attention to as well as to be part of a group, family, or community. Like all social animals, this need likely evolved as a layer above safety, since infant humans cannot survive on their own, requiring dedicated attention from caregivers in order to be fed and protected. Additionally, over evolutionary history, adult humans attempting to survive without a group would have had quite a difficult time protecting and providing for themselves. In this sense, affiliation with a group of people, starting with caregivers in early life and then communities in adulthood, certainly satisfied the need for safety, so much so that the need for affiliation evolved to become its own irreducible need. Now, human beings that are born with basic safety but without care and attention are much more likely to be severely psychologically and even physically impaired. Hence, when we are abandoned or undesirably alone or isolated, the need for affiliation becomes depleted.

Positive Self-Concept   The need for positive self-concept has also been labeled *identity, status, self-esteem, significance, competence, self-worth, value,* and *recognition,* among others. Our self-concept is abstract and multidimensional. It arises from multiple aspects of identity, including one's individual and social identities. When someone perceives that they are not being accepted and valued because of some aspect of their multidimensional identity, their self-concept may be affected negatively and thus this need will be depleted. The extent to which other people can affect a person's self-concept depends on the solidity and coherence of that individual's self-concept and the positive or negative way they generally see themself.

Independence   The need for independence has also been termed *autonomy*, *agency*, *power*, *freedom*, *control*, *orientation*, *self-determination*, and *self-direction*. Human beings have a need to feel control over their lives and that they can make decisions autonomously, especially about important aspects of their lives. A tremendous amount of conflict arises from the perceived threat or impediment to this psychological need. When people feel they are being impeded from making decisions about their health, their money, their families, or other meaningful elements of life, this need will be threatened and will motivate them to take action to remove the threat and satisfy the need.

Engaging Activities   The need for engaging activities has also been called *stimulation, pleasure, leisure, fun, personal fulfillment, eustress, excitation,* and *variety.* This speaks to our drive to occupy our minds with something we find stimulating, even challenging in a positive way. When we are bored, unchallenged, or unstimulated on a regular basis, this need will be diminished.

Noble Pursuits   Finally, the need for noble pursuits has also been called *achievement, growth, self-enhancement, mastery, transcendence, meaning, purpose,* and *self-actualization.* This is the need to feel that we are on a right and meaningful path and that there is some purpose in what we are doing with ourselves. When we lack a sense of purpose, meaning, growth, or goals that we feel are important, this need will be depleted.

Remember our definition of escalated conflict: the perception of a threat or impediment to one's fundamental needs, goals, or values that subsequently produces a stress response. In line with human needs theories, all values are construed and all goals are developed to serve our underlying, irreducible needs. The bottom line: *needs are always the end game.* Therefore, all escalated conflicts—all acute stress responses—erupt from a real or perceived threat to one or more of our basic physical or psychological needs.

For Will Smith at the Oscars, his ASR was most likely associated with a feeling of disrespect, an emotion reducible to the underlying need of positive self-concept. When someone's behavior or language is interpreted as rude or disrespectful, it does not trigger an ASR or fight-flight response unless it hits that underlying basic need. Once it threatens a basic need, however, the survival mechanism is triggered, just as it could be during a threat to one's need for food or water. For reasons we can only speculate, Chris Rock making a joke about Smith's wife on national television had an impact on Smith's basic concept of self in that moment, and he erupted. In general, escalated, even violent conflict is just as likely to emerge when someone disrespects a person with a negative or incoherent self-concept as when someone impedes the food supply of a starving individual.

By understanding this, you can analyze a conflict by looking underneath the parties' surface-level desires, and even beneath their goals and values, to discover which fundamental needs are being perceived as threatened or impeded. We can then find solutions to get those needs met in creative ways (i.e., not just in the way the parties initially desired) and either remove the real threat or reduce the perception of a threat. This will be a theme in the "Tools to Self-Regulate and De-escalate First" section.

Recap: The Arousal System

When we feel emotionally charged during conflict, it's because a basic need has been perceived, whether true or not, as threatened or impeded. This threat perception can occur consciously or, in most cases, without conscious awareness.

As a result, an acute stress response is activated, upregulating our sympathetic nervous system, which motivates us to (1) eliminate the source of threat or impediment, subsequently reducing the pain/discomfort resulting from need depletion and (2) satisfy the need. If we perceive ourselves as helpless and the situation as unchangeable, our sympathetic system downregulates and we withdraw, which is a downstream consequence of the stress response. As long as we continue to perceive the threat and our brain continues to activate the stress response, we will be unable to engage the five Cs and effectively resolve conflict.

In sum, a perceived threat activates the stress response, which limits our conflict resolution capacity, which makes it even harder to reduce the threat peacefully. As you can tell, this is a cycle that spirals and builds on itself, making conflict resolution increasingly difficult as long as we remain escalated. So, how do we interrupt the cycle, stop the spiral, and engage in effective and peaceful solution building? Let's look at some tools.

Tools to Self-Regulate and De-escalate First

For all the reasons explained, it's just about impossible to resolve conflicts effectively when psychologically and physiologically escalated (i.e., experiencing the acute stress response). And one is even more likely to experience an acute stress response if they are chronically stressed and dysregulated. So, if we want to resolve conflicts effectively, we'll have to (1) take steps to minimize chronic stress through self-care and (2) learn tools to self-regulate during acute stress. In a more regulated state, we can then attempt to de-escalate others when necessary. How do we do this? Since escalation is both a physical and psychological state, we'll need to address both; and we do so through directed cognition—deliberate thought and behavior that regulate our own systems and attempt to regulate the systems of others. In essence, we use the conscious mind to affect the sub- and nonconscious parts of us and others. Only then, can we honestly attempt peace-oriented conflict resolution practices, including the five Cs.

Practicing Self-Care

If you're chronically stressed, you'll be more likely to become reactive during conflict. To address elements of chronic stress and dysregulation, we'll need to become committed to self-care. Here are a few important components of chronic stress mitigation.

Sleep   We need good sleep! Yes, I know that can be difficult with a busy life. But adequate sleep is essential for restoring autonomic balance and regulating the brain structures involved in stress and emotional processing. During deep non-REM and REM sleep, the brain reduces activity in the amygdala—the region responsible for threat detection—and enhances connectivity between the prefrontal cortex and limbic system, which supports emotional regulation and adaptive responses. Sleep also reduces baseline levels of cortisol and other stress-related neurochemicals, enabling the HPA axis to reset. Without adequate sleep, the brain becomes more reactive to stressors, prefrontal control weakens, and the sympathetic nervous system remains overactive, increasing the likelihood of dysregulation and acute stress responses. By contrast, high-quality sleep strengthens top-down regulatory networks and dampens chronic overactivation of the stress response system.

To help with sleep, use dimmer light at night, turn off the TV and the phone a couple hours before bed, have some wind-down rituals, and do whatever else necessary to get your body into sleep mode when it's time. If you really want to work on better sleep, read some of Dr. Matthew Walker's books and articles; Walker is a sleep expert and researcher at the University of California, Berkeley.

Diet   To reduce the potential for stress response, we must absolutely feed our bodies and brains well. A healthy, balanced diet supports nervous system regulation and stress resilience by providing the essential nutrients needed for neurotransmitter synthesis, energy metabolism, and anti-inflammatory processes. Nutrients such as omega-3 fatty acids, B vitamins, magnesium, and amino acids like tryptophan and tyrosine play critical roles in supporting brain function, particularly in regions like the prefrontal cortex and hippocampus, which regulate the stress response.

A stable, nutrient-rich diet also helps maintain balanced blood glucose levels, preventing spikes and crashes that can trigger sympathetic arousal and emotional reactivity. Additionally, a healthy gut microbiome—shaped by dietary choices—communicates bidirectionally with the brain via the gut-brain axis, influencing mood, inflammation, and stress hormone regulation. Together, these mechanisms reduce baseline neuroinflammation and support parasympathetic tone, making acute stress responses less frequent and more manageable. Eating well will help your brain and body more effectively manage stressful situations, including conflict.

While there is no single diet I would recommend, since each person's body is different, the vast majority of research does indicate that staying away from highly processed foods is best for the brain and body. Oh, and simple carbs, especially added sugar, appear to be not so good for us. Stick with natural, non-processed food without added sugar, as much as you can, and you'll be on the right track.

Exercise   One of the most important elements of combatting dysregulation and chronic stress is to get our bodies moving regularly. Consistent exercise promotes adaptive changes in both the brain and autonomic nervous system that enhance resilience to future stressors. Physical activity increases vagal tone and parasympathetic activity, which help regulate heart rate variability and shift the body out of chronic sympathetic dominance. Exercise also modulates the HPA axis, leading to more efficient cortisol regulation and reduced baseline stress hormone levels over time.

Neurochemically, exercise boosts the production of endorphins, dopamine, serotonin, and brain-derived neurotrophic factor, which support mood, neuroplasticity, and cognitive flexibility. These changes strengthen top-down regulation from the prefrontal cortex over the amygdala, reducing reactivity to perceived threats and making acute stress responses less likely and less intense.

Again, since each body is different and there are so many competing theories on proper exercise, I'd hesitate to recommend a particular protocol. Though, increasingly more research indicates the general benefits of both strength and regular movement on longevity. One doesn't necessarily have to be in the gym lifting weight multiple times a week; if you simply make it a point to walk for at least 30 minutes a day, do some stretching, some bending, even tending to a garden or getting up and down in your chair regularly, this will be far better for your body and nervous system than being sedentary. Just get moving!

Your Six SAPIEN Needs   Remember, we have at least six basic psychological needs that require attention. If any one of these aren't properly satisfied in your life, you're going to feel unease—somewhere from a little off to highly dysregulated. If multiple needs aren't fulfilled, well, let's just say, chronic stress is almost inevitable. However, meeting our basic psychological needs promotes nervous system regulation and resilience by satisfying the core conditions the brain and body interpret as signals of well-being and stability. When these needs are consistently met, the brain's predictive systems register the environment as nonthreatening, enabling the prefrontal cortex to remain active and parasympathetic dominance to be maintained. This downregulates amygdala reactivity and suppresses unnecessary activation of the HPA axis, reducing baseline cortisol levels and buffering against chronic stress.

For each of these needs, it's worth rating your current level of satisfaction from 1 to 10. Go ahead and rate how satisfied each of your needs is (e.g., ask yourself, "How satisfied is my need for a positive self-concept?"), with 1 being "totally depleted" and 10 being "totally satisfied." Pause reading and rate each need now.

Now, any that you rated below level 7 are worth looking into and possibly modifying elements of your life to get those needs met in a more satisfactory way. For those particular needs, following are a few questions you might ask yourself, followed by affirmations to help jumpstart their satisfaction. Sometimes, repeated affirmations will be all you need.

- **Safety**

  Questions

  "What currently feels unpredictable, uncertain, or unstable in my life?" [Insert Answer] "Is that true? Are those truly unstable/uncertain?" [Answer] How could I reduce uncertainty? How could I increase stability?"

  Affirmations

  "I am safe."

  "Whatever happens, I can handle it."

  "Uncertainty is okay. I trust myself to figure it out."

  "It's okay to make mistakes, no matter what anyone says."

- **Affiliation**

  Questions

  "Where or with whom do I not feel accepted as I am?" [Answer] "Is that true? Am I actually not accepted?" [Answer] "Where do I feel like I truly belong and am accepted? Can I build on that community?"

  Affirmations

  "I am lovable and acceptable, just as I am."

  "People in my life love me, even if I can't always feel it."

  "It is okay to be myself around others."

- **Positive Self-Concept**

  Questions

  "How do I speak to myself? Are there any negative stories I tell myself about *me*?" [Answer] "Are those stories true?" [Answer] "If I started looking at myself in a better light, what would that sound like?"

Affirmations

"I am an amazing being."

"I am loveable and acceptable, just as I am."

"I've learned from my past. What's important is who I am now and how I show up in the world."

"I am a good person. And I will always strive to be better."

■ Independence

Questions

"Where do I feel a lack of control in my life? Where do I feel trapped or like I don't have any choice?" [Answer] "Is that true? Do I actually not have any choice, power, or freedom?" [Answer] "What *can* I control? What if I simply focused on that, believed in myself to make the right decisions, and did my best?"

Affirmations

"Somewhere in this, I have choice."

"I am never trapped. There is a decision here I can make."

"I trust myself. I can make the right decision."

"I am extremely powerful, even if I don't fully understand my power yet."

■ Engaging Activities

Questions

"Where do I feel bored, unstimulated, or underchallenged in life?" [Answer] "What would feel more interesting and stimulating? How could I engage with that more?"

Guidance

This need likely requires more than a mindset shift. So, instead of affirmations, I recommend you take action. Write down every activity you can think of that seems interesting, fun, or challenging (in a positive way). These could be activities you've tried or have just thought about trying. Then, circle the top three you feel would be most interesting. Determine how you could do them, make a reasonable, actionable plan to do so, and commit to it! Let's get this need met.

■ Noble Pursuits

Questions

"What am I currently doing that feels purposeless or meaningless?" [Answer] "Is that true? Are those activities actually meaningless? Do they serve some indirect, downstream purpose?" [Answer] "What would feel more purposeful and meaningful? How could I engage with that more?"

Guidance

Noble pursuits also require action. A lot of people report not finding meaning in their careers. And that may be okay. You can be engaged in purpose-driven activities outside of work or as a side gig. You might also recognize that work pays the bills, which helps you take care of your family or engage in other, more meaningful activities.

This need also feels depleted when people do not have a clear direction for their life in general. If you are not working toward anything specific, you might feel a lack of purpose. If this is the case, I would suggest doing a bit of goal planning. Where do you want your life to be in the next two to three years? You could go as far out as 10 years, but I typically like to keep things a little shorter to make it feel more realistic. Paint the vision for yourself. Three years from now, what are the key elements of your life and lifestyle, your relationships, your work situation, and so on? Make the goals meaningful to you and your family. Then make a grid, putting all of these key points at the end or right side of the grid, and work your way backward by building a timeline with action steps. If the end goals on the right side of the page are three years out, for instance, where would you need to be in two years? And to meet those goals, where would you need to be in one year? In six months? In one month? By next week? Fill in the grid with small steps at each time interval; make them actionable and realistic. I promise that if you have a reasonable action plan to reach your meaningful goals in the next two to three years, broken down by many small steps, you will feel a greater sense of purpose.

Finally, many people find purpose in participating in activities that feel bigger than oneself. These may include gold-directed group causes or spiritual endeavors. If you haven't already, consider if finding a larger mission or a spiritual practice resonates with you.

Life Circumstances   Another important self-care tool is to review and modify your life circumstances when necessary. If you feel like your current life situation is causing ongoing distress, there's no time like now to really think about changing it. Get clear on the circumstances or outside pressures causing ongoing stress in your life, and do your best to either remove or diminish the causes of stress or manage the stress differently. Remember, the definition of distress is when your brain believes you do not have the resources to properly manage the demands of the situation. Those demands could be on your financial, energetic, time, relational, or any other resources. Ask yourself if this is the case in any of your current circumstances.

If so, to change this dynamic and relieve the stress, can you either bolster your resources to meet those demands, recognize that you already have the resources to meet the demands and just aren't using them effectively, or reduce the demands to be more in line with your available resources? If you feel like there's simply nothing you can do, that neither your resources nor the demands will change anytime soon, I highly encourage you to rethink this. There is almost always something you can tweak to either change or lessen the demands, or to change or strengthen your resources. Do some reflective thinking about this, talk to friends and family, get advice from trusted advisors, or otherwise ask for support in figuring out how to make these changes. There's likely something you've just not thought of yet. At the least, you can learn to manage the stress differently by employing some of the techniques in this section or in other material you read on regulating your nervous system to decrease physiological and psychological load.

Additional Practices   The following self-care practices can also help regulate the autonomic nervous system, strengthen top-down control, and reduce chronic activation of the HPA axis, making us more resistant to the dysregulation that leads to acute stress responses.

- **Meditation and mindfulness.** Regular mindfulness practice reduces amygdala activity, strengthens prefrontal cortex regulation, and improves emotional awareness and resilience to stressors.
- **Social connection and support.** Safe, supportive relationships activate the social engagement system and buffer the physiological impact of stress through co-regulation.
- **Time in nature.** Exposure to natural environments (e.g., forests, oceans, nature paths) lowers cortisol levels and increases parasympathetic activation.

- **Somatic practices.** Modalities like yoga, tai chi, Feldenkrais, or somatic experiencing help reconnect body and brain, release stored tension, and enhance self-awareness and self-regulation.
- **Creative expression.** Engaging in creative activities like music, art, dance, or writing can regulate emotional states and provide a nonverbal outlet for stress processing.
- **Healthy boundaries and time management.** Reducing overstimulation and chronic overload by setting limits on demanding activities and prioritizing restorative activities protects against sympathetic overactivation.
- **Therapeutic support.** Practices like cognitive-behavioral therapy, eye movement desensitization and reprocessing, and other trauma-informed therapies help both address unresolved stress patterns and enhance resilience.

Ideally, you are willing to take steps, even small ones, to take good care of yourself. Your body, mind, and feelings deserve care, and no one will be able to dedicate as much time and energy to taking care of them as *you* can. When you do, you'll be in a much better space, mentally and physiologically, to handle conflict, regulate your emotions, and de-escalate others as necessary.

Using Self-Regulation

When we experience distress more acutely in response to a current conflict, and we determine that such a response is not adaptive or productive for solving the conflict, we can take deliberate steps to downregulate our sympathetic response (in the case of our fight-flight reaction) or our parasympathetic response (in the case of our withdrawal/shut-down reaction). This is called *self-regulation*, and fortunately, practical self-regulation tools are plenty. Though, they do take practice and skill building to be increasingly effective. Following are a handful of well-researched self-regulation techniques, but I also encourage you to research more, as there are dozens. Just search for "self-regulation techniques" on YouTube, Google, or any artificial intelligence tool, and you'll find an array of easy, simple, and sometimes strange but worthwhile techniques. The following tools are divided into those recommended during an interaction and those more appropriate to use during a pause.

> **NOTE:** *You can also find a comprehensive list of self-regulation methods on my website at jeremypollack.com/tools/self-regulation. Try several for yourself, see which ones resonate or feel effective, keep practicing, and over time you'll build your self-regulation capacity.*

During an Interaction   You're talking with someone and your blood starts to boil; you feel your heart begin to race, and you're doing everything you can to stay engaged and not blow up or shut down. This is an opportunity to flex your self-regulation muscle. Here are a few practical techniques you can use while interacting with other people in the heat of the moment. Practice these regularly when not escalated, and the next time you feel your stress response get activated during a conversation, you'll have an easier time employing them.

- **Breathe.** Breathing is one of the most foundational practices in self-regulation. It does several things for the nervous system including helping you create a point of focus, get in touch with your body and its sensations, and center you in the present moment. The key to downregulating a stress response is lengthening your exhale, which increases vagal activity and tends to slow your heart rate. This phenomenon is called respiratory sinus arrhythmia (RSA), a natural variation in heart rate that occurs during the breathing cycle. The heart rate increases during inhalation and decreases during exhalation. This variability is mediated by the autonomic nervous system, specifically the parasympathetic influence of the vagus nerve. During inhalation, vagal tone temporarily decreases, enabling the heart rate to rise. During exhalation, vagal tone increases, slowing the heart rate. RSA is considered a marker of vagal tone and overall autonomic flexibility, both of which are associated with emotional regulation and resilience to stress. Try taking a deep breath in for two seconds, then a slow breath out for four seconds. This will slow your heart and downregulate your sympathetic system.
- **Relax the body.** While exhaling, also try to deliberately relax your body. You might especially focus on your shoulders, chest, and face.

If you can let the muscles in those areas drop down while exhaling, you give your brain the message that it's okay to relax, which means essentially that you're *safe* enough to relax. This message counters the threat perception active during a stress response.

■ **Employ mindful awareness.** Mindfulness is the practice of being aware of what is happening inside and outside of your body in the present moment and without any judgment. Whatever is happening, whatever you notice, just notice it. Do not wish it was different or not there; do not label it good, bad, positive, or negative. Just notice. Mindfulness is a practice of becoming extremely present, and it is one of the key practices in relieving anxiety and stress. Anxiety is all about the future prediction of danger based on past experience. So, the more present we can become—the more we can get our brains to stop focusing on past memories and future predictions—the more likely we are to feel safe. Because unless you are being physically attacked in the present or immediate future, your body is actually safe and likely does not need to react with an acute stress response meant for survival. Mindfulness—the practice of being present and just noticing—reminds our brains and bodies that we are safe, right here, right now.

■ **Switch from interoception to exteroception.** Interoception is the focus on and perception of internal bodily states and sensations. Exteroception is the focus on and perception of the world outside of our bodies. When things in the external environment—such as people with whom we're angry or frustrated—make our hearts race, it's because the brain is perceiving a threat. Once the brain creates this response, changing the body's internal state, it reciprocally gives itself the message, for example, that: "We must be in danger because my heart is racing." Never mind that it's the one that actually made the heart race. In other words, threat perception is ultimately an interoceptive state, where the brain both causes and reacts to what's happening in the body. Much of chronic worrying comes from constantly tracking how one feels, what's happening inside oneself, and what might happen to oneself (i.e., neuroticism). To counteract this, when our brains perceive a threat and we notice an acute stress response emerge, we should deliberately shift our focus away from ourselves and toward the other person—from interoception to exteroception. Instead of focusing on *you*, start focusing on what others might be going through. Practice by taking all the focus off yourself and your internal state and placing your entire focus on others in the environment. Become see-through, as though you have no inner self. Be in a state of pure outward focus. This directly counteracts inward attention and self-preservation and is thus likely to downregulate your stress response.

- **Pause.** If you can't seem to calm down, and you feel yourself shutting down or getting ready to explode, do yourself and everyone else a favor: just pause. Take a break. Give yourself permission to ask for a time-out or recess. Even if you're afraid of disappointing the other person or appearing to withdraw from the conversation, it's perfectly reasonable to say, "This conversation is important to me, but would it be okay if we take a pause and get back together in 30 minutes?" You could add, "I'm feeling a bit flustered right now and would just like a moment to gather my thoughts." Or you could instead say, "I have to jump on a call right now, but let's continue as soon as I'm off." Whatever the reason you give, take the time necessary to step away, slow down, and practice self-regulation outside of the heated moment. This is far preferable to not taking a break and allowing your stress response to dictate your behavior.

During a Pause   If you've determined you need a break from the conversation before continuing, good job! That's important. During the pause, to help calm your nervous system, you might try the previous techniques again. Or you can try the following techniques, which are designed more for when you are alone rather than in the midst of an interaction or dialogue.

- **Talk to your brain.** You can literally talk directly to your brain to let it know that it does not have to stay in overdrive and that it can calm down. This is an interesting technique, especially if you're a fan of visualization. Personally, I envision my brain as an engine room with several engineers working on different machines and a foreman to whom I give instructions. He's a friendly, smart, sort of nerdy guy who just wants to be helpful and do the right thing. When I'm feeling escalated and would like to calm down, I close my eyes and envision myself entering the busy, noisy engine room, with the engineers and machinists yelling over loud machines and working together to keep the system running on high. I approach the foreman, who is extremely busy overseeing everyone from an observation and control platform, and start a dialogue that might sound like this:

I say, "Hey buddy, just checking in. It seems like you've got things running a bit high. I don't think we need to be on hyperdrive at the moment."

He seems confused and responds, "Oh, sorry about that, I thought we needed more steam."

"Nope, not right now. But thank you."

"Got it." He nods and turns back to his workers. "Hey guys, let's start powering down. Looks like we don't need to be on overdrive." He turns back to me. "Sorry about that. Got my wires crossed up, I guess." He smiles awkwardly.

I pat him on the shoulder. "No problem, buddy. Thanks for always being there and doing your job. I'll check back in soon." I wait to see and hear the intensity of the machine room slow and quiet down. Once the noise lowers and the machines return to their mundane hum, I head out.

This might seem a bit silly, but try it. Talking to your brain really can work!

- **Objective self-perception.** Imagine being in the corner of the room you're in and staring at yourself from that perspective. Imagine not knowing anything about the person you're staring at other than what you see. Truly visualize this. From this objective perspective, does it seem like that person should feel calm and safe? Without knowing anything about the situation, does anything seem dangerous in the immediate environment? Does a stress response, evolved to defend against survival threats, seem warranted at this moment for the person you're looking at? If not, this objective self-perception can help downregulate the stress response.

- **Satisfy your basic needs.** A violent, physical conflict is a real threat to one's physical and psychological needs and should absolutely be met with a stress response. But since nonviolent, escalated conflict— the majority of our escalated interactions—stems from a *perceived* threat or impediment to our fundamental psychological needs, we can cognitively reframe the situation to help get those needs met and remove the perception of the threat. Additionally, reframing the way the other person likely feels may help lower your defenses and foster compassion. When taking a pause from the conversation, you can close your eyes, breathe, and repeat some of the following affirmations (or come up with your own), whichever resonate. I will only focus on four of the six needs, which I call the *four conflict needs*, as these are the ones most likely to be affected during acute interpersonal conflict.

- **Safety**

  Self-Focused

  "I am safe."

  "I can handle this."

  "I trust myself."

  "I'll be okay."

  Other-Focused

  "They're feeling afraid/unsafe/uncertain."

  "I will help make them feel safe."

- **Affiliation**

  Self-Focused

  "I am lovable and acceptable, just as I am."

  "It is okay to be myself, now and always."

  "I am loved."

  Other-Focused

  "They just want to feel loved and accepted."

  "They feel like they can't be themselves."

  "I will make them feel loved/accepted."

- **Positive Self-Concept**

  Self-Focused

  "I am respected."

  "I am a good person."

  Other-Focused

  "They feel disrespected."

  "They need to know they are good."

  "I will reassure them."

- ■ **Independence**

  Self-Focused

  "I have choice here."

  "I am not trapped. I can make a decision."

  "I am in control of my life."

  Other-Focused

  "They feel they have no choice."

  "They feel trapped and afraid."

  "I will remind them that they also have power and can make decisions for themself."

- ■ **Make a commitment.** A final self-regulation strategy involves creating a rule for yourself and sticking to it. When it comes to escalated responses, I had a pattern: If I perceived a stranger as rude or inconsiderate to me or my loved ones, my reactionary habit was to get aggressive. I would bolster my chest, speak harshly and directly, and sometimes even yell. That's right, at a stranger. Not smart. This was obviously a problem and certainly not serving me or the people around me. So, one day after getting into a yelling match with someone on the street in front of my wife, I decided enough was enough. I created a rule for myself: "When someone is rude or inconsiderate, I am patient and compassionate." I wrote this out and posted it on my office wall above my computer. I read it aloud to myself every day for several weeks, until it became engrained. I committed to it for the sake of not just my own well-being but, especially, for that of my family. This ended up being extremely helpful in regulating my stress response and my behavior. I encourage you to come up with your own rule and commit to it.

Implementing De-escalation

We've gone over some tools to regulate our own nervous systems. Now it's time to regulate someone else's. We're going to use our behavior, namely communication, to affect the inner workings of someone else. Does it sound like sorcery? Well, I have news for you: you do this every day with friends, family, coworkers, strangers, and everyone else with whom you interact. That old psychobabble suggestion that "no one can make you *feel* anything" in response to the notion that someone made you feel angry . . . nonsense.

You make people feel things in every interaction, and they do the same to you. The way we behave and communicate absolutely affects others' nervous systems, including their sensations and emotions. When we do this to effectively help someone calm down, it is called *co-regulation*. We are literally regulating each other's nervous systems.

So, in every moment, you can decide what sort of person you want to be: someone who attempts to dysregulate another's system or to regulate it; someone who makes another person feel aroused in a negative way, aroused in a positive way, or feel safe, calm, and at homeostasis. Sure, we don't make people *do* things as a result of their feelings. The way they behave is up to them—an output of their own ability to self-regulate. But we certainly influence how people *feel*.

That being said, just because we make people feel things doesn't mean we are *responsible* for their feelings. It just means that we should acknowledge that our behavior does have an emotional and neurobiological impact on others. What we do with that knowledge is up to each of us. It also certainly doesn't mean we should alter our ethics or principles in order to not make people feel disappointed or angry. That would be considered codependent. Our job is not to figure out how to make everyone feel good all the time. No, we must do what we believe is right for ourselves or our families regardless of how it makes others feel. But the knowledge that we do affect others' internal states should help us be more deliberate or intentional about the manner, style, and approach we take to each interaction. We might have to give someone hard-to-hear feedback, but we can deliver the feedback intentionally, with respect and grace, to minimize hurt and defensiveness.

Now, we are going to use this natural, sorcerer-like ability in a deliberate, intentional way during escalated conflict to help de-escalate someone's acute stress response. And the way we do it? By paying attention to and trying to meet their basic psychological needs.

Of course, we cannot know what is happening in all aspects of another person's life, including all the complex layers of their subconscious. Heck, most people don't even know that about themselves. But we *can* rely on our understanding that all human beings share a basic set of needs and that when people are escalated, it's because they perceive a threat to those needs.

Hence, a simple assumption we can make in any escalated conflict is that their brains are interpreting a threat. If we hope to de-escalate in order to resolve a conflict, we can use our own brains and behavior to reduce their perception of threat—especially when we (i.e., *you*) are perceived as the source of that threat.

Analyzing which of six different needs may be perceived as threatened in the heat of the moment is, frankly, too heavy a task in most situations. Especially when you don't know the person or their psychology intimately. Instead, during escalated conflict, we're going to go back to the four most common needs affected in interpersonal conflict (i.e., the conflict needs): safety, affiliation, positive self-concept, and independence. In other words, we can assume, without any deeper knowledge of what the individual is going through, that the person is reacting in an escalated fashion because they perceive themselves as unsafe, abandoned/excluded, disrespected, and/ or not in control. So, our de-escalation strategy will be an attempt to directly reduce that perception and get those needs met. And here's how we do it.

Embody Teamship   Teamship is the state and practice of being on someone's team emotionally, psychologically, and behaviorally. Think about what this means. How would you behave toward someone, how would you feel and think about them, if you were truly teammates in this moment? Bring to mind any time you have been on a team with others: the sense that you want them to win along with you; that you'd put yourself out there and risk something of yourself for your teammates, for the good of the team; that as long as you support each other, you can walk away feeling in integrity about your effort, win or lose. That state is teamship, and it is what an escalated person needs from you in their moment of stress, fear, and anger. They need you to be on their team. Win or lose, you're there to meet a challenge and solve the problem *together*.

When you're committed to being on someone's team, you show up to support your partner or colleague's needs, goals, and values. Hence, they are inherently safe, connected, respected, and afforded some control. You would not hurt them; you would not exclude or abandon them; you would not disrespect them; and you would not take away their independence or agency. If you were to do any of those things, it would be because you are in *self-protection* mode, not in *team* mode. When we feel truly supported, our nervous systems relax, we can be ourselves, and we feel safe. This is the product of teamship. The following behaviors aim to communicate teamship, with the goal of downregulating another's stress response.

If you do nothing else but just embody the spirit of teamship, even for just a few moments of an escalated situation, your behavior, thoughts, and feelings will shift in the direction of support.

Use Parallel Positioning   When engaging with someone who is angry or upset, we do not want to seem like their opposition. Remember, we're trying to reduce the perception of threat. Positioning our bodies appropriately can help us nonverbally communicate that we're on their team. So, do not face someone directly chest-to-chest, as this can feel oppositional and challenging. Instead, turn your shoulders and chest, even slightly, so that you are facing the same direction as they are. Facing the same direction is a powerful message of togetherness, where you are both symbolically and physically facing the problem together. You also want to be at the same positional level as they are. Sit if they are sitting; stand if they are standing. If you can get someone to sit next to you, that is often the best position from which to communicate teamship and downregulate a stress response.

Open Your Limbs   When communicating teamship during escalation, we want someone to feel that we are open to hearing them and that we are engaged. Crossing your arms may communicate that you are closed off; so, keep your arms uncrossed. Clenching your fists may communicate that you are angry or aim to intimidate; so, keep your hands open and relaxed. Crossing your legs while sitting in front of someone upset can seem too cavalier or like you are relaxed while they are upset; instead, stay engaged by uncrossing and leaning forward.

Appropriate Touch   This one can be powerful, but be careful. Typically, it's recommended that you know someone and their touch preferences before attempting to touch them, even in a supportive way. Some people, when upset or angry, do not like to be touched, and it may only make them more escalated. If you're not sure, default to *not* touching them. But especially if you know the person well, an appropriate touch when they are upset can help them co-regulate with you. Research shows that appropriate, consensual touch, especially within close or trusted relationships, can have a co-regulatory effect during emotional escalation. A gentle hand on the shoulder or arm may be appropriate. Sometimes, holding someone's hand or a hug can go a long way. Use your discretion on this one. In professional or less familiar contexts, touch should be used with extreme caution, as it can be misinterpreted or unwelcome.

Apologize as Appropriate   Apologizing to someone who is upset and/ or angry can be impactful, but it should be done authentically and correctly. Of course, if you acknowledge that you or the organization you represent made a mistake, you can apologize and take responsibility. Accountability can be important in de-escalation. However, even if you feel you did nothing wrong or the person isn't upset with you directly, you can still use apologetic language for their experience. For example, "I'm so sorry you're going through this." Stay away from apologizing for their feelings, however. "I'm sorry you feel that way" usually sounds condescending and dismissive.

Offer Support, Not Solutions   Supportive or helping language can be incredibly important to communicating teamship. You might say "I'm so sorry you're going through this. How can I help?" or "Is there anything I can do to make this easier for you? I'm also okay just listening." We want them to know we are there for them and willing to support them however we can. In most cases, however, people who are escalated are not ready to solve problems. So, you might offer to help, but do not jump straight to solving their problem or giving advice. In escalated states, people often just need to feel heard and supported.

That being said, if you feel it is appropriate and they are indeed ready for exploring solutions, don't just tell them what to do. Give them agency. Ask them what they think would be a healthy next step. Or you could make a suggestion and ask if that would work. For example, "I suggest we call Amy. I think that would really help. What do you think about that?"

Reassure Their Needs   A final behavior in teamship that's worth highlighting is reassurance. Reassurance lets someone know that we are on their side, we are not a threat, and we want what's best for them. We can reassure someone in several ways, but I suggest getting straight to the individual's psychological needs. What can we say to help address and potentially satisfy those needs? Ideally, after listening to them, it becomes somewhat clear which of the four conflict needs are being affected, and you can reassure those needs directly. When reassuring someone in an escalated state, it helps to use emphatic language—adjectives and adverbs that emphasize and intensify the reassurance. Since they are feeling intensely, it helps to intensify language with words such as *absolutely, completely, totally, truly,* and so forth. Here are some examples of emphatic reassurance for each of the four needs:

- **Safety**
  "I want you to know you're absolutely safe here."
  "I will make sure you have stability."
  "Making a mistake is totally fine."
- **Affiliation**
  "You absolutely belong here."
  "We love having you."
  "I will not leave you."
- **Positive Self-Concept**
  "I respect you greatly."
  "You're an amazing person."
  "You are absolutely right."
- **Independence**
  "You have the option here."
  "It's totally your decision."
  "I'll go with whatever you think is best."

When attempting to de-escalate, do your best at helping someone feel seen, heard, and supported. Whatever you do or say, whether or not you employ the previous tactics, do it as if you're on the person's team. Trust that when you embody teamship, the right words and behaviors will emerge.

Employing team-based de-escalation techniques in the heat of escalated conflict is not easy; it takes skill and patience. Plus, no one is perfect at it, and it doesn't always work—and not because you didn't try your best or do a good job. The truth is not everyone will be ready to receive support from a teammate. Not everyone is willing to calm down. That could be because they may just not be able to emotionally or psychologically register being heard or supported, at least not yet. Whatever happens, try to stay compassionate, remembering that they are escalated and behaving unproductively because they are perceiving a threat and therefore experiencing the pain and discomfort of perceived need depletion. You wouldn't get angry at a rude, agitated patient lying in a hospital bed in pain, would you? Well, an escalated person is experiencing pain just as intensely, in the same brain regions as physical pain, so as long as you can remain self-regulated, give them some grace. Even if de-escalation techniques don't work, and the person isn't able to co-regulate or calm down, give yourself some appreciation for having done your best and showed up as the person you wanted to be.

Moving Forward

We've learned the importance of self-care and self-regulation to reduce the potential for conflict stress. We've also discussed how to de-escalate by communicating teamship, which is meant to help satisfy an individual's four conflict needs. This said, the interesting thing about psychological needs is that their potential satisfiers vary widely and are not as straightforward as the satisfiers of physical needs. Even though human needs are presumably universal, the things that will actually satisfy those needs are specific to each person, group, and culture. This presents a problem and an opportunity. The problem is that we often don't know what support looks like to people we don't know, especially if they're from cultures we aren't familiar with, which makes de-escalation much trickier and potentially less effective.

The opportunity for conflict resolution, though, is that because psychological needs can be satisfied in various ways, we can get creative in our solutions to conflict. If we think outside the box, even outside of what has traditionally worked to satisfy some of these needs, we may find other unique methods of satisfying our own and others' psychological needs. Creative problem-solving and a focus on underlying needs are critical components of conflict resolution and will be addressed in the final principle of this book.

All of this, from de-escalation to creative solution building, takes effort. And there's just about no way to put in this effort if we are not properly motivated to resolve a conflict peacefully. If we think there's no possible positive outcome or solution, or if we simply hate the idea or experience of conflict and confrontation, then our motivation will likely be low and thus our efforts will dwindle. To get motivated, we have to view conflict differently. We have to see it as an opportunity to get creative, to gain clarity, and ideally to grow—for ourselves and for the relationship when applicable. And if we want to change how we view conflict, we'll need a robust understanding of how our brains acquire and wire new information. Get ready for the world of memory and learning.

2 | Learn to Look at Conflict as an Opportunity

"We should look at this as an opportunity." You've probably heard some trope like that before. Sounds great, sure. But come on, is it really possible when it comes to conflict? I mean, opportunities are things we want. How in the world would we *want* to be in conflict?

We may not want conflict. But we need it. We need it to grow, to learn, to really live. I'll prove it. When have you learned your most important lessons? Was it from doing things right or doing things wrong? Think about it. When do people and organizations get the most innovative? Is it when everything is going right? Of course not, it's when something needs to be fixed.

> **NOTE:** *I'm not talking about* escalated *conflict. We don't need that. Escalation limits the opportunities in conflict. That's why we absolutely must de-escalate first. But once we are regulated and ready to problem-solve—what I call being back at* baseline conflict*—it does absolutely present an opportunity.*

Tension. Friction. Opposing forces. This is the energy of life. It's where all creation stems from. From the cellular level to the cosmos. It's also where all destruction comes from. Hence, oppositional energy presents a moment of pure potential, pure possibility, pure opportunity. The opportunity is to escalate and destroy *or* to co-regulate and create. And it's our choice—each of ours—to be destructive or creative with the tension, in every moment and in every interaction.

Our ability to make this choice constructively, however, depends on a couple of important factors. First, it depends on our ability to get out of autopilot and into deliberate decision-making. If we just unconsciously react rather than intentionally respond to conflict, we've likely missed the opportunity. Second, it depends on our view of conflict, both as a general concept and of the particular conflict we're facing. If we see conflict only as negative, uncomfortable, and undesirable, and we simply want to shut it down or run away from it, then again, we've missed the opportunity. Instead, we would need to train ourselves to view conflict as that moment of creative potential. Only then will we be motivated to approach the conflict optimistically rather than approach it aggressively or avoid it altogether. We want to activate our approach mechanisms rather than our avoid response, and we want to approach conflict with curiosity and creative intention.

So, how do we train ourselves to view conflict more optimistically and to be more deliberate about our responses to conflict? How can we not only find the opportunities in conflict but truly *feel* the awe that comes with the creative potential arising from the energy of friction? Can we feel the kind of inspired excitement that a painter gets when viewing a blank canvas or that an avid hiker gets when at the base of a majestic mountain? Yes, we *can* train ourselves to perceive and even feel the experience of conflict this way. In fact, we can pretty much train ourselves to do anything. We just have to understand how our brains learn.

The Memory and Learning Systems

In 2022, I began working with an executive team at a mid-size organization that was experiencing what we in the conflict industry called *conflict avoidance*. This is a common tendency we see in organizations, and in humans in general, that leads people to simply avoid difficult conversations and to essentially withdraw or pretend everything is rosy when there's underlying tension. After meeting with each of the executives privately and hearing some of the issues that they felt were not being discussed, I was a bit confused because it seemed like they all wanted to talk about their challenges and how to address them.

My confusion waned, however, once I met privately with the CEO, Joe, who I quickly discovered was intensely conflict avoidant. I could tell that Joe was deeply invested in being liked and in being perceived as a "nice guy." He was clearly unwilling to have hard conversations, hold people accountable, or confront anyone for fear of being seen as a bully. He was prone to shut down and withdraw during any uncomfortable conversations, and would try to appease others quickly if they confronted him with an issue. Joe's intentions were perhaps rooted in goodness, but the outcomes of his conflict style were quite debilitating and demoralizing for his team. Not only did his conflict avoidance prevent team members from feeling safe enough to express their own perspectives to him but it also prevented Joe from ever receiving feedback from his colleagues—feedback that would have helped him be more successful as a leader. It also often prevented employees, in general, from being held accountable for poor behavior or performance, since accountability conversations can feel uncomfortable.

This dynamic at the top trickled down to the rest of the employees, leading to a hush-hush culture, where people were afraid to speak up for fear they might make their bosses or coworker uncomfortable, lose their favor, and then have their jobs threatened. This kind of culture stifles innovation, hinders growth, and creates an underlying, quiet resentment and frustration. And it certainly was not unique to Joe's team. Conflict avoidance and its downstream effects happen in many organizations as well as in communities and families. That's because those who lead are often not as well trained as they perhaps should be in constructive conflict management and difficult conversations, and because the culture of any human system is heavily influenced by those at the top, such as the CEO, head of household, or anyone perceived to be at the helm of the system. If the one with real or perceived authority indicates that it is not okay to express difficult feelings or topics, then no one will. At least, not out in the open.

Problems in any relationship, be they at work or at home, that go undiscussed for whatever reason tend to fester and grow beneath the surface.

This tension may slowly erode the relational system and possibly explode into escalated conflict. So, to help the organization shift, I had to address the root cause of Joe's avoidance and ideally help him find a way to better manage organizational challenges before they led to more and deeper conflicts.

Over the course of a few weeks, I spent several hours with Joe, getting to know him and building rapport via private coaching sessions. I came to learn about his past, namely his childhood, and it became clear why he was so conflict avoidant. In his childhood home, nothing difficult, sad, scary, or otherwise uncomfortable was ever talked about. If he or his siblings expressed strong feelings about something, especially if it felt like a critique of his parents, his mother would become annoyed and his father would withdraw and go quiet, often leaving the room or focusing on the television or newspaper. In Joe's family, everything and everyone had to be pleasant all the time. So, he learned it was not safe to have conflict. Conflict caused a withdraw of positive attention, love, and acceptance from his primary caregivers.

Those memories became embedded into Joe's psyche, forming the way his brain and nervous system responded to perceptions of interpersonal tension. As an adult, Joe continued the pattern, mostly unconsciously, of always trying to be pleasant. He was unwilling to have hard conversations that might disappoint others or make them feel uncomfortable. Because his brain interpreted conflict as a threat to his needs for safety, affiliation, and positive self-concept, he learned to appease others quickly so as to not make them feel aggravated and withdraw from him.

These traits may sound strange for a CEO, a position typically known for confidence and sometimes arrogance, but I have seen the people-pleasing nice person persona in hundreds of people, including several high-level leaders. In fact, there are all sorts of nuanced perspectives on conflict. Some who perceive it negatively respond with withdrawal or avoidance, like Joe, while others actually seek out conflict and respond aggressively or competitively to get their needs met. We each perceive and respond to conflict based on our individual past experiences of it, and we consciously or unconsciously expect conflict to be experienced similarly in the future. Obviously, a history of stressful conflict leading to avoidance or aggression is not helpful when seeking to resolve conflict effectively. And yet, this comprises most of our experiences and responses to conflict. Rarely have I come across someone who views conflict truly optimistically, with an excitement for how it might lead to more knowledge, understanding, and growth, even though such opportunities exist.

Some people are willing to entertain how rewiring their system so that they could experience and respond to conflict more constructively might benefit their relationships both at home and at work. Though, in my experience, few are willing to do the work necessary to make this systemic shift. It takes effort, persistence, and possibly discomfort to rewire one's system to perceive conflict differently. But for those that do, it opens all sorts of opportunities for the lives of those they affect and for themselves.

Conflict resolution requires optimism—that working through issues constructively will lead to a better relationship, culture, or community. Otherwise, why put in the effort or experience the discomfort that resolution processes often require? To better understand why most of us experience conflict negatively and respond to it unproductively, we ought to be aware of the underlying neurobiological mechanisms driving our perceptions of conflict. With that understanding, we can build more robust and impactful tools for changing our perceptions and, thus, our ability to more effectively resolve conflicts.

Why We Perceive Conflict Negatively

In the early 1900s, Russian physiologist Ivan Pavlov was studying the digestive systems of dogs and stumbled on an intriguing phenomenon by accident. While it was expected for dogs to salivate at the presentation of food, Pavlov noticed they were also salivating in response to things that had nothing to do with food, like footsteps or a lab assistant's coat. The dogs had formed an association between nonfood items and the prediction of food, thus leading to a food-related response (i.e., salivation). Pavlov went on to experiment with this phenomenon, discovering that he could "condition" the dogs to salivate in response to other things, such as tuning forks, buzzers, lights, and even touch. All he had to do was repeatedly pair a nonfood item, like a buzzer, with the presentation of food. After several pairings, the dog's brain would associate the buzzer with food, and voilà! The dog's natural salivatory reflex to food occurred in response to a buzzer, even when food was absent. He called this a *conditioned reflex*, as this association was learned (i.e., not innate or purely biological), whereas the natural salivation response to food was an *unconditioned reflex* (i.e., totally innate and biological).

Later, psychologists would use the *stimulus response* terminology. In Pavlov's example, food was an unconditioned stimulus, and salivation was an unconditioned response, since this stimulus-response relationship was innate and natural. The buzzer was considered to be neutral. However, when salivation came in response to a buzzer, the buzzer became a conditioned stimulus, and salivation became a conditioned response, since this association was learned and not innate.

This stimulus-response conditioning, also called *classical conditioning*, would become the foundation for psychologists, such as John B. Watson in America, to spearhead in the first half of the 20th century a new psychological discipline called *behaviorism*. Behaviorism was focused on how animals' and humans' reflex systems (i.e., their nervous systems) change, learn, and adopt new behaviors through association and conditioning. Behaviorism became the dominant force in the psychological sciences until about the 1950s. At that time, another scientific discipline arose called *social psychology*, which erupted onto the academic scene after the mind-boggling and frightening events of the Holocaust. In some sense, behaviorism lost its dominance in academic psychology, as many cognitive scientists became more interested in studying human conflict and group psychology.

If only social scientists had more carefully integrated the behaviorist insights, including how the nervous system changes through association and conditioning, into social psychology, we might today have a far deeper understanding of how our physiological systems interact with interpersonal and intergroup conflict. It's only since perhaps the turn of the millennium, with the emergence of social and behavioral neuroscience and the advent of more sophisticated neuroimaging instruments, that we have begun to truly study how social conflict affects and is in turn affected by our nervous systems.

To understand how the brain perceives conflict, how this perception affects our behavioral and psychological responses to conflict, and subsequently how we might teach ourselves to view conflict differently, we must start with the basics passed down from the pioneers of behaviorism. We must understand conditioning.

Conditioning: How the Brain Associates Conflict　　As illustrated in Pavlov's experiments, conditioning is a form of learning that involves specifically adopting new responses to stimuli. We have all been conditioned to respond to all sorts of things. In fact, it's reasonable to suggest that almost all our learned behaviors are conditioned. We do, of course, have various innate, unconditioned behavioral responses—like when the doctor hits your knee and your leg rises automatically or a newborn infant's natural ability to cry or pucker their lips for food. But for the most part, just about all of our learned behaviors, especially emotional, social, and habitual responses, are conditioned. Joe didn't avoid conflict because he was born that way. He was conditioned to do so.

Conditioning happens in two general ways: fast and slow. Or to be more technical about it, conditioning happens via one-trial and multi-trial learning. The number of trials refers to the amount of exposure one needs to a stimulus to build a new response. Fast, one-trial learning happens when an experience is highly emotional and physiologically impactful, requiring exposure to the stimulus only once to rewire the brain. This kind of intense emotional learning likely involves activation of the amygdala, which signals emotional salience, and the hippocampus, which encodes contextual memory. This new wiring creates a new predictive model of the stimulus.

Let's say Judy did something that you perceived as a deep betrayal, which was highly impactful, even potentially disorienting, modifying or updating your perception of Judy, your relationship with her, and what her betrayal means about you. Your sympathetic nervous system upregulates, the stress response is activated, and you respond with anger toward her. Then, well, you will likely feel escalated, possibly angry, any time you perceive Judy unless or until this perception gets updated again. The problem is, one-trial learning, occurring from highly impactful events and changing the way our brains and nervous systems are wired, is incredibly difficult to alter. Further, this sort of conditioned response, like your anger toward Judy, becomes even more solidified if the one-trial experience is followed by multi-trial learning (e.g., if there are repeated experiences of betrayal from Judy, including any denial of the initial betrayal), making it increasingly more difficult to rewire and recondition.

Why should our brains have evolved to rewire in such a potentially permanent fashion based on only one experience? Well, because evolution by natural selection generally works via a particular protocol: it's better to be safe than sorry. If an event, person, place, object, or experience affects us deeply, causing psychological disorientation and physiological dysregulation, then the brain says: *Hey, this is really important. We need to remember this in case it ever happens again, so we know what to expect and how to respond in a way that has the best chance of achieving our goals and avoiding danger.* If the impactful experience is positive, like having a moment of pure awe or thrill, our brain remembers it so as to re-create the experience in the future and to watch for opportunities so it does not miss out on future similar experiences. A teen who has an amazing time at her first concert may be drawn to similar concerts for many years after. However, when one-trial learning occurs from a negative experience, like having a moment of sheer terror or rage, the brain can change even more quickly, dramatically, and permanently. If the teen was drugged and robbed at the concert, she may never go to a concert again or possibly avoid crowds and other events similar to concerts. That's because, in line with evolutionary theory, it's apparently much less costly to expect the worst again and it not happen than to *not* expect the worst and it does. Better to be safe than sorry.

The same goes for conflict. Chances are, some of your most emotionally impactful, negative experiences have happened as a result of interpersonal conflict. So, your brain expects the worst from future interpersonal tension, especially with individuals with whom you've previously experienced stressful conflict. The only way to train your brain to see conflict differently, both generally and with particular individuals, is through either highly emotional *positive* experiences with the stimuli (i.e., the person or group) and/or reconditioning via multi-trial learning.

Multi-trial or slow learning comprises most of our conditioning. Since the majority of our everyday experiences are not so deeply emotional or impactful—at least, we should hope not—our brains typically require repeated exposure and practice to form new habits and new conditioned responses. Learning to play baseball, for instance, takes a lot of practice for most people because swinging a bat to hit a fast-flying ball is not an innate behavior; it's a learned behavior that requires repetition and reinforcement. The same goes for Pavlov's dogs: they required repeated pairings (i.e., multiple trials) to learn to salivate when exposed to previously neutral stimuli.

When learning occurs after a neutral stimulus becomes associated with a conditioned stimulus, thus triggering a similar response, as exemplified by pairing food with a buzzer to stimulate salivation, this again is called *classical conditioning*. The baseball player, however, would likely be an example of another form of conditioning called *operant conditioning*. Developed by an incredibly influential behavioral psychologist named B. F. Skinner in the 1930s, operant conditioning occurs when new behaviors or responses are learned through reinforcement (which increases behavior) or punishment (which decreases behavior), based on the consequences of an action. Every time a young baseball player swings and hits more effectively, he presumably receives positive reinforcement, such as better game outcomes, cheering crowds, and coach and teammates' approval. This reinforcement motivates further trials of the behavior and thus more conditioning. To recap: Classical conditioning is stimulus-response pairing; operant conditioning is behavior-consequence association facilitated by reinforcement or punishment.

Certainly, both forms can be applied to how we view conflict. In CEO Joe's case, he was conditioned to experience conflict from both classical and operant frameworks. In a session once, Joe told me that he only ever remembered his parents having argued twice in his life. The first was an intense argument that involved yelling and his mother throwing a pot across the room, hitting the wall and crashing to the ground. He could still recall the sound of the ringing pot hitting the wall, and to this day he has a strong, visceral reaction any time someone drops a pot or pan. The second argument he remembered was also a screaming match, which led to his father leaving the house for several days. The fact that Joe, now in his 60s, could remember these two incidents from early childhood so vividly evidenced their emotional and neural impacts.

No child—or adult, for that matter—enjoys or thrives in a consistently unsafe, unpredictable environment. Such environments lead to a natural fear response (i.e., acute stress response). This stimulus-response relationship is unconditioned; we're wired from birth to be afraid of chaotic, unstable settings. While some people become conditioned to accept or live in such environments, we're surely not innately wired that way. Since two of Joe's first instances of interpersonal conflict (a neutral stimulus) were paired with an unpredictable environment (meaningful stimulus) and distress (response), conflict became a conditioned stimulus and distress became a conditioned response. The fact that it only took one or two instances to condition this was an example of one-trial learning, which makes sense given the emotional impact. He was also conditioned over many repeated instances (i.e., multi-trial learning) to believe that a total lack of confrontation or expression of difficult feelings was associated with a safe, predictable environment, leading to a regulated nervous system. These conditioned responses are examples of classical conditioning.

From an operant conditioning perspective, Joe and his siblings learned that if they stayed quiet or agreeable, they would receive positive attention (reinforcement), whereas if they brought up difficult feelings, their parents would become aggravated or withdrawn (punishment). Of course, all children crave positive attention and adjust their behaviors to avoid emotional and physical withdraw from their primary caregivers. So, Joe learned that conflict led to rejection and abandonment while being "nice" led to acceptance and safety.

To be clear, humans do have a basic psychological need for affiliation or connection, which means we are innately wired to feel distress from abandonment, rejection, or aggression. This is natural and does not require conditioning. Though, we should question why nonviolent, interpersonal conflict, typically manifesting as one person's expression of uncomfortable thoughts or feelings toward another, is perceived as a threat to our basic needs, thus triggering the stress response. And could we perceive it differently? When conflict arises, does it need to be directly associated with rejection, abandonment, attack, or other negatively associated concepts? Not necessarily.

The reason conflict is perceived to associate with these concepts, leading to dysregulation and distress, is that (1) it's a fundamentally logical association that would have to be deliberately recognized and addressed and (2) no one ever taught us how to recognize our negative associations with conflict, why it would be better to change those associations, or how to go about such a task. So, throughout our lives, we've experienced conflict as stressful and unwanted, both via one-trial, emotionally impactful events and multi-trial, ongoing small moments of tension and stress. Our memory is full of these trials, these experiences, thus conditioning our brains to expect the same in the future and inevitably re-creating and reinforcing the negative experiences of conflict. So, if we hope to alter our experience of conflict, we need to change our predictions about it. And that means, we need to create new, more positive memories of conflict.

Memory: Where Conditioning Comes From   Memory is inherent in learning and conditioning. From both a psychological and neurobiological perspective, our brain's memory functionality is generally thought of in three main categories: sensory, short-term, and long-term memories. Sensory memories last only fractions of a second up to few seconds and are generated by incoming sensory information. One example is *iconic memory* from visual stimuli, like when our eyes see a flash of light and then we continue to see that light spot in our vision for a few seconds; another example is *echoic memory* from auditory information, when we hear a sound and it lasts for a second in our minds. The majority of sensory information is filtered out, and we pay no attention to it. Still, it is considered a memory since it takes a second or so for the brain to determine whether it's important enough to pay attention to.

Once the brain determines that particular sensory information is important enough, it converts the memory to short-term memory, which lasts for about 30 seconds. These are memories that are useful in the moment, like remembering how much a bill is so you can calculate a tip. Short-term memory combines with long-term memories (e.g., remembering how to add and subtract) into what is called *working memory*: memories that are being actively used in each moment to complete the task at hand, like calculating and paying the bill. Most short-term memories are quickly discarded, as they typically reinforce our understanding of the world and thus do not add any new or impactful information. Hence, they don't warrant much more attention.

When the brain determines that a short-term memory is worth storing, perhaps because it contains significant new information, important reinforcing information, or impactful experiences, the memory can be converted and stored into long-term memory. As you might infer, conditioning and learning are built on long-term memories. This is where information gets stored for future prediction, rewiring the brain or bolstering its current wiring, so as to continuously predict the world more in line with what it experienced in the past.

Long-term memories are further categorized into *explicit* and *implicit* memories. Implicit memories are mostly learned through experience and are embedded into the unconscious or deep subconscious, rewiring how the nervous system works and enabling us to understand elements of the world without consciously bringing them to mind. They're connected directly to our autonomic processes and play a role in basic motor skills. Riding a bike or driving a car are examples of implicit memories, specifically called *procedural memories.* You don't have to consciously recall exactly how to ride a bike to perform this complex task; your body and brain just know how to do it unconsciously, so much so that you are likely thinking about other things while bicycling.

Explicit memory, however, requires the mind to bring forth into working memory explicit experiences. This can happen automatically, without you thinking about the memories, like when your brain remembers how to do addition so you can add up the bill. And, of course, explicit memories can be engaged more consciously, whenever you deliberately try to remember something, like how much the bill was the last time you were at this restaurant so you can compare the charges. Explicit memories about facts and concepts are called *semantic memories,* whereas those about particular events and experiences are called *episodic memories.*

Our experiences with conflict, especially those that were emotionally salient and highly impactful, create both implicit and explicit memories. On the one hand, these memories become encoded into our neural wiring, conditioning the way we perceive, interpret, and respond to interpersonal tension; this is totally unconscious and thus implicit. On the other hand, such memories also become stored in the subconscious for later explicit retrieval.

After Judy betrayed you, for example, your brain might determine that it's important to recall the betrayal whenever interacting with Judy, so you can predict how she will treat you going forward. And, by the way, an emotionally relevant stimulus doesn't require that it necessarily happened to *you.* Judy might have betrayed a close friend, or you might have simply heard about the betrayal of someone whom you don't even know. The context matters only to the extent that it becomes emotionally and physiologically impactful. Once your brain flags an experience as significant—whether it's your personal experience or one that you only heard about—and your sympathetic nervous system upregulates in response, that experience creates a memory that updates your predictions. These emotionally significant memories are often encoded with the help of the amygdala, which tags them as emotionally important, and the hippocampus, which stores their contextual details, together reinforcing long-term predictions about similar future situations. Until this memory is overridden with new experiences and associations, the betrayal will continue to color the way you see Judy and your relationship with her.

Memories can be viewed as the psychological foundation of *why* we associate certain stimuli with particular responses, while conditioning is mostly dealt with as a behavioral framework for understanding *how* we respond as a result of those associations. As we go through life and experience conflict in all its different forms, we generate memories of these experiences, especially the emotionally charged ones, and thus become conditioned to experience, make predictions about, and respond to conflicts in particular ways.

Our memories both cause conditioned responses and are increasingly reinforced by those responses, thereby contributing to additional, reinforcing memories and thus predictions around conflict. The more Joe predicts he will feel uncomfortable in a conflict, the more he avoids it, which reinforces the memory associating safety with status quo "niceness," leading him to behave in ways that re-create the experienced association of comfort with niceness and discomfort with confrontation. In other words, memories and conditioning compound and reinforce themselves, creating ongoing experiences throughout life that build on and reinforce how we view conflict.

This cycle of: experience → memory → prediction → behavioral response → experience → memory → [repeat] contributes to our *internal working model*. This concept originates in psychologist John Bowlby's attachment theory and describes a system of neural representations formed by past experiences that encode: what to expect from the world (e.g., is it safe or dangerous?), how others typically behave (e.g., trustworthy or threatening?), and who I am (e.g., capable or helpless in conflict?).

Our internal working models, formed by memories of our experiences, illuminate why our brains categorize particular events or stimuli into categories such as good or bad, right or wrong, and so forth. The senses perceive an event (i.e., a stimuli) and send the perceptual information as electrochemical signals to the brain via networks of sensory neurons. The brain encodes and interprets the signals, categorizes them into appropriate categories based on past experiences and associations (part of the internal working model), checks them against predictions generated from memories of similar experiences, and then sends response signals to the rest of the body via motor neurons for the body to respond. This creates a real-time, instantaneous feedback loop whereby the brain senses and predicts, the body responds through behavior, the senses take in the response of our response (i.e., further stimuli), which the brain checks against its initial predictions of the situation, then responds again, and the cycle continues.

The good news is that our brains are quite moldable, or what neuroscientists call *plastic*, and we can override habitual predictions with more accurate ones if we are properly motivated. Numerous studies in social neuroscience and social and evolutionary psychology have shown that even deeply ingrained associations and conditioned responses, such as those related to threat, bias, or stereotype, can be significantly altered through exposure to repeated, contradictory experiences that update the brain's predictions. With enough repetition of a new association—pairing positive experiences and interactions with a previously negatively associated concept or person—people create new experiences, new memories, and thus new perceptions, predictions, and conditioned responses to stimuli. This is the essence of reconditioning or reassociation, since we are teaching the brain to perceive someone or something differently than we were conditioned to do so previously. And all of this, from memories to conditioning to reconditioning, are possible because of a powerful neurobiological mechanism called *neuroplasticity*—the biological foundation of all learning. If we understand the basics of conditioning, memory, and neuroplasticity, we will have a much clearer picture of all levels of learned conflict responses and will, therefore, be better equipped to create effective protocols for changing negative predictions about conflict.

Neuroplasticity: The Neural Underpinnings of Conditioning and Memory   Neuroplasticity refers to the brain's ability to change its structure and function in response to experience, learning, or injury. It is the mechanism by which new neural pathways are formed and existing ones are strengthened or weakened, all of which update cognition and behavior over the lifespan. Our capacity to change how we think, feel, and act lies in the biological reality that the brain can be reshaped. This is the promise and power of neuroplasticity.

Conditioning is the behavioral expression of neuroplastic change. In classical conditioning, when a neutral stimulus (e.g., a buzzer) is repeatedly paired with an unconditioned stimulus (e.g., food), synaptic connections form between sensory neurons (e.g., hearing the buzzer) and motor/autonomic neurons (e.g., salivating). These associations are encoded via Hebbian learning, based on Canadian psychologist Donald Hebb's neuropsychological theory, which is described as synaptic plasticity and often paraphrased as: "Neurons that fire together, wire together."

Hebbian learning describes how repeated co-activation of neurons (e.g., between sensory input and emotional or physiological response) strengthens their connection. This principle is believed to be implemented biologically via a process called *long-term potentiation (LTP)*, which is particularly prominent in brain areas critical for learning and memory, such as the hippocampus, amygdala, and prefrontal cortex. This synaptic strengthening forms the neural basis of learned responses. With his dogs, Pavlov was activating and strengthening synaptic connections between auditory sensory pathways and salivatory reflex circuits. Repeated simultaneous activation of these circuits eventually led to one circuit triggering the other, even in the absence of the original stimulus (i.e., food).

In operant conditioning, when a behavior leads to a reward or punishment, dopaminergic circuits in the basal ganglia and prefrontal cortex update to increase or decrease the likelihood of that behavior. The brain reorganizes to prioritize the avoidance of behaviors that are associated with punishment (i.e., activating pain and/or fear circuitry) and secondarily to enact behaviors that are predicted to cause reward (i.e., activating pleasure and/or comfort circuitry).

Now, here's a fascinating component: the pairing can be bidirectional. There is evidence that once paired, either neural circuit can activate the other. This is referred to as *reciprocal conditioning*, circular causality, or more technically, bidirectional associative learning. Once paired, Pavlov's dogs might mentally anticipate or even "hear" the buzzer any time they salivate. Similarly, after a stress-inducing experience of vertigo, my brain associated dizziness with danger, so any time I felt dizzy, I would feel anxious; reciprocally, any time I felt anxious, I would also feel dizzy. The brain is amazing! Sometimes scary, but certainly amazing.

Another intriguing element of neuroplasticity is the state in which neural wiring starts to change versus when new changes settle into place. Neuroplastic change begins during wakefulness, especially during sympathetic arousal because of the neurochemicals associated with that process. For example, when an experience activates the stress response, causing someone to feel frightened or enraged, like when Joe witnessed his parents arguing or when you discovered that Judy betrayed you, a number of changes happen in the brain: acetylcholine is released, which increases signal-to-noise ratio in the cortex, causing the brain to focus and pay attention to what's happening and simultaneously marking specific synapses for neuroplastic change; norepinephrine is released by the locus coeruleus, enhancing alertness and emotional salience; dopamine is released to signal novelty and stamping in behaviorally relevant experiences; cortisol is released through the HPA axis, flooding the system, which can either strengthen or impair encoding of emotional memories, particularly by modulating amygdala-hippocampal interactions; and glutamate, the main excitatory neurotransmitter that drives LTP, is released, strengthening new synaptic connections. As a result, the brain recognizes that this event is significant and enables temporary changes in synaptic strength, tagging those synapses for later change.

Then, the neural circuit changes consolidate and solidify during upregulation of the parasympathetic system—during deep sleep and nonsleep deep rest. This is when the actual reconfiguration and rewiring of the brain occurs. In this phase, gamma-aminobutyric acid, an inhibitory neurotransmitter, is released, which facilitates deep sleep and helps reduce neural noise; growth hormone is released, particularly during slow-wave sleep, which supports tissue repair and indirectly assists in neural recovery; brain-derived neurotrophic factor is released, supporting synaptic growth, dendritic branching, and neural repair; and thalamocortical rhythms are activated, which help replay and integrate newly encoded experiences into long-term circuits.

So, let's recap how this works. The organism (that's you) has an experience. That experience activates various brain networks that are biologically innate (i.e., unconditioned). For example, we have one natural neural network that activates stress circuitry, another network that activates avoidance behavior, another that encodes memories, and another that senses visual information from the outside world and transmits that data to the brain. These separate networks don't necessarily fire together. But when you *see* an animal with fangs that scares you, activating the stress circuit, and a behavioral response to avoid the animal relieves the fear and downregulates the stress response, the brain has created the potentiation for co-wiring these networks. Your high-alert state modified synaptic strength temporarily, which may then become more permanent during deep rest.

Going forward, the network associated with fear is now co-wired and co-activated with the network that remembers the fanged animal, immediately activating the network for avoidance. All three networks have now become associated: perception of the animal, stress, and avoidant behavior. This neural wiring is the basis for a new internal working model, all based on your brain's prediction of the animal's behavior and how your own behavior should be directed in response.

When neural signal strength is high enough—that is, when the neuron-to-neuron electrochemical charge is intense enough across synapses throughout the neural circuit—leading to hyperarousal, the potentiation for one-trial learning is heightened. This is true for experiences that activate fear and pain networks. But remember, sympathetic arousal is not only a result of fear and pain. Heightened alertness and hyperarousal are also stimulated by intensely pleasurable or awe-inspiring experiences. So, either valence can change how the brain wires and subsequently how we perceive and experience the world and ourselves within it.

When it comes to upregulation toward the stress response, however, something marvelously neurotic tends to occur. Our brains and bodies do not just predict or respond to dangers perceived outside of the body; they also become the source of perceived danger. Our brains actually respond with stress to its own stress response, as if to say, "Uh oh, I'm stressed out. That must mean we're in danger. Activate more stress!" Our brain's perception of our own internal state is again called *interoception*, and this neural loop (i.e., stress response in reaction to an internal state of stress) amplifies or compounds the stress response and perpetuates the entire association between threat and stimulus. Interoception involves brain regions like the insula and anterior cingulate cortex, and this stress amplification loop is often referred to as *anxiety sensitivity*. In order to change this, we'd need to both calm the body and get the brain to reinterpret interoceptive signals from the body so as to make them less threatening.

So, if we take our schematic (experience → co-wiring → memory → prediction → stress response → amplified stress response → behavioral response → experience → [repeat]) and apply it to a conflict, the brain's process might look like this:

1. **Experience.** Difficult conversation with Helen.
2. **Co-wiring.** Stress network activated + facial recognition of Helen activated.
3. **Memory.** Helen is remembered as stressful.
4. **Prediction.** Helen will be stressful in the future.
5. **Stress response.** Stress chemicals released; body feels it.
6. **Amplified stress response.** The body is reacting. I must be in danger.
7. **Behavior.** Better to avoid conversations with Helen.
8. **Experience.** Helen confronts me about avoidance.
9. *[Repeat and possibly reinforce wiring, memory, and prediction.]*

You can see how an initial conflict that causes stress and that is not effectively processed and resolved at both an interpersonal and neurobiological level can create an ongoing or chronic conflict loop. Our memory, prediction, and behavior continue in a cycle that reinforces itself. This occurs not just with particular conflicts but with the experience or concept of conflict in general. The more often we experience conflict as negative, the more our brains are wired to predict all conflict will be negative in the future.

For those neuroscience buffs out there, I will stipulate that this is an incredibly simplified overview of how neural activity, memory, and conditioning work. There are many complex networks interacting in all sorts of ways, and many more nuanced layers of neurochemical activity at the cellular and molecular levels. But for purposes of this material, this high-level illustration will get us where we need to go. At least, that's my intention.

So, if we are properly motivated, how might we change the way we are wired? Before we answer that, I think the final question ought to be, how do we get motivated to do so? Obviously, rewiring will take some effort, maybe even discomfort. So, why exactly would we want to go to the trouble of rewiring our neural circuitry and changing our perception of conflict? Let's briefly discuss the benefits of perceiving conflict as an opportunity, and then we'll go over practical tools to rewire our brains toward a more optimistic view of conflict.

Benefits of Perceiving Conflict as an Opportunity

In general, optimism about the outcomes of any endeavor—whether it's a business opportunity or a conversation—makes success more likely. That's probably obvious, and I'm sure we all have anecdotal evidence to prove such a hypothesis. Nonetheless, plenty of scientists thought it important to support such an idea with data; indeed, there's a whole lot of research to back it up. Across a variety of tasks and contexts, reasonable optimism (as opposed to unrealistic optimism or overconfidence), when compared with the absence of optimism or pessimism, has been shown to enhance goal pursuit and persistence; predict business and entrepreneurial success; improve interpersonal outcomes, including in conversations and negotiations; improve creative problem-solving and adaptability; and protect against stress and burnout, which enhances long-term performance and well-being.

These findings align with a body of research in positive psychology. For example, Martin Seligman's work on learned optimism shows that cultivating optimistic explanatory styles improves resilience and well-being. Barbara Fredrickson's broaden-and-build theory further demonstrates that positive emotions, such as hope and curiosity, expand our cognitive and social resources, making us more adaptable in conflict and better able to generate creative solutions.

From a neurobiological perspective, optimism activates dopaminergic pathways, particularly in the mesolimbic system, including the ventral tegmental area and nucleus accumbens, which are associated with motivation, reward anticipation, and goal-directed behavior. When we expect positive outcomes, dopamine release increases, which leads to numerous benefits: we become more likely to approach the situation rather than avoid it; we're more open-minded; and, as can be expected, we're more driven and persistent. Positive expectations also reduce amygdala reactivity. Remember that the amygdala is our salience and valence system, helping to tag experiences as emotionally significant. Reducing amygdala reactivity typically reduces emotional arousal and dampens threat perception, thereby lowering stress responses. This shift also allows for greater prefrontal cortex engagement, which further supports emotional regulation and social interaction.

So, what does this mean for conflict resolution processes? Well, you might be able to surmise that all of the aforementioned benefits of optimism (e.g., willingness to approach, open-mindedness, persistence, decreased threat perception, greater emotional regulation, and heightened capacity for social interaction) help people in conflict find mutually acceptable solutions more easily. That would make sense. So, does research support the use of optimism in conflict as well? Absolutely.

Studies have shown that when conflicting parties expect a positive outcome from negotiation or conflict resolution processes, they are more likely to engage in open dialogue and exhibit empathy. Those who approach conflict with an expectation of growth and positive change are also more likely to collaborate and communicate effectively. Research also suggests that optimism, positive framing, and belief in mutual gain increase the likelihood of negotiation success, even in entrenched or violent conflicts. In organizational settings, team cultures that frame conflict as an opportunity tend to foster continuous learning and adaptive systems, ultimately enhancing both individual and collective performance.

To test this yourself, simply imagine a world wherein you feel more positive about the particular conflicts you're currently witnessing or experiencing. Think of a specific conflict. Go ahead, stop reading for a moment, and bring the conflict to mind.

Now imagine, just for a moment, that you became excited when thinking about it. And not excited in an "I'm excited to beat them" sort of way; but rather, excited in an "I think this is going lead to a better world" sort of way. Would you be more inclined to approach the situation in a productive manner?

I realize this visualization might be a large ask. Regarding any ongoing conflict, whether it's with a family member, friend, or coworker, or even one of the many larger intergroup or social conflicts we hear about and see images of every day, how could we possibly see these as beneficial? How could we see these as anything other than stressful, uncomfortable, and possibly tragic situations that we just want to eliminate as soon as possible? The answers lie in our brain's predictive plasticity and our ability to learn and recondition—techniques for which we will discuss in our "Tools to Perceive Conflict as an Opportunity" section.

Getting stuck in ongoing cycles of conflict, including cynical perceptions and pessimistic predictions of others, is quite common. Behaviors to eliminate conflict as quickly as possible, such as those associated with conflict avoidance or aggression, are also normal. But our goal, if we're looking for healthier relationships and ultimately less stress, is to resolve conflicts more constructively. Getting to this goal is all the more difficult if we do not believe there is any possibility for a positive outcome—for ourselves, others involved, or the world.

Based on everything we know about the benefits of optimism, including for conflicts, do your best, just for a few moments, to put aside your memories, judgments, and predictions about the conflict you brought to mind earlier. And imagine feeling confident that this conflict, if managed properly, will truly lead to several beneficial outcomes. For example, addressing the conflict effectively could result in greater understanding of all the people involved, more clarity about the relationship(s) and what to expect moving forward, everyone getting their needs met in ways they have not before, deeper knowledge about relationships and the world in general, and any other benefits you can imagine. If you suspend your historic experiences and simply choose to feel confident and optimistic about resolving the conflict productively, would you be more motivated to address the conflict proactively than you have been in the past? Would you feel less stress and anxiety about the prospect of addressing it?

I hope your answers are yes. If not, you may be a bit too stuck in your memories and habitual predictions (don't worry, we can work on that). But if you do see the benefit of believing that positive things can come of this situation if approached constructively, then it's time to discuss how exactly we might shift our memories and predictions of conflict, including the underlying neural wiring that generates them, toward a more optimistic outcome.

Recap: The Memory and Learning Systems

Recall the bidirectional (i.e., top-down and bottom-up) structure of brain functionality. From our neocortical and limbic regions (top), our brains make predictions about what the body will experience and what resources it will need in each moment. These predictions are founded on long-term memories of past similar experiences and interpretations. Simultaneously, our sensory neurons (bottom) are transmitting sense data to our brains that are checked against the predictions. This information may or may not override the predictions.

Experiences encoded as memories and subsequently used for predictive processing drive regulatory functions, including autonomic processes such as up- or downregulation of our sympathetic system. When sympathetic arousal, including the stress response, is paired with an experience, our brain may wire together previously non-associated neural networks.

Many of us have had experiences with conflict that lead to pessimistic predictions, which drive upregulation of the sympathetic system, namely the stress response. Through one-trial learning, this alone can condition a stress response to conflict. And when we experience chronic escalation from a conflicting stimulus, such as a person or concept, we can become dysregulated and compound the negative association. The more stress we experience repetitively with conflict, the more stress we're likely to feel in the future, and the more avoidant or aggressive we'll likely become when faced with the stimulus.

So, how do we interrupt the pattern and change these predictions of conflict from negative, cynical associations to more positive, optimistic associations with creative potential and opportunity? We need to interrupt the long-term memories being pulled into working memory during conflict, and the way we do that is through experience. Indeed, we can direct our own experiences of the world, even though it may often feel like we are at the mercy of the powers that be. In fact, we have more control over our experiences than we might realize. Yes, there is plenty we cannot control. But our choices in how we behave, think, and regulate ourselves can change our experiences of the world, including in response to all the elements outside of our control. We can direct our own conditioning. We can be our own Pavlov's dog. We just need a few tools.

Tools to Perceive Conflict as an Opportunity

Before an object becomes a conditioned stimulus, it is considered a neutral stimulus. For example, the buzzer in Pavlov's experiments was a neutral stimulus, relative to the salivatory response, prior to being paired with food. It was considered neutral because it did not naturally induce a salivatory response. My suggestion is that while threats of rejection, abandonment, or aggression are natural, meaningful stimuli to an acute stress response, interpersonal conflict should be thought of as a neutral stimulus. It was only the pairing of conflict with these perceived threats that created the relationship with a stress response. If this is so, we can learn to change this stimulus-response relationship.

In order to *decondition* a conditioned response, driven by modifying the neural circuits and networks that are wired together, we essentially want to bring a stimulus back to neutral. For our purposes, we would teach our brains to experience conflict without a stress response. Ideally, the neural networks perceiving conflict would no longer activate the neural networks associated with threat perception and distress. Or, at the least, we would quickly become aware of this association and be able to downregulate our stress response. This type of deconditioning might also be referred to in the psychological literature as *extinction*, and it's a critical step on the road to changing our appraisals and predictions of conflict.

While extinction weakens the conditioned response, it doesn't erase the original memory. An important memory sticks around. So, the real trick to changing our experience of a particular stimulus is in *reconditioning*, which is composed of various processes such as reconsolidation, reassociation, and reintegration. Reconditioning does not simply involve taking a stimulus back to neutral so that it no longer activates a particular response; it also involves creating a brand-new association and response. Reconditioning allows for editing of the original memory's effect.

At the very least, it is likely beneficial for our brains not to activate stress circuitry in response to perceived conflict and thus for us not to respond aggressively or withdraw avoidantly. However, even more productive would be to wire the networks perceiving conflict with the networks associated with engagement, interest, curiosity, and optimism. This way, we'd be more likely to approach the conflict with opportunity in mind—an opportunity to learn, grow, understand, and create. This type of rewiring activates our sympathetic system but toward the positive or engaged spectrum of arousal, which activates the dopaminergic system, increasing motivation and approach behavior.

Reconditioning

Let's employ a protocol to help decondition or neutralize the stimulus, and then to recondition and reassociate conflict. This protocol generally aligns with memory reconsolidation theory, conditioning theories, and associative learning, which yield well-established protocols for changing our experience of memories and subsequently modifying our predictions and responses. You can run this protocol with a particular conflict you're experiencing or witnessing. But for now, we'll start with how you hold the idea of conflict in general.

Step 1: Activation and Awareness   How do you generally feel about conflict as a concept? Do you want to get away from it? Would you rather avoid it? Do you love the drama of it, and want to spark more of it? Do you have particular stories, feelings, and sensations when you think of interpersonal or group-level tension? If you're interested in changing your associated thoughts, feelings, and sensations about conflict, possibly even feeling excited, fascinated, or opportunistic about it, there is a method. The method starts with activating and becoming aware of your associations. Let's do some reflection and writing. Please grab a piece of paper and pen or pencil.

First, I'd like you to write down some stories you have about conflict in general. These are your cognitive appraisals. Common stories sound like the following:

- "I don't like conflict."
- "Conflict is painful and uncomfortable."
- "I'd rather avoid conflict."
- "Nothing good can come of this tension."
- "One of us will lose."
- "I'll be abandoned/rejected/excluded."
- "This will lead to loss."

Please write your own. And be honest with yourself. No one will see this.

Next, write down the feelings you have when thinking about conflict. These are your emotional outputs that may be driving or resulting from your cognitive appraisals. Feelings people commonly report include these:

- Uncomfortable
- Frustrated
- Angry
- Stressed
- Helpless

- Stuck
- Avoidant
- Defeated

Write down your own.

Finally, write down the physical sensations you experience when thinking about conflict. You might write things like the following:

- Chest feels tight
- Hard to breathe
- Sweaty
- Shaky
- Hot/cold
- Bloated
- Headache
- Back pain
- Numb

Write down your sensations.

Now, read back through your thoughts, emotions, and sensations. Study them. Get to know them well. Become acutely aware of them. Practicing self-awareness is like putting your brain through a new type of school, teaching it to catch your habitual neural patterns. Self-awareness on activation is the first critical step in interrupting our habitual patterns so that we know *when* to insert a reconditioning protocol. The next time you're aware of these feelings and sensations as a consequence of conflict, you'll know the conditioned associations between neural networks have been activated.

Step 2: Metacognitive Separation   Now, it's time to separate the experiences you are aware of from the stimuli to which they are attributed. Most of the time, we attribute our thoughts, feelings, sensations, and even behavior to events, people, and situations outside of ourselves. The truth is that none of our experiences are based on anything that is necessarily real or true about the world. They are produced purely in our brains and felt in our nervous systems. In this sense, we don't actually experience the world directly; we don't experience some *reality* as it truly is. We experience our brains and nervous systems. More precisely, our experiences are products of our brains' predictive processing, which is based on implicit and explicit memories, which are driven by neural wiring that occurred as a result of past experiences. Our predictions are checked against sensory information, but that sensory information is filtered through all sorts of mental heuristics or biases, so even the information we are sensing is colored in unique ways based on our individual internal working models.

Recognizing this is part of a process I call *metacognitive separation*. *Metacognition* is the ability to think about our own thoughts. As far as we know, human beings are the only animals that can achieve such a complex cognitive task. And *separation* refers to the ability to separate the subject of our thoughts from the process of thinking. In creating a new experience of the world, including conflicts, it can be important to separate our experiences and responses from their habitually attributed stimuli. This might be as simple as repeating a mantra to yourself whenever exposed to the stimuli, such as "What I'm feeling is not because of what's happening outside of me. My feelings and experience are coming from my brain."

If we want to change our current experience of conflict, we can change circumstances outside of ourselves, certainly. Sometimes, modifying or dissolving a relationship or situation does the trick. But we're still left with our brains; and trust me, there will be conflicts in the future somewhere. To alter our experience of conflict in general, we need to deliberately and metacognitively change our understanding and experiences, which modifies neural wiring, which stores new memories, which creates new predictions and ultimately generates new experiences.

Our next step, then, is going to build on activation and separation and integrate the tools we learned in Principle 1 about self-regulation. We are going to pair self-regulation with the stimulus (i.e., conflict). Ready for some fun? Take a deep breath, and let's get started.

Step 3: Reconsolidation   Once we're aware of our general patterned responses to conflict and we've gotten a bit of separation from them by recognizing where these patterns are generated (i.e., in our brains), it's time to interrupt the patterns. We're going to try our best to get the neural circuits associated with a stress response to stop firing so intensely when exposed to conflict. In the study of memory, this has been called *reconsolidation*: activation of a past emotional memory or conditioned response is reactivated (e.g., fear of conflict), a mismatch or prediction error occurs (i.e., something happens that contradicts the expected outcome), the brain flags the memory as changeable and thus ready to be updated. This is the open window where the original learning becomes editable. And the method we're going to use is called *exposure with self-regulation.*

Here's what I want you to do: Find a podcast, YouTube host, or news anchor that typically sets you off. Someone that really frustrates, angers, or scares you because of the perspectives they take, the guests they feature, and/ or their strong opinions. For now, you might start with someone who isn't extremely emotionally triggering for you. Perhaps start with a mild stimulus and work your way up to a more intense one later. Don't turn it on yet. Just find the channel.

Currently, this podcaster or news anchor, or their ideas, is the conditioned stimulus. And your conditioned response is to react with anger, fear, disgust, and/or some otherwise escalated reaction. We all typically feel justified in whom we dislike or refuse to listen to. That's okay. The following is only an experiment for purposes of reconditioning, a technique that you can then use as you see fit.

First, we're going to practice activation with awareness during exposure. Go ahead, press play and really listen/watch until you feel a deep sense of aggravation. It may only take 30 seconds. Once you feel it, stop.

Let's do a bit more writing now. Write down:

- The thoughts going through your head when exposed to this stimulus
- How you feel emotionally
- The sensations you experience
- The behavior you are inclined to take (Are you wanting to turn it off? To turn something else on instead, maybe a channel you agree with? Maybe yell at the screen?)
- Any secondary thoughts you have about this entire exercise, such as any justification for your conditioned responses (e.g., "Yeah, but I *should* feel this way about this host/channel.")

Now, we're going to hit play again, but this time, I want you to metacognitively separate. As you experience your thoughts, feelings, and sensations, repeat a mantra to yourself: *What I'm feeling is not about what I'm hearing. My experience is coming from my brain, including its memories and its predictions.* During the exposure, repeat it as often as you need. Play the program for at least 60 seconds. Allow yourself to experience all your thoughts and feelings—do not suppress them. Simply, experience them while reminding yourself where they come from. Okay, hit play!

How was that round? While attempting this, your brain might come up with stories that resist the protocol. Stories like *But he really is dangerous*, or *We can't let them get away with that*. I'm not here to tell you whether you are right or your stories are true. I'm simply reminding you that all your thoughts, feelings, and experiences are produced in one place: your brain (i.e., your neural networks). And if you have a sense that these stories are no longer serving you or leading to anything productive, and you'd like to find a better way of addressing the conflict, then it's worth changing your experience so you can respond differently.

Now it's time to reconsolidate via a pattern interruption or prediction error: a mismatch between what your brain expects it needs to respond to the stimulus and the response you consciously induce. When you hit play on the next round, I want you to continue repeating the separation mantra while practicing self-regulation. Take slow, deep breaths; relax your shoulders and facial muscles on each exhale; become acutely aware of tension in your body and consciously relax those areas.

We are now taking both a psychological and physiological approach to self-regulation, since distress involves both mental and biological processes. Another cognitive element that is important in reconsolidation is the sense of agency or control over the stimulus. In this case, since you are the one turning on and off the stimulus, you're already practicing with agency. In real-world situations, you can remind yourself that you are in control of being around the other person, you can make the choice to leave at any time, and you can choose exactly how to respond in each situation. Putting yourself back in the driver's seat, discarding any notion of being trapped, is extremely useful in downregulating a stress response.

Additionally, you may add another mantra or two that (1) directly contradicts the initial stories you wrote down and (2) helps to satisfy a basic psychological need. For example, if one of the thoughts you wrote down was "He's dangerous," then you know your basic need for safety is being perceived as threatened. So, your new mantra during self-regulation would be something like: "I am safe right here, right now." Because it's true! No one is physically threatening you right here and now. You may project some imagined threat happening in the future or some incident happening to other people somewhere else in the world, but I want you to focus solely on the here and now—no predictions or projections of the future or elsewhere. Create a mantra or two for yourself. Make them simple, so you can easily recite them.

When you're ready, hit play again, and try to stay with it for five minutes or until you become unbearably uncomfortable, whichever comes first. Remember your mantras, and remember your self-regulation techniques. Okay, go!

How was that round? Were you able to calm your mind and body during the exposure? Were you able to create a new type of experience in the presence of the conditioned stimulus? If you keep doing this over and over, there is a good chance that you will decondition and reconsolidate the stimulus-response relationship—that you would no longer experience or respond to this particular host or channel in the same way . . . if that's something you're interested in. It's not that you should suddenly agree with the host's perspectives or that you no longer care about their message. Rather, it's that while recognizing that the perspective or information is still conflicting with your own, it does not stimulate or activate your stress response, at least not to the same extent. This way, you can approach the conflict more constructively and strategically rather than in an emotionally escalated state.

Before moving on, I would recommend practicing this reconsolidation protocol repetitively until you are able to feel calmer when exposing yourself to stimuli that would typically escalate you. This is part of a process called *habituation*, which involves diminishing behavioral responses to repeated nonmeaningful exposure to a stimulus. Neurobiologically, habituation is linked to reduced synaptic strength in circuits that process the repeated stimulus. Fewer neurotransmitters are released, and the postsynaptic response decreases.

Once you've completed this process enough times and you feel that your acute stress response is dampening when exposed to the stimulus, or you are at least able to stay aware of your response and separate it consciously from the stimuli, we can attempt the next step.

Step 4: Reassociation   Once a mismatch occurs and the prediction error message is flashing in your brain, your neural circuits should be in a more malleable state, ready for neuroplastic modification. This may not happen after one trial, but repetitive trials on a consistent basis will make your brain and its responses increasingly more changeable when exposed to the stimuli. In this malleable state, we will introduce a new pairing to update the association of neural networks, replacing or overwriting the old one.

Using principles of classical conditioning to reassociate the stimulus, we are going to pair the previously conditioned, now mostly neutralized stimulus with a different stimulus that is associated with a more positive, engaged response. Please think of a physical activity that you regularly pair with sensory information (e.g., auditory, olfactory, visual) that makes you feel super engaged and present. Remember, neuroplasticity first occurs during aroused states, so we do not want an activity that makes you feel too relaxed or sleepy. Also, the activity should be something that does not require much cognitive load or thinking (e.g., reading, working, or problem-solving), as we are about to fill that space up. If your activity involves music, it's best to find music without lyrics. Some examples of applicable stimuli include the following:

- Dancing to electronic music
- Cooking to classical music, while sipping on tasty wine
- Working out to hip hop in a different language
- Playing guitar
- Walking on the beach during sunrise, listening to cinematic music
- Walking on a nature path and listening to the forest

Think of something visceral to engage your body and senses. Got it?

In a few moments, you are going to start your activity. When you're in it, I want you to practice present moment awareness and hyperarousal. Really feel your body and movement. Really listen to the sounds, taste the flavors, smell the aromas, or take in the scenery. While feeling and sensing, notice how alive you feel, how present you are, how excited you become. Consciously upregulate your sympathetic system so you feel a sense of thrill and ultra pleasure. In this moment, there is no past or future, no memories or predictions. Be totally free from expectations. Just live in this moment.

Once you feel it for a minute or two, then we're going to start our reassociation protocol. Introduce the conditioned stimulus—the podcast/news host. I know, I'm killing the vibe. But, you should not be attempting reassociation until you've at least mostly neutralized the stimulus through reconsolidation. That is, you've been able to downregulate your sympathetic response and stay mostly calm while listening to the host. We don't want to ruin or negatively associate your intensely pleasurable activity. On the contrary, we want to enliven and positively associate the habitually uncomfortable stimulus. And although it's theoretically possible, reconditioning a stimulus that has not first been set back to neutral proves to be quite difficult.

Now you're experiencing your engaging activity and simultaneously being exposed to sensory information you've historically disliked. Continue your activity, don't stop. But really listen now to what the host is saying. This is not an attempt to get you to like the host or to adopt or agree with their ideas. Rather, it's an attempt to get you to find excitement and aliveness in the presence of perceived or felt conflict. So, it's not only okay but *preferable* that you continue to find this host's perspective conflicting. That's what we're going for here!

Let the host's words and ideas seep in. We'll now reappraise the experience of hearing challenging information and a conflicting perspective. You choose the right words that work for you, but they should sound something like these:

- "I sense tension. Yes! Let's get into it."
- "Ooh, a different perspective. I love hearing new things."
- "What a fantastic opportunity to recognize differences."
- "Ah, this is the perfect time to practice empathy."
- "This conflict is a tremendous opportunity, even if I don't yet see it."
- "This tension is the start of greater clarity."

Whatever words you choose, they should help you feel engaged, interested, excited, and wanting to hear more. They should not, of course, be sarcastic, vindicative, condescending, or manipulative. To believe your new perspective about such historically jarring information, two elements are important: confidence and humility. The confidence that you can handle being faced with a conflicting perspective and the humility that you are willing to stay open to others' feelings, thoughts, and nervous systems without immediate judgment or condemnation. Stay confident and humble, and you will be able to engage optimism and excitement in the presence of a conflicting persona.

Don't just go through the motions of this exercise. Reassociation—rewiring neural circuits that have not previously fired together much if at all—will only work if you really feel engaged and believe what you're saying. And it will likely only work after multiple trials and repeated pairings. So, if you want to experience conflict with more excitement and curiosity, do this exercise multiple times with a targeted stimulus. Then, make sure to get some good rest that night, as neuroplastic change solidifies during deep rest and sleep.

I realize this may be a different, possibly uncomfortable method of interacting with information or perspectives that you've previously experienced as a threat. But true change and growth only happens through challenge, disruption, and discomfort. Changing your brain is just like changing your body. These are psychophysiological exercises. Just as you need to repetitively challenge or push your body in the gym to strengthen and grow muscle, your brain requires repetition, challenge, and discomfort to strengthen new neural connections. These exercises should feel like effort, just like the work you do at the gym, and you will only see the benefits if you're persistent and consistent.

Over multiple trials, this new experience of the conditioned stimulus will contradict old predictive processes and modify your neural wiring, updating your memory of the conflict and creating new predictive models for this stimulus. As a recap, we're using neuroplasticity to first neutralize the conditioned stimulus and then to reassociate it. Fun, right? Let's have some real fun and update our entire internal working model, including our self-concept.

Step 5: Reintegration   After a new association is formed, the brain and body need to reorganize. What does it mean to respond to conflict this way? Who are you relative to this habitual conflict experience and response? Once you reassociate and teach yourself to respond differently to a conflict, the new response becomes part of your autobiographical narrative, which is a central element of your internal working model. So, if you were to approach conflict with the thrill of growth and learning, what might your updated narrative or core belief sound like? Here are a few examples:

- "I'm safe in the face of opposing views."
- "I can handle conflict."
- "Conflict brings opportunity."
- "I'm going to learn a lot from conflict."

In parallel to this updated model, your nervous system relaxes its hypervigilance for conflict, helping you feel less anxious/angry/frustrated and more opportunistic/optimistic when conflict occurs. Your new experience creates new memories, which create new predictions and more new experiences, ultimately creating a new version of you. This is the final synthesis where reconditioning moves from a neural modification to a new experience of self. You're not just creating a new response to conflict but also a new experience of being *you* in the world.

Once we start changing the neural pathways to downregulate our escalated responses to conflict and instead feel more optimistic, curious, and approach inclined, we're ready to practice with people in our lives. If there is someone in your life around whom you regularly feel distress, discomfort, anger, frustration, or disgust, and you'd like to change this dynamic into an opportunity, then let's apply this protocol. The following outline is how it might look with a conflict counterpart we'll call Ralph. I encourage you to fill in the sections for your own scenario, with your Ralph.

Practice Example

Step 1: Activation and Awareness

- ➤ Think about Ralph.
- ➤ What thoughts come to mind?
  - "He seems to single me out at work. He doesn't acknowledge me. He doesn't like me. He's rude and vindictive. I want to expose him."

- ➤ What feelings?
  - ■ Anger. Hurt. Sadness. Jealousy. Rage.
- ➤ What sensations in my body?
  - ■ Heart racing. Shoulders raised. Jaw clenched.
- ➤ What am I inclined to do when I see him?
  - ■ Avoid him. Get away!
- ➤ Write these down, and remember them the next time I see him.

Step 2: Metacognitive Separation

- ➤ "I realize all my experiences, including my thoughts, feelings, sensations, and behavior, are generated in my brain."
- ➤ "It might feel like I'm reacting to Ralph, but really my brain is responding to a prediction based on a memory about the way I experienced situations that I associated with Ralph."

Step 3: Reconsolidation

- ➤ Think about Ralph again. Let's see if I can calm my mind and body.
  - ■ Breathe, relax, keep thinking about Ralph as I do so.
  - ■ Notice my heart rate slow down. Lower my shoulders. Relax my face.
- ➤ Keep thinking about Ralph. Remind myself:
  - ■ "I am safe."
  - ■ "I am valuable."
  - ■ "I am acceptable just the way I am."
  - ■ "I'm not sure what others are thinking."
  - ■ "Other people don't determine my worth."
- ➤ Repeat this practice every day for two weeks.
- ➤ Every time I am around Ralph, repeat this practice. Keep practicing with each exposure to the stimulus.
- ➤ Behave differently. Approach him and say hello. Ask him how his weekend was.
  - ■ Create a new experience with Ralph.
  - ■ Complete this step, practicing daily for at least two weeks, before moving on.

Step 4: Reassociation

➤ Put on some good music. Prepare a meal. Get present. Feel the aliveness of this moment. Enjoy the ritual. Take in the aromas.
  - Now, think of Ralph. Stay present. Enjoy the moment. Think of Ralph.
  - Repeat several times.
➤ Keep thinking about Ralph. Update the narrative. Come up with a mantra, similar to the following:
  - "I wonder what Ralph's life is like. I hope he's happy."
  - "The tension I feel is a fantastic opportunity to look within myself. Why does it bother me so much? Who does Ralph remind me of from my past? What do I still need to process or work through in myself?"
  - "Ralph is a great teacher for me. He's teaching me my triggers and helping me recognize where I still need healing."
  - "I'm going to have a better relationship with Ralph. If I can do that, it will show me something about my resilience, wisdom, and ability to evolve."
  - "Ralph's not doing anything *to* me. He's doing everything *for* me."
  - "I love learning about myself through the relationships I have."
➤ Repeat and practice these narratives while staying present. Every time I think of Ralph. Every time I'm around him.

Step 5: Reintegration

Recite a new self-concept story repetitively. Become a new version of me: a me who expects conflict to be fruitful. Examples of a new story:

➤ "I am a person who grows through conflict."
➤ "I am someone who welcomes challenging situations. It's the only way to learn and evolve."
➤ "I appreciate all of my teachers, especially the ones who challenge me the most."
➤ "Without my teachers, I wouldn't be the amazing person I am."

Practice, practice, practice. Repeat, repeat, repeat.

Moving Forward

Conflict always presents an opportunity for growth. I have learned some of the greatest lessons of my life by working through nervous system activity, understanding that when I am extremely anxious or my dizziness symptoms return, it's because my nervous system is ramped up. And that only happens when a conflict exists internally that I have not yet fully processed or worked through. I'm not perfect. I can spiral, just like anyone can. But I've found that when I have taken the time to interrupt the pattern and focus on learning and growing through difficult experiences, it has led to profound moments that change the way I show up for others and the way I think about myself in the world from that point forward.

My challenge to you (and to me) is to be grateful for all the opportunities that conflict brings. There are simply no greater teachers in our lives than those who challenge us and push us outside our comfort zones. Can we learn from these teachers? Can we shift the neural wiring, the narratives, the feelings, the behaviors—from avoidance or aggression to optimism, appreciation, and approach? There are and will be plenty of opportunities throughout our lives to practice reconditioning around conflict. Both interpersonal conflict and larger, systemic conflict. All of it—yes, even the most challenging situations—are opportunities if we learn to experience them in the spirit of wisdom-building and personal evolution.

One major hurdle to change exists, however. An element that can bolster our habitual patterns and lead us to resist change and growth. This hurdle is a constant theme and often a crutch to peacebuilding and conflict resolution processes. It is our tendency, our need, our addiction to being *right*. If we hope to be effective conflict resolvers, we absolutely must dismantle our illusion of certainty. And that requires we understand how perception works and recognize that things aren't quite as certain as they seem.

3 | Certainty Is an Illusion; Remain Curious

We've learned that a regulated nervous system is important for resolving conflict and that our systems become dysregulated in response to particular stimuli due to neural wiring that has been conditioned through experience. Through reconditioning, we can teach our nervous systems to become regulated around these stimuli and our minds to frame conflict as an opportunity. Our aim is to create new experiences of conflict and stress-inducing stimuli. Of course, all of our experiences are driven by our perceptions. What or who we pay attention to and the way we interpret those elements lead to our experiences of them.

Therefore, while changing our neural and behavioral responses to conditioned stimuli requires new experiences with those stimuli, changing those experiences requires that we change our perceptions. But that's tricky because our perceptions seem like accurate pictures of the world. In fact, most of us are certain that what we perceive, and the experiences those perceptions lead to, are true and real, so much so that any questioning of the way we have perceived and experienced situations is usually discarded and/ or defended against. Indeed, we are often absolutely convinced about the legitimacy of our own perceptions. We are certain that what we've experienced and subsequently now remember, know, and predict about the world is legitimate, and that if others' experiences, perceptions, memories, or predictions contradict our own, then they must be wrong. So, in a sense, the certainty we feel about the way we perceive the world is an addiction to being *right*. And there are lots of interesting mental tricks our brains play that keep this addictive programming in place, maintaining certainty that our experiences are true, right, and real while any contradictory experiences must be false, wrong, or fake.

This attachment to certainty and, ultimately, to being right are significant neuropsychological hindrances to self-regulation and reconditioning around conflict. The pesky pattern stems from our basic psychological needs for safety and a positive self-concept, and from the brain's underlying basic functionality involving memory and prediction. Per the running theme of this book, we would not want to alter the basic functionality of our brains; rather, we can use its functionality to modify neural programming, including the way we perceive people and situations and our attachment to certainty and rightness.

Reflect for a moment on a conflict you are currently experiencing or experienced in the past. You could even look at a current social-political conflict and reflect on where you stand on a contentious issue. How convinced are you that you or your side are right? How uncomfortable would it feel to open yourself to the possibility that you may not be totally right? Or that there is more than one right, ethical, or moral way of perceiving the situation or topic?

If you've identified a situation or topic that triggers a feeling of defensiveness when questioning your own certainty or rightness, that's good! That's our goal. We're about to explore the nuances of perception, certainty, and rightness, and it's great to have a particular stimulus in mind when experimenting with these concepts in your mental laboratory. Welcome to the world of perception.

The Perceptual Systems

In 2023, I began working with a senior manager at a manufacturing company named Jared, who apparently couldn't find a way to get along with his boss, Diana. He had numerous stories about how Diana had treated him for the last several years. A prominent theme was how she repeatedly failed to give him clear directions and had then gotten mad at him for not meeting her expectations. At this point, Jared believed that Diana had it in for him and was targeting him regularly with hostility. This indeed sounded frustrating. I asked him for a few concrete examples of her harsh treatment.

Jared showed me an email from Diana, which read,

"Hi Jared, just checking in on the materials order. Any updates?"

"Can you believe the way she talks to me?" he asked me.

Since I was reading this without any context, memories, or predictions about Diana, the message seemed totally benign and normal to me. But, of course, I'm not Jared, with his unique experiences, which have conditioned his brain to apply particular filters to interactions with Diana.

I asked Jared what he thought it meant. How was he interpreting the message?

"Obviously, she's trying to build a case against me," he said. "She wants to see me fail. She knows the materials aren't in yet. She just wants a paper trail, so she can cover her ass and fire me when she's ready."

I felt compassion for Jared. To live daily with this lens and the resulting internal dysregulation must have been difficult. Later that week, I had a chance to attend some of their team meetings and observe Jared and Diana's interactions in a real-world setting. Personally, I found Diana to be quite pleasant and professional, but I could see why their personalities conflicted. Diana was a bit indecisive, not willing to make clear plans, at least not quickly. Jared was the opposite. He wanted directives to be straightforward, simple, and fast.

Getting to know Jared better over the next few weeks, I learned he was quite opinionated on a number of topics. He had strong social-political views and had intense, somewhat volatile relationships in his personal life. He was divorced with two kids, and he had a lot of stories about how his ex-wife had also wronged him in multiple ways. In some sense, he was both the victim and the hero of his relationship narratives. Yet, he never seemed to want pity or compassion. He just wanted to feel validated and justified in his positions, experiences, and perspectives. It took me quite a number of coaching sessions to build enough trust with Jared before I could even begin to question what he believed. But, as I explained to him, if he wanted to start having better relationships at work and in life, and ultimately lower his stress levels resulting from interpersonal tension, he would have to open his perceptual aperture to consider other points of view as potentially valid. This was not easy for him, but I greatly respected Jared for being willing to get uncomfortable and eventually open to a wider lens of reality.

Jared was the perfect example of our human tendency toward perceptual certainty and rightness. He was perhaps an extreme representative of the pattern, but, of course, all of us have this tendency. Some of us are like Jared—extremely one-sided and opinionated—when it comes to particular topics or people, and some of us are a bit more open to others' ideas and perspectives. But I bet there is at least one event, relationship, experience, political topic, or other area of life that each of us feels absolutely certain, justified, and ethically or morally in the right. If you don't, you're a more open-minded person than I am.

Our need for certainty stems from our basic psychological need for safety and the neurological functionality of prediction. The brain is constantly generating and updating mental maps of the world to predict where sources of danger/pain and safety/pleasure exist. This drive toward predictability, paired with our basic psychological need for a positive self-concept, manifests in conflict as the need for rightness. If I know I am right, then (1) the world becomes much more predictable and (2) I can feel good about myself for knowing how to act and respond to the world in the *right* way. If I'm not so certain about what is right, true, or real, then the world seems more unpredictable and the concept of myself as a good, moral, ethical person is not so clear.

In my experience as a mediator and coach, individuals can become especially triggered if their strongly held position or beliefs—their certainty or rightness—is challenged. And yet, this challenge is inherent in the nature of conflict. Conflicts only emerge when at least two sides oppose what one another believes is true about the past and/or right for the future. And conflicts only resolve when all sides let go of their attachments to being right and get authentically curious about the experiences and perspectives of one another.

> **NOTE:** *As we move through this chapter and learn to question our own perceptions, and thus our sense of certainty and rightness, I promise to tread delicately as I did with Jared. I realize that probing our certainty, rightness, beliefs, and experiences can feel a bit unsettling if not totally jarring. But wait a minute . . . that's why we're here, right? I did say this book was meant to be provocative. Okay, let's dive in, maybe not so delicately after all.*

Interpretive Machines: What Is Real and True?

Perception emerges in the human mind from two primary, integrated channels: what we pay attention to and the way we interpret the objects of our attention. The objects include all of the people, places, and situations outside of our bodies (using exteroception) and all of the sensations inside of our bodies (using interoception). We don't typically control much of what we pay attention to or how we interpret the world. Most of this is done at either a totally unconscious (i.e., neurobiological) or deep subconscious (i.e., psychological) level. Let's break down how perception works and just how complicated this whole phenomenon is. We'll begin with sensory transmission:

1. First, our receptors (e.g., photoreceptors in our eyeballs, mechanoreceptors in our ears, skin, and organs) convert environmental energy into neural signals. This creates a huge amount of raw data.

2. At the first relay stations (e.g., retina to lateral geniculate nucleus for vision, cochlear nuclei for hearing), large amounts of redundant or non-salient information are suppressed. The remaining sensory data is then sent via electrochemical signals that travel through sensory neurons to the central nervous system (i.e., the brain and spinal cord).

3. The thalamus in the brain acts as a central filter, letting through only information deemed relevant based on our attention, the context, and top-down predictions.

You can see, at only the level of sensory input, we are increasingly removed from an objective reality. Each layer of transmission shrouds the original data in neuropsychological processing. It's like a complicated game of telephone, where we can only hope that the original message being sent actually reaches the final receiver with some degree of accuracy—that real-world things are transduced into bioelectric signals and transmitted through biological wires with limited distortion.

At this stage, it's already reasonable to question how could "real" things be transformed purely into electric and chemical signals, and how could we be sure of the accuracy of such transformations. Electrical and chemical pulses are, after all, the only languages the brain can speak. Pretty incredible how this complex intertwining of signals can create a multidimensional human experience. But electrochemical transduction or bottom-up processing is not the only perceptual game involved.

The other important process here is top-down processing, much of which we've covered in the previous chapter. Through neuroplastic changes, our brains store memories from experience, which create predictions about what sensory information will be inputted depending on a variety of factors, including the stimulus, the environment, the situation, and even our current affective or emotional state. In the perception literature, this is often referred to as *perceptual set*, the psychological tendency to perceive things in a particular way based on expectations, prior knowledge, context, or emotions, which effectively biases how incoming sensory information is interpreted.

Our brains expect what to see, hear, taste, smell, and feel before such sensory information is even transmitted to the brain. These predictions, traveling from our brains (top) are then checked against signals coming from our senses (the bottom) to determine if the predictions are accurate. If predictions are determined to be accurate, some scientists think that sensory information is basically discarded, which means we would be experiencing the environment based purely on top-down predictions coming from our brains. It's important to note that in most cases, sensory input isn't discarded entirely but rather down-weighted or filtered, so that only the most relevant or prediction-challenging elements are emphasized in conscious awareness. In other words, our brains continuously balance raw input with expectations, giving priority to predicted information while still monitoring for unexpected signals that may require an update.

If the predictions are deemed inaccurate, then they may be overridden and updated, creating a different perception and possibly a new experience. When this occurs, the brain likely processes mostly the error signal—the difference between prediction and sensory data—rather than the full raw stream of sensory information. More often than not, however, even inaccurate predictions hold firm and are not overridden or updated. Consequently, we are not experiencing or responding to sense data in real-time, and thus not truly experiencing or appropriately responding to what is really happening in the outside world. At least, this is the theory, supported by a growing body of neuroscience research.

Depending on the level of processing needed, brain scientists believe that *somewhere between 90 and 99 percent of raw sensory data is discarded or ignored* before it reaches conscious awareness.[1] Some estimates suggest a million-fold reduction of perceived data compared to receptor-level transduction rates.

Suffice it to say that we live in a world of experiences produced almost solely in the brain and only sometimes by what we sense in the world. And even when we are experiencing the situations we sense inside and outside of our bodies, these experiences are driven by our attention (i.e., selective elements of the situation, rather than the entire situation) and our interpretations (i.e., the situation filtered through our memories and predictions based on similar past experiences). In other words, we are not experiencing the world as it is. We are experiencing our versions of it.

Since perception relies on what we pay attention to, two people might find themselves in conflict when discussing their experiences of the same event or situation because each paid attention to different elements of it and so cannot agree on exactly what occurred. However, since perception also relies on interpretation, two people might agree on what occurred but place totally different meanings on the situation and thus will have experienced it totally differently. In conflict, we're often so convinced that our version of events is the only true and real version. To suggest we might be wrong or that there is more than one right version is often taken as an insult if not an outright attack.

Our sense of being right in conflict relies on a layer of certainty that what we've experienced and remember is real and true, and that certainty relies on a deeper layer of belief that what we perceived is an accurate representation of some objective reality. But if we know our perception is composed of electrochemical signals transduced from only particular, attended-to aspects of the world, which are then filtered through our unique experiences, memories, predictions, and interpretations, how could we be sure that what we perceived was the whole truth and nothing but the truth? And if we can't be certain of that, how could we know absolutely that there is only one version of right and that *we* hold it?

The fact is, based on everything we know about perception, each of us is walking around with an entirely unique, astonishing, immersive universe inside our own head and body. Each of our internal universes is constantly interacting with and reacting to our environments, including and especially all the other universes in all the other heads and bodies around us. You could imagine a crowd of people and visualize their heads replaced with little, contained galaxies bobbling atop their necks.

Yes, we humans might agree on several "truths" and find common ground with others, especially with our closest friends and family members. But in the end, there's no one else who experiences the world exactly like you do. That's because no one else has your nuanced, complex configuration of a brain and nervous system, which was generated from a combination of your distinct biological makeup and all of your experiences and subsequent memories and predictions. Your nervous system is your experiential fingerprint. There's only one of them in the whole world and in all of history.

This fact makes each of us unique and incredibly special. However, of course, it also presents all sorts of interesting challenges in social life. Navigating interactions and relationships every day, from simple head nods between strangers to emotional conversations with a spouse, each of us is one nervous system interacting with a completely unique other nervous system, trying to align on what exactly is real and true about our human experiences. And no matter how we cut it, people's experiences are generated from their one-of-a-kind nervous systems creating their one-of-a-kind perceptions—not a direct experience of an objective truth or reality.

This leads us to some fundamental questions about the nature of reality, about which most of us are certain most of the time:

- Is there such thing as objective reality?
- Should there be such a thing as a universal moral rightness?
- Do I live by the most moral and ethical code?
- Do I really know who I am?
- Is my memory and experience of events accurate?

These and similar questions are fundamental to the human experience and have likely been asked by humans since our brains could process such metacognitive reflections. They've certainly been the subject of philosophers all around the world and psychologists from a variety of disciplines, perhaps especially those who study perception.

If we can recognize the complexity of perception and the essential questions that such complexity reveals, then the question remains: how in the world could we be sure that we are *right*? If I am the only one who actually experiences the world the way I perceive it, including my interpretation of events outside and within my own body, then how could I really be certain that anything is true for anyone other than myself? I'll tell you how. By employing some interesting mental tricks called *cognitive biases*, which both reinforce and are reinforced by our attention and interpretations of the world.

Cognitive Biases

We hear the word *biases* a lot these days. However, unless someone has training in psychology or has read more deeply into the topic, most people probably have a judgment about the word and don't clearly understand what it actually refers to. We can use the term *bias* in the pejorative way that is often used in pop culture (e.g., "They're biased against me."). But in psychology and neuroscience the word *bias* refers to a complex neuropsychological mechanism typically referred to as a *mental heuristic*. These are filters or shortcuts that the brain has evolved in order to make some sense of the world.

There is far too much information available to our sensory systems to actually pay attention to everything the world has to offer. Only a tiny percentage of raw environmental information is actually getting through. Once the information gets past early sensory and thalamic filters, our brains' predictive models produce a range of biases to further filter and interpret the data. If our brains didn't have these filtering mechanisms, we would be overwhelmed and flooded by sensory information constantly. We wouldn't know what to pay attention to, the world would seem chaotic, and we would not be able to make sense of things. We need our biases—our filters— that tell us what to pay attention to and what to ignore. We wouldn't and couldn't have it any other way.

While there are dozens of cognitive biases that have been thoroughly researched by psychologists, the following few are some of the most common heuristics I have seen at play in conflict. They tend to bolster our certainty of what we perceive and experience, leading to a sense of being right and that others are wrong, and ultimately making conflict resolution and peacebuilding ever more difficult.

Selective attention is often thought of in the psychological literature as a cognitive bias even though at its core, selective attention is a fundamental feature of the brain. Since the brain can only process a finite amount of information, it must discard much of the raw data transduced by the senses. It can also be thought of as an overarching bias, however, since it is in fact a sort of mental shortcut, helping us to pay attention to only what our brains deem relevant and important. Attention bias leads to many other nuanced forms of neuropsychological processing, such as negativity bias and confirmation bias.

Negativity bias is a fundamental heuristic that instructs our brains to pay attention to things that might be dangerous now or in the future. Our brains evolved to prioritize information that is most likely to keep us safe and help us procreate. By remaining vigilant about potential sources of pain or danger, the brain is more likely to keep the body safe so the organism can reproduce its genetic material. And remember that old program the brain runs: better to be safe than sorry. The problem with a heuristic, however, is that it often overperforms its job. Negativity bias leads to us looking for problems proactively and hypervigilantly, and to interpreting problems as more meaningful and consequential than they probably are. When we've had distressing experiences as a result of interacting with particular stimuli, we'll tend to be hypervigilant about those stimuli in the future, expecting the worst and allocating metabolic resources to upregulate the sympathetic fight-flight system in the presence of such stimuli. Hence, negativity bias can become especially activated in conflicts with people or situations that we've had issues with in the past.

Confirmation bias is another form of attentional bias. This is a neuropsychological phenomenon that leads our brains to pay attention only to information that confirms our beliefs and to ignore or filter out any information that might contradict or invalidate those beliefs. For example, if you had a conflict with Peter that didn't get properly resolved, and now you believe Peter is a difficult person, then it's likely your brain will only pay attention to elements of his behavior that confirm he is, indeed, difficult, and it will discount or dismiss elements that may contradict that perception.

There are also a variety of biases related to an overarching concept that psychologists call *attribution*. Attribution describes the way we attribute intentions or causality to behaviors and events. If Peter smiles at you, your brain will automatically attribute some meaning or intention behind the smile. This is closely related to theory of mind, a foundational concept in psychology, which explains humans' innate capacity to infer, whether true or not, what other people are thinking based on their behavior. In other words, we're all armchair psychologists, constantly making sense of our social environments by surmising what one another is thinking, planning, and intending. One of the more prominent attribution biases in conflict tends to be hostile attribution bias.

Hostile attribution bias is closely related to both negativity bias and confirmation bias in that it places a filter of hostility on particular stimuli. If you begin seeing every action that Peter takes as potentially hostile, so much so that it would be hard for him to do anything right in your eyes at this point, you're likely experiencing hostile attribution bias.

Another attribution bias is called **fundamental attribution error**, which quickly places intentional, character-level meanings behind behaviors, ignoring situational factors. For example, if Peter showed up late to a meeting with you, you might think, "He doesn't respect my time, and he's trying to prove he can show up when he wants without consequence. He thinks he's more important than me." When in reality, you might discover that traffic was the real cause of his tardiness, and he actually had no intention of disrespect. The interesting flipside of this error emerges from **self-serving bias**, which leads people to focus on situational factors rather than on character or intention when they have made a mistake. If you were late to the meeting instead of Peter, your brain would likely not suggest that it's because you don't respect Peter or are trying to prove something but rather it was because of the situation (i.e., traffic).

All of these biases are incredibly well studied with hundreds of scientific experiments and academic papers supporting their existence cross-culturally. These and other biases are central to human neuropsychological architecture. That's because, again, they help us make sense of the world so we can make important decisions efficiently, without getting bogged down by analysis. Heuristics have proven to be essential filters for our brains to create predictable mental models in order to remain safe and get our needs met.

Just because they are useful, however, doesn't mean they are optimal. Biases evolved for efficiency, speed, and survival; they were never optimized for accuracy. And they certainly have been shown, both in research and in everyday anecdotal evidence, to produce a significant number of errors in our perception, memory, and judgment.

Understanding both how our brains function (e.g., top-down and bottom-up processing) and how our minds operate with regard to perception (e.g., mental heuristics coloring our conscious awareness) can help illuminate exactly why we're often so certain of our perspectives and why we feel so right about contentious issues and situations. We're literally wired for it.

Why We're Wired for Certainty

Certainty is the nemesis of peace. Our drive toward certainty, which underlies our subconscious and conscious desires to be right, is antithetical to our capacities for flexibility, open-mindedness, and collaboration with those we perceive as sources of conflict. And the unfortunate news is that our brains are certainty-seeking machines.

At a neuropsychological level, the brain is constantly generating mental models of the world to anticipate sensory input and reduce the "prediction error" between expectation and reality. When the world is experienced as predicted and the error is low, dopamine signaling in reward circuits, such as the ventral striatum, reinforces the perception of control and safety. Conversely, high uncertainty activates the amygdala and anterior insula, brain regions involved in threat detection and interoceptive awareness, increasing our stress response. Another key player is cortisol, a stress hormone released by the hypothalamic-pituitary-adrenal axis. Cortisol strongly influences how emotional memories are encoded in the hippocampus and amygdala, which helps explain why conflict experiences can feel especially vivid and enduring. Stress hormones not only heighten the salience of conflict but also reinforce the certainty we attach to our interpretations of these events.

At a physiological level, the brain and nervous system are working to regulate the body's internal state to activate rest or movement depending on the situation. However, those regulatory mechanisms are all dependent on what the brain predicts the body will need in the upcoming moments. So, reducing uncertainty about what will happen and what resources the body will need is a crucial function of the brain. The way it reduces uncertainty is through the top-down or predictive processing model discussed throughout this book.

Predictive Coding   Dr. Lisa Feldman Barrett, a prominent neuroscientist and one of the most outspoken proponents of top-down processing or predictive coding models, calls the brain a "guessing machine" that has a massive, constant inverse problem. In a 2023 podcast with Dr. Andrew Huberman, another prominent neuroscientist, Barrett suggested that since transduced signals coming from our sensory receptors must first pass through various elements of our bodies, our brains are really reacting to the body rather than to the outside world.[2] In other words, the brain only knows about the world through the filter of the body (i.e., the signals it receives from the body). Then, the brain essentially has to guess what those signals were transduced from (i.e., what environmental energies were picked up by our sensory receptors) and what they mean. It does this by instantly placing the qualities of those electrochemical signals (e.g., signal frequencies, amplitudes, receptor networks involved, etc.) into categories that have been established from previous experiences. The brain, she says, is a "constant category constructor."

In this way, the brain does not experience the world directly; it only experiences signals coming from our body, makes its best guess or interpretation about what the signals are representing, and generates instructions for the body to respond. The output is not an intellectual response but rather a motor plan. The plan is to change the internal state of the body in order to activate various systems and skeletal motor movements. This motor plan, again, comes from past experiences—learning or conditioning hardwired into the brain, pulling from categories of particular motor plans or outputs in response to combinations of sensory signals or inputs.

This complex system of bottom-up (i.e., sensory) and top-down (i.e., predictive) processing evolved presumably because it was the most efficient and effective system for keeping humans alive and able to reproduce. The ancient message transmitted from our evolved nervous system is that the more certain we are about what's about to happen and what we'll need to meet the demands of the environment, the better off we'll be. That's because uncertainty is incredibly costly. If all possibilities are open, and nothing is certain or predictable, then the body's entire suite of metabolic processes would have to be available at all times for all purposes—a metabolically unsustainable state. Ultimately, a brain that cannot sufficiently predict what resources the body will need to meet the demands of its environment will likely not survive long, and life will be extremely difficult. Reducing uncertainty and prediction error is crucial for a well-regulated body and success over the lifespan.

If the brain is a regulation-prediction machine (i.e., predicting how to regulate the body appropriately based on what it predicts), the question is, how accurate is each of our brains in each moment? In situations of conflict especially, when appropriate responses make all the difference, is your brain interpreting the transduced body signals appropriately, assembling the most categorically relevant memories to make the most accurate predictions and subsequent behavioral responses for the present and immediately arriving reality?

In hindsight, after a difficult conversation or intense interaction with someone, we might decide that our nervous systems reacted in a way that was energetically wasteful, functionally disruptive, emotionally unpleasant, and/or psychologically uncomfortable. There may have been a mismatch between how we responded and what the reality of the situation called for. Why did this happen? Was it because our nervous systems weren't working as well as they should be?

On average, our nervous systems work extremely well. They are responding incredibly accurately based on what our brains perceive and predict. Any mismatch between appropriate response and reality is not due to the operation of the brain but rather to the errors between perception and subsequent prediction. The information the brain pays attention to, the way it interprets sense data arriving from transduced signals inside the body, and what exactly it predicts will happen next may be inaccurate. So, the nervous system reacts inappropriately not because something is wrong with its output or function but rather because the interpretation of the inputs are incorrect. In other words, we are often responding totally accurately to situations based on how we perceive them; the problem is in the way we perceive the situations. And when our nervous systems react inappropriately to what is needed, creating costly energetic outputs, this is a classic example of dysregulation and a setup for escalated conflict.

Why might our brains inaccurately perceive, categorize, and initiate inappropriate responses to conflict? We learned in Principle 2 why we are often conditioned to respond defensively to conflict. But uncertainty is one element we did not dive into, specifically, how we perceive and respond to uncertainty.

The brain's wiring to predict and create mental maps of the world is a core function we're not attempting to alter. Instead, we may attempt to modify *what* exactly it predicts, and thus how we respond, when we are faced with uncertainty, ambiguity, or contradictory perspectives. These are core elements that emerge during conflicts, to which the nervous system may activate our sympathetic, fight-flight response. Remember that our nervous systems escalate during nonviolent conflict to defend against a perceived threat or impediment to our basic psychological need(s). So, contradicting perspectives that inherently challenge our own sense of certainty or rightness may be triggering a threat to these needs.

Our Psychological Needs and the Drive Toward Rightness When someone challenges our viewpoint in conflict, it creates prediction error—a mismatch between our mental model ("I'm right") and our perception of the outside world ("They're saying I'm wrong"). The brain's predictive coding system is built to minimize these errors. A large error resulting from a disagreement over a topic could introduce uncertainty about our memories, our beliefs, our social standing, and/or the world in general. This uncertainty threatens our four conflict needs, triggering the amygdala and insula, which signal potential danger. As a result, our brains will desperately seek certainty and predictability—something safe to hold onto—in order to meet these needs. This seeking leads to entrenched positioning and an insistence on being right. Ultimately, our brains are trying to reduce ambiguity, restore a sense of predictability, and downregulate the body's threat response. Uncertainty is experienced as dangerous. Being certain, having predictability, and feeling right is experienced as safe.

Our psychological need for safety is perhaps our most fundamental and irreducible of our basic needs. It's a need we share with virtually every other animal with survival instincts and stems directly from the predictive coding nature of our brains. To feel safe, and for our bodies to remain in an appropriately regulated state for the environment, we need to have some level of certainty or predictability about how events will unfold and how we should respond. So, this need is an obvious target for uncertainty's threat.

Disagreement, especially over values or worldviews, can also be experienced as exclusion or rejection, threatening our affiliation need. In conflict, defending our correctness may help us avoid social rejection, which historically carried survival costs, and reaffirm our membership in a moral or social order. Further, research into theories such as *social identity theory*, *uncertainty-identity theory*, and *worldview defense hypothesis* have shown that people seek ingroup affiliation, becoming more entrenched in their social group identities, when faced with uncertainty, ambiguity, or challenges to their worldviews. Such uncertainty poses an existential threat to the brain's predictive system which, according to *terror management theory*, drives people to more fiercely defend and adhere to their worldviews.

Conflict can also challenge our sense of agency, control, or independence. When we perceive a contradiction, which generates uncertainty, it may feel like we are losing control of the situation. On the contrary, being right helps us feel that we have regained control or influence, rather than being at the mercy of someone else's perspective. Stating, defending, or proving our position restores a feeling of agency: "I can influence this outcome."

The need for control is also linked to the drive for what psychologists call *cognitive closure*: a motivational initiative to arrive at a firm answer and avoid ambiguity. The need for control becomes stronger under stress, time pressure, or perceived threat, as it reduces mental load and helps us conserve cognitive resources.

Finally, the need for a positive self-concept is one of the most affected core needs when it comes to uncertainty or any challenge to our rightness. Self-concept is our mental model of "who I am," which includes one's beliefs, values, and abilities. Being "right" is often tied to being consistent with that model. In conflict, challenges to our correctness are often perceived as challenges to our self-concept. The medial prefrontal cortex (mPFC) is involved in self-referential thinking; when our beliefs are attacked, the mPFC activates to protect our self-concept. Several psychological components may be at play around this particular need, including self-serving narrative, self-esteem, and identity.

With regard to narrative, humans are story-driven animals. We make sense of events by weaving them into stories with characters, motives, and plots. In conflict, these narratives often cast us in two roles: the victim and/or the hero. When we play the victim, being wronged justifies our emotional reactions and absolves us of any blame. It reinforces our moral high ground. We might think, "I didn't cause this. Someone did this to me. It's all their fault." The victim role also generates sympathy and support from others, fulfilling desires for belonging and validation. On the contrary, playing the hero presents us as principled, courageous, and acting in defense of what's right. It reinforces a self-image of integrity and competence, often giving us the sense that we're restoring justice. In conflict, we might play both the victim and the hero: the one who was wronged and the one who is defending what is right. These roles create a psychological anchor around which to form an identity. Abandoning our "rightness" would mean rewriting who we are in the story, possibly turning ourselves into a partial villain, which feels threatening to our identity.

Self-esteem is also an aspect of self-concept that can be threatened when our correctness is in question. Self-esteem is our overall evaluation of our worth, and conflict that challenges our perspective can threaten that worth. Admitting faults or errors risks lowering our self-esteem unless it's in a safe, non-shaming environment. Holding on to being right helps preserve self-esteem by showing ourselves and others that we are competent, moral, and justified.

When it comes to identity, any challenge to our sense of being right can be aggressively defended against. That's because when someone challenges a belief, especially one that's central to our identity (e.g., political values, moral code, expertise), conceding can feel like a mini-identity collapse. It may throw us into a state of confusion and disorientation, causing us to lose a sense of who we are in the world. The irony is that when people update their beliefs, they often experience a sense of inspiration and renewed motivation. Nonetheless, the brain resists what it categorizes as a monumental shift. The more central the belief, the larger the shift appears to be and the stronger the resistance to updating it. This is why conflicts over identity, values, or worldview can be especially escalatory: the threat isn't just intellectual, it feels existential.

The desire to be right in conflict is a multilayered protective strategy. At the biological level, it reduces threat arousal (safety). At the social level, it safeguards inclusion (affiliation). At the motivational level, it reasserts agency (independence). At the identity level, it protects self-esteem and our place in the conflict story (positive self-concept). This is why being wrong can feel so destabilizing and why stating facts alone rarely shifts anyone's entrenched positions. Being wrong isn't perceived as simply a lack of information but as our most basic human needs being put at risk.

Typically in conflict, when people become entrenched in their positions or perspectives, it's because any challenge to being right makes them feel uncertain, which triggers all sorts of psychological threats and creates a stress response. We humans do our best to avoid threats like that. On the contrary, when we reestablish certainty by winning an argument, proving a point, or defending our narrative, the brain gets a dopamine hit. This reward strengthens the neural circuits that associate being right with emotional relief and social power. Over time, such reinforcement can become habitual. Our brains learn that "the way out of uncertainty is to dig in and defend my position."

So, we double down on our viewpoints. We become convinced that our own perspectives, memories, or experiences are the right, true, and/or moral ones and that anyone who disagrees or has a different perspective must be necessarily wrong, ignorant, or immoral. When we are absolutely certain about our own rightness, however, and that any contradictory perspective must be wrong, then we have effectively shut down the capacity for curiosity—one of the five Cs of conflict resolution (discussed in Principle 1). Curiosity is the exact opposite of certainty because it is only available in a state of embracing uncertainty. To resolve a difficult conflict, you'll need to get curious.

Benefits of Curiosity for Conflict Resolution

When I first started my conflict resolution consulting firm, a colleague and direct report of mine came to me with a difficult issue. She was upset about the way I handled a previous conversation with her, and I could tell it had taken a lot of courage for her to bring this to me. My immediate inclination was to defend myself. I was acutely aware of my heart rate elevating and my stomach tightening. I felt a slight rush of adrenaline, and my brain said, "Defend! Prove her wrong." I desperately wanted to prove that that I had handled the earlier conversation just fine, and that she was being overly sensitive. It was a story I had experienced many times before in my life: "I'm right. They're wrong. How dare they suggest otherwise."

Thankfully, I was able to catch myself before letting my adrenaline lead the charge. I remember listening to what she was saying while also practicing self-regulation, telling myself it was my job to listen calmly, breathe, and stay curious. What was really bothering her? What underlying needs were affected by that previous conversation? What might I have done ineffectively? What could I do better or differently to support her in the future?

Like anyone, I'm not perfect at self-regulating. There have been plenty of times that I haven't caught myself and regulated my nervous system appropriately. But fortunately, this time, I really put all the lessons I teach into practice. I wasn't automatically right. There was something in what she was saying that would be valuable to me and to our relationship. I just had to listen with curiosity.

When she was done telling me what she had experienced, I remember following the steps of a protocol that she and I codeveloped for receiving feedback: I owned the parts of my behavior she called out and that I recognized; I asked clarifying questions to dig deeper; I reassured her, addressing her basic psychological needs directly; and I asked if we could cocreate an actionable plan for the next time we have a similar conversation.

I found that by staying calm and curious, even though I desperately wanted to be right, the capacity to receive difficult feedback built an entirely new level of trust between me and her. From that point forward, all of our conversations, including difficult ones, have been easier. Today, several years later, we still work together. In my perspective, we have a great relationship full of mutual respect and admiration (at least, I hope so). She still comes to me with difficult feedback when she needs to, and I feel proud of us every time for having the courage and curiosity to have these conversations in a constructive way. After every difficult conversation, we walk away with greater trust, feeling increasingly safe to bring up difficult situations with each other without the threat of retaliation, humiliation, rejection, or abandonment. This is critical for the health of any relationship—at home or at work—and it really starts with a calm nervous system and a curious mind.

A plethora of research into the benefits of curiosity has supported my anecdotal experiences. One study[3] found that individuals curious about an upcoming, scary task felt more positively challenged, less threatened, and presented longer physiological engagement than less curious individuals, indicating curiosity's positive effect on stress-inducing situations. In lab studies, curiosity has been shown to enhance learning and induce participants to expend greater effort and delay gratification, which improves downstream decision-making. These effects are important for conflict resolution processes and healthy relationships in general.

Research from the field of positive psychology also identifies curiosity as one of the core character strengths most strongly linked to life satisfaction, resilience, and positive social relationships. This suggests that cultivating curiosity not only helps resolve conflicts but also contributes to overall well-being and thriving, making it a foundational skill for both peacebuilding and personal flourishing.

Studies have also shown curiosity can help reframe and transform conflicts through social problem-solving and collaboration. This has been supported in a variety of contexts from classrooms to boardrooms to high-stakes negotiations. Since genuine curiosity requires some level of uncertainty in one's perspective, or at least that one's own experience is not the only one that counts, it's worth understanding what the academic literature reports about uncertainty's effect on conflict resolution processes.

Indeed, the ability to embrace uncertainty has also been examined in the psychological and conflict resolution fields. Various experiments have shown that reducing the need for cognitive closure (i.e., certainty) fosters openness to new information and compromise during negotiations. Also, those with a high need for cognitive closure have stronger tendencies to use cognitive heuristics (i.e., biases) when making judgments and decisions in negotiation. Studies have also shown that learning to be comfortable with uncertainty reduces the threat response, which often fuels escalated conflict.

In a series of studies comparing the effects of empathy versus perspective taking on negotiation, researchers using both individual differences measures and experimental manipulations found that the willingness to cognitively consider others' perspectives increased participants' abilities to discover hidden agreements and to both create and accept points of common ground during negotiations. Interestingly, empathy, which the researchers defined as the ability to connect emotionally with another person, did not prove nearly as beneficial and, in some instances, was detrimental to finding agreement. Empathy can indeed be an important element of conflict resolution, but perspective taking seems even more impactful during dispute resolution. True perspective taking can only be facilitated by a state of uncertainty and curiosity.

In organizations, the willingness to embrace complexity and uncertainty has been shown to improve leadership capacity, which reduces the potential for workplace conflicts. Additionally, individuals with a higher tolerance for ambiguity tend to perform well in their jobs, demonstrate greater creativity, and make better decisions in the workplace. Studies also report that a "paradox mindset," characterized by the ability to embrace and leverage competing demands, can positively affect performance and innovation, while a lack of such mindset can hinder these outcomes. Embracing uncertainty has benefits not only for conflict processes but for each individual who practices it.

If we're certain about something, we've closed our minds to other possibilities. If we're absolutely right, then there's no way for us to be curious about other perspectives. For those of us interested in resolving conflict more effectively, a curious mindset is highly beneficial. The "Tools to Embrace Uncertainty and Get Curious" section will dive into several interesting techniques you might use to get curious, and in doing so to embrace uncertainty with a positive mindset.

Recap: The Perceptual Systems

Professionally, I have been involved in hundreds of disputes. And in my personal life, like most of us, I have experienced or witnessed countless conflicts, from small disagreements to multinational wars. Unfortunately, such is to be expected in a complex social landscape inhabited by perceptually unique universes, such as the ones atop each of our heads, that are regularly changing and constantly interacting with one another. One thing I hope we can all agree on is when people in conflict stop trying to be right, magical things can happen. People begin to really listen to each other, drop their guards a bit, and open up to new information and experiences outside of their own. In that moment, the spark of possibility ignites. The brain stops its habitual wiring and opens to the potential for neuroplastic change. The brain gets ready to rewire, which leads to a widening of the perceptual aperture, enabling us to see into the enigma of uncertainty we may not have previously been willing to imagine.

Listening to someone else's perspective with genuine curiosity takes courage. It requires that we stop believing so steadfastly in our own narratives, that we stop tying our self-esteem or self-worth to some version of a truth to which we've been committed, that we find a new shore in which to anchor our self-concept other than in the rigid waters of rightness, and that we let go of certainty—certainty that what we perceive is based on the absolutely true, real, and good version of an objective reality.

It's hard to deny that there is, in fact, at least something that is true and real beyond each of our own perceptions. After all, you and (ideally) many others like you are reading the same words on this page. That's real, isn't it? Well, sort of. While the words on the page are real in that they do exist outside of you— they're not something you generated in your mind—the way you perceive these words is incredibly distinct. You are not, in fact, experiencing the "real" outside world directly. You are experiencing an astonishingly complex, integrated somatosensory, cognitive, emotional experience created by your nervous system, which is following instructions from your brain, which has combined your memories and expectations with electrical and chemical pulses from multiple sensory relay stations inside the body, which originally received transduced signals from sensory receptors that picked up various forms of light waves that were emitted from this page or screen. The real world has traversed many electrical, chemical, physiological, emotional, and psychological layers to give you the experience of reality that you are having.

We should be grateful for and in reverence of this amazing experience of human consciousness. And yet, we should also realize just how special and distinct our experiences and perceptions of reality are. Only then, might we be able to glimpse the mystery of human perception—the unknown that exists outside of every one of our perceptual gazes. Only then might we be willing to concede that there are possibilities of experience and perception outside of our own, that not everything we're certain is true actually is, and that there is a possibility we are not right, or at least not absolutely and completely right, about the entire situation. In that space, there is room for movement, there is space to resolve conflicts, even complex ones. The following are a few tools we can use to help create that space with curious, constructive intention.

Tools to Embrace Uncertainty and Get Curious

Curiosity requires that we embrace uncertainty on some level. Being curious inherently means we don't fully grasp the entirety of a situation, including other people's perceptions and experiences. This is an extremely healthy state for resolving conflicts. The following are a few exercises to cultivate a new level of comfort with uncertainty and with the notion you might not be totally *right*. Then, we'll highlight some practical techniques for fostering curiosity during conflict.

Embracing Uncertainty

The feeling of uncertainty can be scary, both consciously and unconsciously. Heck, it's why the brain evolved as a prediction machine. To embrace uncertainty is to counteract our default tendency to feel safe in certainty. Although difficult, it can be done—through a bit of self-regulation and reconditioning.

Lower Threat Perception   As discussed, our brains and mental programs innately search for certainty and predictability. When uncertainty arises, our systems might naturally perceive danger, specifically a threat to our needs for safety, affiliation, positive self-concept, and independence. If we do not attend to these needs when faced with uncertainty, our survival mechanisms will likely drive us to seek certainty by digging into our versions of truth and rightness, all in order to regulate our nervous systems. If we hope to interrupt this cycle, we'll need to help quell our threat perceptions. The best way to do this is through self-talk. Just like we've done previously in this book, we'll use the conscious mind to surface and ideally calm our subconscious fears.

Think of a situation when you have been uncertain—a time when what you thought was right or true was in question or when you were concerned with how a particular situation was unfolding, including what it might mean and lead to. It could be when you were up for a promotion, waiting to hear about getting a job or being admitted into a program, uncertain whether someone had reciprocal feelings for you, or any other experience of uncertainty. If there is some situation currently that feels uncertain, even better. Bring it to the top of mind and see if you can feel the uneasiness of uncertainty.

Now, determine what you would need to know or hear to feel just bit calmer in the face of this vague, indeterminate experience. What could you remind yourself to lower your threat perception and downregulate your sympathetic arousal? It might sound like the following:

- "I trust myself. I'll be okay, whatever happens."
- "I'll take care of myself, no matter what."

- "I have support from my family/friends/colleagues. They'll stand by me."
- "I am a good, valuable person, regardless of what happens."
- "I did my best, and it's okay to make mistakes."
- "I choose what I do next. No one else can choose for me."

Whatever your messages of safety sound like, hold them in your mind when faced with uncertainty. Repeat them while using self-regulation techniques (e.g., deep breathing while consciously relaxing your body). And really try to feel the truth of these messages in your body. What would it feel like to genuinely believe the message? Over time, and possibly not long, you will teach your brain that uncertainty is not as threatening as it might have seemed. Keep repeating these statements and experiencing how they feel until they become your reality.

Recondition Uncertainty Want to get more comfortable with the unknown? Be with it in a new way! Find something that is a bit of a mystery to you—a situation that feels unfamiliar and/or somewhat unpredictable. Nothing dangerous, but something that heightens your senses and elevates your heart rate just a bit. Some examples:

- Riding on an airplane or boat
- Attending a new networking event
- Going on a first date
- Speaking in front of a group

During the experience, notice the sensations in your body. Practice your self-regulation techniques and your messages of safety. Attend to your psychological needs. This is the deconditioning part (i.e., turning the physiologically arousing stimuli into neutral stimuli).

Then, to recondition, you'll implement some updated messages about uncertainty. You're no longer simply trying to calm yourself and neutralize the stimuli. You're now teaching yourself to look at uncertainty in a whole new light. For example, you might tell yourself the following:

- "I'm not sure how this is going to go, and that's totally okay."
- "Wow, my heart's beating fast. Uncertainty is exciting!"

- "This is new, and new is fun."
- "Not knowing is part of the adventure. And I love adventure."

You can practice this over and over, with various unfamiliar situations. Eventually, you'll start feeling differently when faced with uncertainty.

Allowing for Non-Rightness

The following exercises are not meant to suggest you might necessarily be wrong, but only that you are not the arbiter of the only right or true version of reality. Not being right is not the same as being wrong. Though, sometimes you may, in fact, be wrong. Either way, for us to detach from the need to be right, we need to adopt a different narrative about what being right or wrong means.

Reframe Wrongness   One method of allowing for non-rightness, is to not frame yourself or your ideas as wrong. Instead, frame the situation as: "I didn't have all the information, and it's totally okay to update my position." In all moments, based on each of our unique brains, nervous systems, experiences, knowledge, perceptions, and circumstances, we are all simply doing our best. It may not appear that way to others; and when others are doing their best, it may not appear that way to you. But we *are*, all of us. Remind yourself of that.

When you find yourself in conflict, steeped in your position or perspective, and have even a small inkling that you'd like to find your way to peace and productivity with the other person or group, let yourself off the hook for having to be right. Perhaps you don't or didn't have all the information. Indeed, none of us have all of it . . . ever. That would require knowing every nuance of every person involved, including their histories, experiences, and nervous systems. None of us know all of that. Even the smartest artificial intelligence doesn't. So, based on what you knew in the moments you took a strong position, you (and everyone else) were simply doing your best. But now, you may have new information. That information might consist of facts about the world you weren't aware of, or of someone else's experiences or feelings, which they shared with you and which you did not know before. And it's okay for new information, in whatever form, to change your perspective.

Not only is it okay but it's also worth appreciating your own willingness to take in new information, to modify or widen your perspective, and to consider others' perceptions. If you do this, you've done so despite all the mental shortcuts and biases making it difficult for your brain to admit you might not be totally and completely right. So, be proud of yourself for letting go of rightness and learning something new. On the contrary, ignoring new information in order to stick to your original perspective, judgment, or evaluation of the situation is a sure way to remain in conflict. To do so also likely reflects the very thing that frustrates you about the "other side" of the conflict.

There will inevitably be moments in life when we are, in fact, wrong. Fortunately, many of us can admit our mistakes when they are glaring. But most if not all of us have had the experience of recognizing we made a mistake or were wrong and still had a lot of trouble admitting it. Because to do so takes courage. It's scary to admit we're wrong. We might be afraid of abandonment or rejection. Or admitting mistakes could be construed as taking blame or responsibility for something that we fear might have negative consequences, with relational, professional, legal, or financial implications. That's why it's important, of course, to be strategic about how we go about taking ownership over mistakes, when it's appropriate, and in what manner.

When you determine that you were wrong and you strategically discern that admitting so is unlikely to lead to extremely detrimental consequences, at least if you take responsibility in the appropriate way, then it's important to reframe errors as opportunities. Reperceiving wrongness in a more positive light, even if simply admitting you didn't have all the information at the time, will make admitting mistakes or updating your position much easier.

Admitting to mistakes, acknowledging that we're wrong, and/or updating our positions, has a number of positive benefits. Doing so relieves psychological burden for you and others involved, since hiding your truth or sticking to a path you know isn't right will be quite cognitively and emotionally distressing, it enables others to not feel "crazy" or gaslit as often happens when someone defends their rightness even when they were obviously wrong, and it almost always increases trust between people. Admitting we're wrong tells others that it's safe to make mistakes and own up to them or that's it's absolutely okay to update one's position. This creates a psychologically safe environment for being vulnerable and taking risks in the relationship.

Every time we recognize we were wrong or didn't have all the information, it is an opportunity for growth, learning, curiosity, and humility. Once again, when you can embrace this sort of experience, you can be proud of yourself for being open and humble enough to own your mistakes or previous lack of knowledge.

Separate Self-Concept from Rightness   One of the major resistance points to letting go of rightness is the identification with being right. As discussed earlier in this principle, our self-concept, including our self-narrative and self-esteem, can be tied to rightness, and any threat of being wrong or not the only right one could be construed as a threat to who we are. So, it would serve us to separate our self-concept from the notion of being right. The best way to do this is by creating new narratives that you repeat to yourself regularly, especially during conflict, until you believe them and live them. Here are a few examples. If none resonate with you, I encourage you to come up with some that do.

- "Others might be right also, and that's okay."
- "I don't have to be right all the time. I'm still a good person."
- "I'm not the victim or the hero here. We're all doing our best."
- "I know what's right and true for me. And that's enough."
- "Right and wrong have nothing to do with who I am as a person."

Admitting you're not necessarily right does not have to destroy your self-image. Separate the two so you can maintain a coherent, positive self-concept regardless of being right.

Argue for the Other Side   When in a difficult conversation or conflict, it is a great practice to invite error checking and steelmanning, which is when you don't just repeat what you heard but also attempt to articulate the other person's arguments. What that means operationally is to have each individual involved list how they might be wrong and summarize the strongest opposing argument before stating their own. Doing so helps create a psychologically safe environment for testing alternative ideas and viewpoints and often helps people save face when owning a mistake or admitting to incorrect facts.

Fostering Curiosity During Conflict

Now that we've worked on embracing uncertainty and letting go of rightness, let's take it a step further. How can we cultivate curiosity during conflict, to widen our lens, allow space for other perspectives, and take in new information? Here are a few ideas.

Metacognitive Perceptual Widening   This is best done with your eyes closed. Visualize your field of perception as though your eyes are two flashlights, shining light on a finite, brightened space in front of you. The light shines out from your head and widens out into the world to encompass all that you perceive. Notice all the bright, colorful elements of the world in your field of light.

Then, become aware of the outskirts of your light field, where there is darkness, obscurity, things you do not yet see. There is something there. It's not empty. You just can't perceive it yet. See if you can get curious, perhaps even excited about the mystery of the space you have not yet perceived. What could be there? What have you not yet experienced? What information lies just outside of the light? If you were to slowly illuminate that area, what would emerge into reality? What other experiences, perspectives, stories, and concepts might appear?

See if you can brighten that area just a bit. It will not become completely vivid because there is still much you cannot see. But try to perceive just a bit more. The more you see, the wider your gaze of light becomes, and yet there will always be darkness on the outskirts. The available perceptual field is an infinite plane: no matter how far your light field widens, there will always be more to learn, more you have not yet understood, experienced, or perceived. Let's get curious about the infinite plane. Let's get excited about the enigma that lies outside of our perceptual awareness.

Deliberate Curiosity   Becoming truly curious about someone does wonders for a conversation, which does wonders for a relationship. Curiosity leads to natural questioning that digs deeper into the topic or story the person is divulging. But can and should we force ourselves to be curious?

Many years ago, I was listening to an interesting lecture by renowned businessperson-turned-speaker Brian Tracy that completely enhanced my ability to form relationships through conversation. And it was extremely simple. The basic gist: You can *make* yourself interested in what someone is saying, no matter the topic or perspective. I found it to be true and incredibly powerful. I've used it frequently throughout my life. It's not only helped me form relationships but also kept me interested in topics and perspectives that I might not have otherwise been open to.

For example, there are some people whose main form of conversation is storytelling about their own life experiences. Many of us know someone like that (or maybe it's you!). This form of conversation can be quite tiresome for those listening, especially if it's someone's typical mode of dialogue, because it's not really a conversation—it's just a storytelling session. But if you're up for the challenge, and you're not exhausted or already frustrated, I bet you can actually activate a curious mindset. It may only last for a few minutes, if there's no true back-and-forth in the conversation. But it's great practice.

During conflict, you will probably be much more engaged than during mundane storytelling sessions. Though, you may also be escalated and defensive. The minute you put yourself into a curious state, however, you will immediately lower defensiveness and escalation. That's because defensiveness and curiosity are activated by different neural networks and can't fully operate at the same time. You cannot be authentically curious about someone's perspective and also motivated to defend your own. True curiosity leads to humility. And when you're clearly curious, it will typically help others in the conflict become curious as well. When one person drops their guard, stops trying to be right, and opens up to new information or perspectives, it sets the tone for others to do the same.

You have the power to deliberately become interested and curious about someone at any moment. I encourage you to try it at the next conversation. No matter what they're talking about, even the most mundane, uninteresting topic, put yourself deliberately into a state of curiosity. Make yourself feel interested. I promise, if you're motivated, you can do it, and it will be authentic, even though you pushed yourself into the state.

Compassionate Curiosity Prompting During conflicts, it can be incredibly important to pause and do some reflection before attempting to solve a contentious issue. One method that can shift conflicting parties is called *curiosity prompting*. So, you might ask yourself questions such as these:

- "What am I feeling right now?"
- "What am I *not* feeling right now?"
- "What am I afraid of? Why is that scary? And if that happens, then what am I afraid of?"
- "What would have to be true, and what would I have to know, see, or hear to change my mind?"
- "What about this situation or the other party am I probably not seeing or taking into account?"

Now, ask the same questions about the other person or group. See if you can answer them.

- "What are they probably feeling right now?"
- "What are they probably *not* feeling right now?"
- "What are they likely afraid of? Why would that be scary? And if that happens, then what would be scary for them?"
- "What would have to be true, and what would they likely have to know, see, or hear to change their mind(s)?"
- "What about this situation or me are they probably not seeing or taking into account?"

Answering these questions can really help widen your perceptual lens and foster curiosity about both your deeper psychology and that of the other party. If appropriate, you may want to ask the other party these questions directly to get their answers, especially if you have trouble answering them on your own. You could make them comfortable by first sharing the answers to your self-questions. Such clarity on perspective for all sides of the conflict can be eye-opening and transformative.

Reassociate Contradiction with Curiosity   You can again use reframing and narrative generation to reframe conflicting perspectives and foster curiosity. Here are a few examples you might repeat to yourself in the face of contradiction:

- "Wow, this is so different from what I believe. How interesting."
- "Now that's something I've never heard before. Very interested to explore this alternative perspective."
- "I'm so curious why they have that viewpoint. Let me find out more."
- "Ooh! Okay, here's a chance for me to learn about someone else's mindset."

Pair these curiosity-driven stories enough times with a challenging stimulus, and you'll condition an updated neuropsychological response to conflicting viewpoints.

Moving Forward

Perhaps you've heard of some of the amazing, superpower-like perceptual capabilities of other species. Sharks and rays, for example, have special sensory organs that detect electrical fields produced by the muscle contractions of prey, which is called *electroreception*. Bees use polarization patterns in the sky, which are invisible to us, as a celestial compass for navigation. Migratory animals such as birds and sea turtles can sense the earth's magnetic field to guide their long journeys; to do this, birds are believed to have magnetically sensitive proteins in their eyes that allow them to literally see magnetic fields. Other animals like bats, dolphins, and some whales use echolocation, which enables them to build a three-dimensional sound map of their environments using high-frequency sounds. Even our common household pets are extraordinary: dogs' sense of smell is anywhere from 10,000 to 100,000 times more powerful than ours; and while cat's sense of smell is only about 10 to 15 times stronger than ours, they have a Jacobson's organ (vomeronasal organ), letting them detect pheromones and chemical signals we can't sense at all. This is all to say that the world is absolutely rich with energy fields, waves, and molecules invisible to humans but still perceptible to different types of nervous systems.

This same concept applies between human beings. There are many invisible forces at work all around and inside of each of us, including our mental experiences generated from epigenetic expressions—experiences arising from unique amalgamations of innate biology, memories, and predictions all shaping our individual nervous systems, coloring our perceptions, and directing our brains to precisely what we end up paying attention to. This makes our perceptions of the world completely exclusive to each one of us.

With this in mind, it always serves us to question how certain we can be about contentious issues and how right we believe we are during conflict—possibly even to question the entire paradigm that there is a right and wrong in conflict, at least much of the time. If there is one thing I have learned after intervening in countless conflicts, it's that there are always two sides to the same story, which suggests it's not the same story at all but rather completely different narratives and experiences.

Now that we've ideally opened our minds to the possibility that other perceptions may be valid and that deliberate curiosity would serve our conflict resolution processes, it's time to get talking, and, more important, listening. Using all the human superpowers we've discussed so far—self- and co-regulation, learning to view conflict optimistically, and embodying authentic curiosity—we're set up for the right approach to communicate our way to peace.

4 | Peace Starts in Small Ways

Communication might be thought of as neural telepathy. It's a way to reach into the brains of other organisms and affect their nervous systems and thoughts. We do this with each other and with social animals that are familiar to us, like our household pets. Of course, human beings are the only species, as far as we know, that can generate complex, symbolic, and syntactically structured vocal communication systems called language.

Language is the most powerful mind-influencing system ever created. It powers all that we produce, create, and solve, especially when it comes to conflict resolution and peacebuilding. And the metabolic resources needed to power our socially oriented, language processing neural networks are significant. Some researchers believe our social and language capacities are the reasons we have such large brains and dense cortical regions, evolving human babies to be born before the brain and head grow too big, which leads to us being totally un-self-reliable for many years of our early life. No other species on earth is so dependent on caregivers for as long as humans are. But that's what you get when you have a metabolically expensive brain to grow.

Social communication and language are, on the one hand, biologically innate and, on the other, socially wired. That is, they are epigenetic phenomena—genetic mechanisms that are naturally wired for potential expression but require social learning to be expressed. That's why we don't come out of the womb all speaking the same language, but also why all normally functioning human beings are able to learn to speak in the first years of life without any formal training or education. Researchers also believe that the ability to use language gives humans the unique capacity for abstract thought, a crucial element of creativity, which is critical for conflict resolution.

Complex communication, including the use of language, is processed in several neural networks across various elaborate circuits and brain regions. A fascinating element of our communication is the nuance in which it occurs—nuance that ends up being forgotten when lost within an integrated, everyday experience. This makes sense, of course. We can't slow down to recognize all the tiny components of communication while we're trying to talk, listen, read, or write. It would take way too long. So, our cognitive heuristics jump in to help smooth out the experience. For our purposes, though, it's important to slow things down and learn the important lessons our communication systems can teach us about how to communicate during conflict. As you'll see, it's the small stuff that matters. Peace almost always begins in small interactions, broken down into smaller gestures, utterances, and moments of silence. So, let's get deliberate about how we build peace in small ways.

The Language and Communication Systems

In 2024, my team and I were called to help clients in the entertainment industry resolve an ongoing conflict between two companies that partnered on a multibillion-dollar project. Apparently, the company responsible for creative and their counterpart responsible for finance and operations, each of which employed hundreds of people, were not communicating productively, which was threatening the entire project. When they came to us, they were on the verge of just calling it quits, completely blowing up what the partnership had already spent tens of millions of dollars building. Of course, no one wanted this. During our discovery phase, it became clear that at least 60 people were going to be involved in the initial peacebuilding process, and then perhaps another 100 or so in later stages. Involving this many people in a peace process is no easy task.

My co-facilitators and I knew we would get nowhere fast unless we broke this whole process down into smaller parts, beginning with senior leaders. So, we brought in the three most senior executives, representing creative, finance, and operations, respectively, and began an alignment process. Instead of simply letting their legal personnel write threatening letters to each other's companies, we got these leaders talking and listening to each other. It became quickly clear that although they had some seemingly competing methods of completing the project on time and on budget, these department heads actually had the same goals and shared similar values regarding the project. When we cut out the noise from everyday frustrations and interrupted habitual behaviors, clarity began to emerge.

During this process, something dawned on me about conflict resolution and communication: the smaller we break things down, the easier peace tends to come. Yes, breaking large groups into smaller cohorts of counterparts to get them talking is the first step. But even at the interpersonal level, when two or three people are trying to resolve an issue with each other, it's the little moments, the tiny gestures, expressions, tones, words, and pauses that start to shift things. I noticed how the head of finance lifted his eyebrows and just slightly opened his mouth while listening to the head of creative, indicating a mix of surprise and empathy. And how the head of operations' subtle lowering of vocal tone and slowing of speech made the head of creative visibly relax his face—a sign that his sympathetic nervous system was downregulating. It was like watching an interaction with X-ray vision, where I could see upshifts and downshifts in these individuals' frustration, compassion, and understanding in reaction to each sentence, each facial expression, each body position and vocal tone. I was witnessing in real time how tiny moments in communication lead to large movements in clarity and alignment.

Only when these three senior leaders got aligned with each other did we call in the rest of their teams. We then broke these large teams down into smaller cohorts of counterparts—three or four people per group, with one to two from each company who most closely interacted with each other on a daily basis. So, the large peace process turned into a bunch of small dialogues. An intergroup conflict was transformed into several interpersonal discussions. And once each of these small groups got aligned and arrived at an action plan to communicate and collaborate more effectively, we brought everyone back into a large group to share what they had come up with. This was a multiday process we called an *alignment summit,* and the results were excellent. Both teams, including senior leaders, walked away feeling empowered, renewed, and ready to get back to work. A year later, the project was back on track and moving forward as scheduled. Things weren't perfect (they never are), but the teams had new tools and new commitments that helped them stay on track with how they communicated.

Group conflict is quite common, of course. Conflict happens in its most extreme expression as protracted, escalated, violent conflict between large groups of people, such as in international wars. These types of conflicts can be extremely difficult to resolve through diplomacy and may take dozens of dialogues between multiple cohorts over several years to do so. If we view the prospect of resolution from this standpoint, it's like being at the base of a mountain, knowing we must climb it to get to the other side but wondering how in the world we'll ever reach the top. To maintain optimism and keep our nervous systems regulated, we need to perceive the peace process differently: we need to break it down into small steps, small groups of people, small timelines, and small behaviors. In large conflicts, we might focus on the few, influential individuals who are willing and able meet together this month, and what little step or action or point of alignment we can accomplish in just one meeting. We concentrate on the next step in front of us, not on the top of the mountain. Taking one step is not that difficult. Getting to the top of mountain, however, can feel daunting.

The same thing is true for ongoing interpersonal conflicts. If there's someone in your life with whom just can't seem to communicate well or resolve a long-lasting conflict, it's time to break things down into smaller steps. Throughout this chapter, I'll ask you to think about the tiny moments of communication you can focus on. You don't need to solve it all tomorrow. But you can pick one or two small elements to improve. You can slow down the next conversation, just to see how that feels. Or lower the tone of your voice, or just breathe while listening, or simply try paraphrasing what you hear. Just a tiny gesture, a few words, a subtle, minute shift in communication can set a new path for the relationship.

Remember, don't look at the top of the mountain. Don't expect things to change tomorrow. Just focus on the next step in front of you and take it. Adjust your expectations and trust the process: If you take enough small steps forward, even if you occasionally pause or stray from the path, little by little, eventually you'll arrive at the precipice of peace.

The Magic of Electrochemical Influence

It's quite an extraordinary experience to be a social creature alive on this planet. We get to use our bodies in all sorts of strange ways to influence the electrical and chemical signals inside other animals' bodies. Even nonsocial animals do this, like when one animal runs from another that's trying to hunt it. But we social organisms have the privilege of doing so in mutually beneficial ways. And humans, especially, get to do it with each other in a special exchange that can accomplish something presumably no other animals can: We can communicate with each other to create long-lasting friendships, fruitful partnerships, deeply intimate relationships, brand new ideas, and the collaborative manifestation of tangible things in the real world. All of which would never have been possible without communication.

The creative and relational capacities of our connections are truly greater than that of each individual on our own. And the medium through which we connect is communication—an incredibly complex and nuanced process of using our own bodies to affect the electrochemical processes inside another person's body. Let's break down how communication works so we can marvel at the fascinating conglomeration of phenomena that take place thousands of times a day with each other—phenomena we almost always take for granted. By becoming more aware of these little steps in the communication process, we'll get to deliberately choose one or two small actions to focus on improving during difficult conversations or conflict resolution processes.

Theory of System (ToS)

All observable behavior, whether consciously motivated or unconscious/non-motivated, is communicating something to those who are observing it. From the tiniest eyebrow lift to the clearing of your throat to the total lack of movement, all of it conjures in the mind of an observer what may be happening in your mind. Others are attributing an intention to your behavior (i.e., attribution theory), and they may be doing this with or without conscious awareness. But there's even more than that going on: if you're intentionally communicating something, it means you're also inferring what's happening in the minds of your observers and how you might reinforce, influence, or modify such happenings. When you purchase a stick of gum from a cashier, no words or even looks have to be exchanged for the transaction to occur. By simply placing the gum on the counter, with an understanding of the clerk's role and what placing gum on the counter means to both of you, you're counting on the clerk to understand what you want; and that's enough observable behavior for the clerk to take an action that you intended for that individual to take. There is shared, reciprocal recognition of intentionality leading to changes in each of your minds, activating motor neurons, which drives behaviors that satisfy the desired effect for both parties in the exchange.

Many social animals can do this, since it's a fundamental requirement of communication. If we want to communicate anything to any other conscious agent, we better believe that we can reach in and influence their mental stuff, often in a way that influences their behavior. Most of us who have dogs, for example, can give our furry friends a simple look, and they know exactly what our intentions are. My dog knows I want to play versus go on a walk based on a few, simple facial cues, let alone verbal cues. All animals, humans or otherwise, that communicate with one another have some capacity for attribution.

Humans, however, are the only species, at least as far as we know based on various experiments with all sorts of animals, to recognize that other people and animals have thoughts, beliefs, desires, and perspectives that are different from our own. This capacity is a foundational concept in psychology called *theory of mind (ToM)*. ToM, which emerges in normally functionally humans about age four or five, is the complex social cognitive function that enables us to recognize that others may know something we don't and that others may not know what we know, which stimulates further communication to help people align. However, it also helps people intentionally misalign. That is, ToM enables us to lie to one another—to manipulate other minds into believing things we know are false. This adds an entirely new, complex layer to human communication. Not only are we consistently trying to infer the intentions of others based on their behavior and influence the minds of others through our own behaviors but we're also constantly calculating whether the individual's behaviors are authentic or deliberately misleading and whether we want to be truthful or misleading with our own behavior.

In addition to ToM, we also have theory of a general system. Based on one another's behavior, we're not only able to infer, often accurately, what's happening in someone's mental space but also what's happening in the emotional and physiological space. We can tell when someone is angry, sad, frustrated, stressed, surprised, or joyful; and inferring such emotions does not require an idea of their thoughts. You might not have any idea what just happened to someone or what they're thinking about but can clearly tell they're upset. This inherently enables us to attribute a physiological state to them as well. We can perceive when someone is nervous, uncomfortable, sweating, shaky, or numb, and we feel that in our own nervous systems. All of these observations lead to a theory of predicted behavior—what we believe the person is about to do, including if we predict their behavior to be totally erratic and unpredictable. This layered capacity for attributing mental, emotional, psychological, and behavioral states we could call *theory of system (ToS)* because it's not just the mental or even emotional stuff we're inferring but all the rest of it, too.

Your ToS, stemming from observable and sometimes unobservable cues from another person, emerges from your unique perceptual landscape, which comes from your internal working model, which is based on your memories and predictions (or lack thereof) about the person, the environment, the context, and the behaviors you observe, all of which instruct the regulatory mechanisms of your nervous system to respond appropriately.

While typical, everyday communication is experienced as an effortless flow of back-and-forth interactions, it's clearly an incredibly complex, multisensory phenomenon involving a range of cognitive, behavioral, and neurological processes. Becoming aware of the parts involved in these processes can lend insight into where peace must begin: the little places that set a rich foundation from where cooperation can grow when harvested appropriately.

So, beyond our ToS, what else exactly is happening when we're communicating?

Sender–Channel–Receiver

There are three high-level components involved in all communication: the sender, the transmission channel, and the receiver. Each of these components can be further divided into subcomponents of communication, which illuminate the many small and fascinating steps involved in even a simple interaction.

Sender　When we are the ones delivering a communication—be it via spoken language, written text, a grunt, a smile, or an eyebrow lift—we're employing several important neuropsychological and behavioral resources.

Intention and Motivation　First thing's first, as the sender, we need to do our best to (1) be aware of our own intention behind what we'd like to communicate (the *why*), (2) decide on the most appropriate form and tone to communicate our intended message (the *how*), (3) determine which person(s) need to receive our message (the *who*), (4) develop the correct content or lack thereof to have the best chance of accurately placing our intended message into the mind of the intended receiver (the *what*), and (5) decide on the most appropriate context for delivery, including timing and the environment, to ensure our intention is interpreted accurately by the receiver (the *where* and *when*).

These intentional elements are generated from many distinct neural networks and brain regions all working together, such as our prefrontal cortex (PFC), hippocampus, anterior cingulate cortex, limbic system, default mode network, basal ganglia, and insula, among others. Together, they take into consideration all of the described decision points and help form intention and motivation that are filtered and layered with memories, predictions, and our ToS. So, already, we've got many moving parts . . . and we haven't even begun communicating yet!

Message Construction　Next, the brain employs symbolic encoding in order to choose the correct words, symbols, or gestures to communicate the intended message. When we choose language as the appropriate communication medium, language centers in the brain's left hemisphere—including Broca's area (inferior frontal gyrus) for syntax and Wernicke's area (posterior superior temporal gyrus) for semantics—integrate the message content (e.g., ideas, facts, requests), message structure (e.g., sentence order, emphasis), and lexical choice (e.g., formal versus casual, technical versus simple). At the same time, particularly during spoken language as opposed to written, the brain begins paralinguistic encoding, involving right hemisphere regions and limbic system structures to modulate tone, emotional inflection, pitch, rhythm, volume, and emphasis. In parallel, syntactic and phonological encoding are directed by Broca's area, which generates grammatical structure and phonemes—the smallest possible units of sound in a spoken language that make words perceptually distinct from one another (e.g., *p*, *b*, *d*, and *t* in the English words *pod*, *pot*, *bod*, and *bot*).

To produce speech, our primary motor cortex directs muscles of lips, tongue, larynx, and respiratory system; the cerebellum and basal ganglia coordinate timing, rhythm, and fluency of speech; and the brain stem and cranial nerves V, VII, IX, X, and XII carry motor commands to articulatory muscles.

Whether using spoken language or not, our brains also process nonverbal encoding. This is especially important, of course, when we can be seen by the receiver but may happen naturally whether we are seen or not. Areas including our motor cortex, premotor cortex, brain stem, and cerebellum send signals to our muscles that control our facial expressions, gestures, body posture, eye contact, and haptics (use of touch); our parietal cortex contributes to proxemics (use of space); and our autonomic nervous system directs elements such as micro-expressions and physiological cues (e.g., blushing, pupil dilation).

All of these nuanced components combine instantaneously and without conscious awareness to construct and relay our messages. Any little shift in any one of these mechanisms can completely alter the way a message sends and/or lands. In between sending and landing is the communication channel.

Channel   The first place our messages travel, of course, is through some transmission channel before reaching the receiver. In spoken language or other communicative sound production, we produce physical sound waves (i.e., air vibrations) that may travel through the air directly to someone's ear or may first be converted into digital signals, which travel through cellular radio waves or fiber optics, or into analog signals traveling through copper wires, for example, used by traditional phone lines.

If we're able to be seen while communicating, then the light waves reflecting off our bodies and faces produce light patterns and light wave frequencies, which are ultimately processed by the receiver's visual system. If we're unable to be seen or heard, then we may be using written communication that is converted into digital signals via text, symbols, or images. Or perhaps we're old-school and sending good ole-fashioned letters. In any case, all forms of written or visual information ultimately produce light patterns processed by the visual system.

Whether through sound, light, or neither, we may also be using our physical bodies through space (i.e., proxemics), via the use of mechanical forces, to make physical contact with someone.

Regardless of the transmission channel, once communication travels through time and space in the form of sound, light, or touch, it becomes vulnerable to noise. Noise in communication or psychology refers to potentially confounding elements in the environment that may distort or distract an intended signal. Noise can come in the form of distracting or loud sounds, disruptive light patterns or visual stimuli, technical issues such as poor signal strength, lack of clarity in semantics or language, or physiological or psychological stress on the part of the receiver, among others.

Lots of systems and mediums have to align for an intended communication to reach the sensory receptors of its intended receiver without massive distortion. Once the message reaches those receptors, a whole other process begins.

Receiver   The first thing that happens when we are on the receiving end of a communication is, as just stated, that a receiver's sensory receptors pick up the sender's signals via the transmission channel.

Auditory Sensory Processing   When we receive communication via sound, whether through spoken language, visceral noises like grunts, or other sounds like car horns or music, our auditory mechanisms decode the data. Remember, this is not just about language processing. In fact, most of what we infer from communication comes not from the symbolic content of words but from the tone, volume, and top-down processing (i.e., predictions) of messages.

When receiving auditory data, sound waves via air vibrations enter the ear through the external auditory canal until they hit the tympanic membrane (i.e., eardrum); the pressure waves then pass through the ossicles (i.e., the malleus, incus, and stapes), which vibrate in sequence, causing the stapes to press against the oval window of the cochlea. The oval window's motion pushes fluid inside the cochlea (i.e., inner ear), converting air vibrations into fluid waves. The cochlea—specifically the fluid inside it and the hair cells of the organ of Corti—directly transduce the pressure waves into neural signals. Those electrical impulses then travel a sophisticated pathway, including through the brain stem, pons, and thalamus, before reaching the primary auditory cortex (in Heschl's gyrus of the superior temporal lobe) where it analyzes sound features (e.g., pitch, intensity, timing) and then the secondary auditory cortex (A2, belt and parabelt regions), where it extracts more complex features of sound (e.g., patterns, phonemes, melodies) and begins distinguishing speech from nonspeech sounds.

Language Processing To process language specifically, the Wernicke's area (i.e., posterior superior temporal gyrus) decodes words, semantics, and sentence-level meaning. Meanwhile, the arcuate fasciculus (i.e., white matter tract) connects Wernicke's area to Broca's area, enabling linguistic comprehension to link with speech production, which is important for conversation. The right superior temporal regions decode tone of voice, intonation, sarcasm, and emotional coloring, working with the insula and amygdala to apply affect and meaning to speech. To integrate language with context and memory, the angular gyrus and supramarginal gyrus link sound and language to concepts, while the hippocampus and medial temporal lobe layer in memory context.

Visual Sensory Processing When we can see the sender delivering a message, our visual processing of their face, body language, and the surrounding environment plays a significant role in interpretating communication. Of course, we also use visual processing any time we receive written or image-based messages.

To receive and decode visual data, light waves bouncing off external objects (e.g., faces, bodies, environments, paper, digital screens, etc.) are captured by the eye cornea and lens, which focus those light waves onto the retina. The retina contains photoreceptors that transduce light waves into neural signals. Specifically, the rods pick up dim light, motion, and black and white light wavelengths, while the cones are sensitive to color frequencies (i.e., red, green, and blue wavelengths). Once transduced, these neural signals are preprocessed by the bipolar and ganglion cells, the latter of which have axons that form the optic nerve.

These now-transduced electrical pulses traverse from the retina through the optic nerve and then optic tract to the brain, landing in the lateral geniculate nucleus inside the thalamus, which acts as a main relay station for visual input, organizing visual data into layers for motion, detail, and color. In parallel, data is transmitted to the superior colliculus in the midbrain for fast, reflexive visual processing, including orienting the eyes and head toward a stimulus (i.e., visual grasp reflex), coordinating saccadic eye movements, and detecting sudden movement in the periphery, which is important for survival.

After hitting the thalamic relay station, the thalamus sends the electrical data to the primary visual cortex in the brain's occipital lobe. This first cortical stop processes edges, orientation, spatial frequency, and basic patterning. Then, data gets sent to the secondary visual cortices, which integrate contours, depth, more detailed color, shape perception, and motion perception.

The signals then travel from the occipital lobe to the inferior temporal lobe and the parietal lobe simultaneously, which are two major streams of visual processing. The ventral stream in the temporal lobe identifies and makes meaning of objects, faces, and words, while the dorsal stream in the parietal lobe processes spatial location, movement, and visually guided actions, including gesture recognition, hand-eye coordination, and proxemics in communication.

Phew! That's a hefty process to comprehend. Now, keep in mind as we continue: All of this processing purely involves electrical and chemical signals, at various frequencies and intensities, being translated by your brain and producing an experience of consciousness that feels like seeing.

Somatosensory Processing   An additional and important element of communication, when present, is the interpretation of touch from the sender. While this isn't always a part of communication, or appropriate, when it is employed, touch certainly influences our construal of the message.

To process touch during communication, a variety of mechanoreceptors in the skin transduce physical pressure, vibration, and stretch into neural signals. When someone touches us, these receptors de-form and open ion channels, producing action potentials (i.e., neural signals) in sensory neurons. The signals then travel along afferent nerve fibers to the spinal cord, where they enter the dorsal root ganglia and ascend through the dorsal column medial lemniscal pathway to reach the brain.

First-order neurons synapse in the dorsal column nuclei (e.g., gracile and cuneate nuclei, medulla), while second-order neurons decussate (i.e., cross) to the opposite side and ascend via the medial lemniscus to the thalamus. The thalamus once again acts as a central switchboard, refining and routing signals to cortical (i.e., higher order processing) areas.

Signals reach the primary somatosensory cortex, specifically S1 of the postcentral gyrus in the parietal lobe, which charts the touch signals into a somatotopic map or homunculus. Here, the brain processes basic features like location, pressure, texture, and intensity of the touch. Signals also get processed in the secondary somatosensory cortex (S2 or parietal operculum) and associated cortical areas, which together integrate bilateral touch, generate object recognition by touch (i.e., haptic recognition), and incorporate touch with vision and proprioception (i.e., the body's ability to sense its position, movement, and action in space). All of these capacities are important for gesture and body language awareness and interpretation.

Valence and Interpretation Ultimately, whether from auditory, visual, and/or somatosensory data, the signals reach the higher cortical areas and limbic regions for experiential integration, interpretation, and prediction. The amygdala and associated limbic structures apply rapid emotional evaluation of faces, tones, touch, gestures, and other elements of the interaction (e.g., threatening versus friendly). Meanwhile, our PFC, especially the medial PFC, infers intention and pragmatic meaning (e.g., "They said x, but they meant y" or "They touched my arm to reassure me, not to push me away"). And, due to our predictive coding functionality, the brain is essentially constructing meaning of messages, images, or touch even before inputting all this sensory information.

Combined with all these sensing and decoding mechanisms, our valence and memory processing systems are evaluating and judging the sender, including the context of the interaction and the relationship in general. For example, the amygdala and orbitofrontal cortex evaluate the sender's trustworthiness and emotional valence, including threat versus safety cues; the insula integrates bodily states with emotional tone, supporting empathy and affective interpretation; the angular gyrus connects both written and spoken language with broader concepts related to the sender and the world, supporting metaphor deconstruction, narrative meaning, and perspective taking as well as linking language with conceptual knowledge; the hippocampus and medial temporal lobes retrieve past conversations, autobiographical memories, and cultural schemas that shape interpretation; the prefrontal regions assess credibility of the sender as well as consistency within the context; and the ToM network (e.g., medial PFC, superior temporal sulcus, temporoparietal junction) infers the sender's intentions and perspective.

Reciprocation Finally, the receiver's PFC formulates a response based on the their interpretation, goals, and social norms. The communication process then reverses and repeats. Because, of course, interpersonal communication is not usually a one-way street but a dynamic neuropsychological interplay that includes feedback loops. The sender monitors their own communication, detects errors, and adapts in real time, while the receiver's verbal and nonverbal responses inform the sender's adjustments.

In short, the entire process can be high-level mapped as follows:

> Sender: Intention → Encoding (verbal, nonverbal, paralinguistic) → Message Production → Medium → Noise → Receiver: Sensory perception → Neural transduction → Integration with memory/prediction → Evaluation (trust, context, emotion) → Meaning construction → Response (*Receiver becomes the sender.*)

All of these incredibly complex and nuanced processes typically go back and forth, quickly and effortlessly. That's because in normally functioning brains, communication is deeply hardwired as implicit, procedural memory, like walking. You needed to learn and practice it initially, but doing so was easy, requiring little if any conscious effort. We learned communication when we were young, when our brains were tremendously plastic, and because, frankly, our brains were built for this stuff.

As you can tell, there are so many tiny processes and components, all playing their parts, all working together in an incredibly fascinating and complex neuropsychological fusion that creates a virtually seamless and integrated multidimensional experience in time and space of the other person and their intentions. Given the complexity of communication, it's a wonderful miracle that we have any idea at all what one another is attempting to communicate.

With so many little elements influencing interactions, it's no wonder that conflicts often erupt from miscommunication and misinterpretation. Which highlights the importance of communication and reinterpretation to help resolve conflicts. If poor communication causes most interpersonal conflicts, then it would serve us to get better at it. Indeed, with the capacity to influence others' minds and bodies, and for them to influence ours, in a way that can either align or misalign us, the significance of communication in conflict resolution cannot be understated.

The Importance of Communication in Conflict Resolution

You don't have to have a PhD in conflict analysis to recognize that conflicts get resolved peacefully primarily through communication. In fact, it sort of goes without saying that nonviolent, interpersonal conflict typically requires healthy, mutually respectful conversations to resolve. But hey, why not say it anyway—because it's worth reinforcing. We absolutely will not solve our disagreements or interpersonal tensions without some form of effective communication, be it direct dialogue or some other communicative method. Sure, we might be able to ignore the tension for a bit. Sometimes it might even disappear if we just pretend it's not there. But in most conflicts, especially long-standing or complex ones, there needs to be some communication about the real, underlying issues and/or our shared preferences about the relationship moving forward, if we're to have any hope of resolving the issues and improving the relational dynamic. This is especially evident when considering the consequences of conflict resolution methods that do not use communication.

Conflict Resolution Without Communication

One common noncommunicative approach to managing conflict is avoidance, where people simply avoid interacting with each other as much as possible. In some cases, when completely avoiding the other person or group is sustainable, this may actually resolve the conflict and bring both parties more peace. In other cases, when the individuals have no choice but to have at least minimal interaction, such as with coworkers or former romantic partners who are co-parenting, avoidance might also feel more peaceful. In fact, many people end up using the avoidance method after they have tried unsuccessfully to communicate about their issues. Sometimes, parties have given up on trying to communicate effectively, especially when no one believes their counterparts will listen, change, or address the real problems.

These situations are unfortunate because whether avoidance feels like the easiest route or the only option left, there may always be tension bubbling just beneath the surface. And festering tension has the potential to erupt. In work settings, I have seen such avoidance stifle opportunities to collaborate and innovate; it also makes other coworkers, who have relationships with the people avoiding each other, feel uncomfortable and sometimes demoralized, causing stress for the wider team. This is obviously not ideal for organizational success. In families, the avoidance approach tends to have a similar effect, causing discomfort and stress for surrounding family members, including children. Again, not ideal.

The other extreme form of noncommunicative conflict resolution is the control approach. Rather than avoid the other person or group, we try to control their behaviors, thereby debilitating their abilities to conflict with us. We may attempt to control through a variety of ways. We could become aggressive and try to intimidate someone into submission. If we have greater authority or resources than our counterpart, or greater influence on someone who does have the authority or resources, we could impose rules and regulations that would constrain their behavior. We could use the law or court system in a way that limits them. We could also forcefully or underhandedly direct them into education or training programs that aim to change and control their beliefs and behavior.

At the group level specifically, since avoidance is typically not sustainable and communication is often difficult, the control approach is regularly used. With intragroup conflict (i.e., issues arising within a particular group of people), the group may choose to control group members by way of explicit laws or regulations and/or implicit rules, such as cultural norms that would impose shame or embarrassment for breaking with standards. With intergroup conflict, especially between conflicting nations, one or both groups may feel they have exhausted all communication attempts and so must take the control approach, as complete avoidance is virtually impossible, especially if they share a border. To implement control, one nation might take measures to bolster security across their border or, at extreme levels, invade the other country in order to constrain them; or one or both countries might agree to an intermediary body that can help manage and police the relationship, ensuring boundaries are enforced and both parties are held accountable for their actions.

From a strategic perspective, both the avoidance and control approaches have their merits whether for group-level or interpersonal conflicts. Perhaps communication has been attempted multiple times in various ways and has led to little progress. Perhaps the parties don't have the ability or motivation to effectively communicate, in which case communication may make the conflict even worse. Maybe the conflict needs to be resolved or at least managed quickly because it has a risk of leading to extreme circumstances, such as the loss of a major business deal or group violence; and since communicative approaches can take longer to resolve conflict, at least one of the parties involved feels avoidance or control is the safest or most strategic approach. They could even decide that a noncommunicative approach is best now but plan to take a more communicative approach in the future.

At the end of the day, there is no necessarily right or wrong way to resolve conflict. Remember, conflict is a neutral energy—a field of pure potential. We can be constructive or destructive with it; our strategy depends on our goals. Do we want to find peace? If so, do we think peace requires that we improve the relationship with the other person(s)? Or can we simply avoid or control them? Which is likely the most sustainable and least costly way of building and maintaining peace? All of these questions ought to be thought through when deciding whether or not to use avoidance, control, or communication in attempting to resolve conflict.

You'll notice one commonality between the avoidance and control approaches: Neither addresses the needs, goals, or values of the other person or group, and so neither presents an opportunity for a better relationship between the conflicting parties. Again, this is not necessarily bad or wrong. But if we want a better relationship with someone whom we find difficult or challenging—if we want to find opportunities for growth, collaboration, and mutual benefit—there is no better way than through communication. Both control and avoidance have different trajectories than relational enhancement. The best and perhaps only way to improve the relationship while resolving conflict is through effective communication.

Conflict Resolution with Communication

Communication is the only method that I have seen anecdotally and that has been proven empirically to improve relationships. There are two general methods of successfully communicating through conflict: the problem-solving approach (i.e., direct communication about the problems) or the common ground approach (i.e., communication that focuses on areas of alignment and circumvents the problems). The most effective method depends on the nature of the relationship and the goals of the people involved.

I have a friend who has, throughout his life, experienced tension with his father. They simply don't see eye to eye on several topics. Yet, they both care deeply about each other and want a good relationship. Over the years, they have attempted to communicate about their conflicting beliefs directly, but it never led anywhere productive. In fact, my friend believes that such conversations only regressed the relationship. So, they have quietly decided to stop talking about their points of disagreement. They never deliberately said they would avoid the topics; they just started avoiding them. Instead, they talk about subjects they align on, like football, family, and travel. So, this is not an avoidant peace strategy; rather, it is a strategic approach to building trust and maintaining the relationship by focusing on commonality rather than on differences.

Like many people who have chosen to avoid discussing politics or religion with those whom they disagree, my friend and his father developed an implicit boundary around the subjects they're willing to discuss. And it works. As long as they both adhere to the quiet rule, they enjoy being around each other and satisfy their desire for connection with one another. While they *could* find an opportunity for growth and even deeper connection if they were to engage a skilled mediator or counselor to help them talk through their issues directly, there is no guarantee that would work or that it would be worth the trouble. In fact, they have adhered to their implicit boundaries long enough to establish increasingly greater trust with each other, and over time they've finally reached a place where their connection and their feelings for one another far outweigh any of the issues they disagree on, making such issues totally unnecessary to address. My friend and his dad have had enough pleasant interactions over a long enough period of time to transform how they feel about one another, leaving their tension in the distant past.

This common ground approach has also been proven quite an effective method of resolving conflict and transforming relationships in the intergroup conflict literature. In 1954, renowned social psychologist Gordon Allport developed one of the most influential and foundational frameworks still used in conflict resolution called *intergroup contact theory*. Allport posited that when groups in conflict have frequent, positive contact with each other, they would begin to see each other more positively and break down old prejudices. He suggested there were a few important requirements for contact to work, none of them directly addressing their issues of disagreement or conflict.

More than 500 published studies, across different cultures and contexts all around the world, have supported the fact that positive contact, even if only imagined, does help members of historically conflicting groups perceive and treat each other more positively. Despite Allport's suggestion that there were particular requirements, a meta-analysis of hundreds of studies indicates that positive contact alone is enough for a robust positive effect, but that several of Allport's conditions can enhance this effect. One modulator, which Allport hypothesized, is when the groups are given common, interdependent tasks or goals; instead of talking about their issues directly, group members focus on a shared goal that requires they work together to achieve it.

Another powerful modulator is superordinate identity salience, which is a fancy way of describing a focus on shared identity. For example, groups in conflict within a nation might focus on their shared nationality rather than on their disparate groups; and members of different nations in conflict might focus on their shared humanity rather than on their national identities. Without trying to solve their points of disagreement directly, the relationships can transform and conflicts can diminish simply by having repeated, positive contact and enhancing such contact with these and other modulating strategies.

The same framework can be mapped onto interpersonal conflict. When direct problem-solving isn't successful or appropriate, individuals in conflict can instead make efforts to simply have frequent, consistently positive contact with each other. They can focus on shared identity, values, and needs and on common, interdependent goals rather than on their differences or areas of disagreement. Coworkers who have not seen eye to eye might choose to instead focus on shared values or collaborative projects in which they do agree. By doing so, over time, they can rebuild trust and re-perceive one another in a more positive light.

These effects can set a healthy relational foundation for the parties to eventually feel safe and trusting enough to dialogue about the issues directly, should they feel that would be constructive at some point. Ultimately, the common ground communication approach requires two important elements to be successful: (1) that all parties agree with the approach (i.e., they agree, explicitly or implicitly, to focus on commonalities and not discuss contentious issues) and (2) that everyone is motivated to improve or maintain their relationship. If we're motivated to get along and we agree to focus on areas of alignment and not bring up topics of high tension, we might just build enough trust to improve the relationship over time.

The other central communicative approach to conflict resolution is problem-solving, which is the method most often discussed in conflict resolution and mediation practices. In this strategy, finding common ground is also an effective practice, but it is used to build a bridge between parties' underlying needs so they can directly address their issues more effectively, as opposed to purposefully circumventing their points of contention.

In practice, people dialogue about their issues either on their own or with an intermediary who is not involved in the conflict, such as a mediator, counselor, negotiation consultant, respected leader, or employee relations representative. With or without a mediator, conversations about complex or long-standing conflicts are often most productive when the parties have first had at least some training or coaching on communication best practices, such as how to effectively deliver and receive hard-to-hear feedback, how to disagree respectfully, how to hold others accountable in peaceful ways, and basic conflict resolution and communication skills.

Effective communication during conflict often requires digging underneath surface-level complaints and concerns to uncover deeper, underlying needs, goals, and values at play. The more clarity each party has regarding their counterparts' perceived threats to their psychological needs, the more likely they are to understand and relate to one another. All of us have the same core needs, and many of us have similar core values and goals. It just takes a little digging to find common ground.

Being intentional about our communication style is also incredibly important for problem-solving during conflict. Appropriate styles may include empathic behaviors, perspective taking, appropriate apologies, optimism, and focusing on modifying behavior and tasks rather than on personality or character. Since there are indeed so many little, dynamic elements involved in communication, discussing issues with intention, clarity, understanding, and empathy may take practice. But the more intentional we are about what and how we'd like to communicate, the more likely we are to gain understanding and reach solutions that will solve the real issues, decrease threat perception, improve the relationship, and maintain peace over the long run.

Empirical research has also shown the positive effects of solution-focused communication on relationships and peace process outcomes. In fact, entire books have been written on the subject, presenting both qualitative and quantitative evidence of the efficacy of dialogue for solving conflict at both the interpersonal and group levels. Studies have been applied between marital partners, family members, groups representing international opponents, arbitrary experimental groups, and in workplaces. In organizational research, highly cited meta-analyses, which calculate the results of several previous studies, showed that clarity in communication can help keep conflicts solution-focused rather than character-focused, that effective dialogue can diminish the negative effects of conflict on relationships, and that communication style often determines whether conflict is constructive or destructive.

If our goal is to use conflict as an opportunity to build trust, learn, grow, and heal relationships, communication is ultimately the only way forward.

And every small element of communication holds the potential for large effects. After a recap, we'll look at some tools to translate these small components into actionable practices.

Recap: The Language and Communication Systems

Sending and receiving, speaking and listening, behaving and observing—this stuff we call communication is really quite fascinating and inspiring. It happens between individuals, groups, and even species. It is the way we regulate (or dysregulate) one another's nervous systems and influence each other's thoughts, emotions, and behaviors. In this sense, communication can also be thought of as intersystem circuitry: a way for signals in one nervous system to activate signals in another. Over time, as we get to know people and predict how they will behave and communicate, our neural system may, in a figurative sense, wire together with another person's system. This intersystem circuitry is part of co-regulation and conditioning, and it all starts and sustains with communication.

To be more deliberate about the ways we co-regulate with others' systems, we'll need to implement effective communication practices, both as senders and receivers. As you become more aware of your communication techniques and styles, keep intersystem circuitry in mind. You may just find yourself wiring with others in more peace-oriented ways. Now, to our tools.

Tools to Build Peace in Small Ways

Peace begins, solidifies, and sustains from all the tiny factors that together create the experience of human-to-human interaction. The style in which we speak and listen to each other; the context in which it happens; the gestures, body language, and tone we employ; the interpretations and predictions our brains invoke—each and every part of it carries a small, moment-to-moment opportunity for peace. We should not take these nuanced communication particles for granted. Rather, we should recognize and cultivate them with intention. In this section, we'll discuss ways we can become more deliberate and strategic about *how* we communicate. These tools can help us improve communication, whether we're taking the problem-solving or common ground approach to conflict resolution.

> **NOTE:** *We're not yet going to dive into the content of messages (i.e., what exactly we should be communicating during conflict resolution). We'll tackle that in Principle 5. For now, we'll simply discuss best practices for peace-oriented communication, including the small mechanical and contextual elements we should be aware of and cultivate to build peace.*

Communicating as a Sender

Communication is typically a fluid role exchange between sender and receiver. In most conversations, we play both roles rapidly and frequently, almost without distinction. That said, here are some exercises we can practice or consider when sending messages during a communication. With greater awareness and capacity, we'll be able to use communication more effectively to resolve conflicts.

First, I want you to think of a person with whom you'd like a better relational dynamic, whether that means a closer friendship, a more collaborative working relationship, or simply being more pleasant and polite to each other. To achieve this, let's start planning the next conversation you'd like to have with them. The dialogue could be directly about the issues themselves (i.e., the problem-solving approach) or it could be circumventing the issues to focus on simply having a positive interaction about shared values, needs, or goals (i.e., the common ground approach). Bring the situation to mind, and let's start planning.

Adjust Expectations to Small Steps Relationships are built on many small moments of communication, from a friendly smile to a light touch on the hand. The first thing to keep in mind when attempting to rebuild peace and adjust a relationship is not to go for the big win every time. One conversation isn't likely to change everything. Change will take many small moments over some period of time. But recognize that these tiny, positive moments are not insignificant. They can lead to a positive sense of that particular interaction, and many positive interactions over time can change the relationship. Be patient with peace. Adjust your expectations about how fast trust and relationships can be established or reestablished after past conflict. Having more realistic expectations is likely to prevent intense frustration and instead support a more optimistic and teamship-oriented approach to peacebuilding.

Be Ultra Clear About Your Intention   Most people don't think a whole lot before speaking; they just blurt out what comes to mind, ideally after some appropriate filtering for the context. Some people don't even filter well—you know, the folks who are known for "not having a filter." So, at this first step, without some clear intentional direction, communication may already be doomed. Before communicating with someone who you find difficult, you'll want to be purposeful about the interaction. Having a clear intention requires a level of self-awareness and self-reflection. Regarding your upcoming conversation, here are some questions to ask yourself beforehand:

- "If I could reach into their mind and plant a message directly, what would it be?"
- "To achieve that, what's the most appropriate and clear way of articulating the message?"
- "What's likely the best timing of the message? Is it immediately, or should I wait for a more conducive period for the message to be received accurately? How can I tell?"
- "What is an appropriate setting for this particular message? Is the current environment sufficient, or should I wait or ask for a different setting?"
- "What words, tone, and body language would be most effective for the time and place of the message?"
- "Does the other person seem like they're in the right emotional state to receive the message?"
- "Am I in the right emotional state to send this in a respectful and clear way?"
- "Who should be around? Should we be alone or around other people? If the latter, then which others?"

- ■ "What outcome am I truly hoping for? Is it understanding, agreement, compromise, or simply to be heard?"
- ■ "What might they need from me in order to feel safe enough to engage (e.g., reassurance, validation, patience)?"
- ■ "How might they perceive my message differently than I intend? What assumptions could they make?"
- ■ "What is my backup plan if the conversation becomes tense or derails? How will I respond without escalating?"
- ■ "Am I willing to really listen and adjust, or am I only focused on being heard?"
- ■ "If I were them, what questions would I want answered before I could hear this message?"

These questions should be answered thoughtfully so as to afford the greatest likelihood of your message being received and interpreted in the manner you intend. And for you to be ready to listen and respond appropriately to various potential responses from the receiver. Of course, we have no control over anyone else's interpretations. Nonetheless, there's no point in sending a message unless we believe it's got a good chance of being received and understood the way we intended. So, do your best to be mindful and intentional prior to communicating.

Let Your Expression Lead Your Tone   Research has shown that changes in facial gestures, such as smiling, actually influence vocal tone in the direction of one's expression. It has also been shown to influence word choice when sending written messages. If you want to convey concern, wear a concerned face. If you want to evoke positivity or happiness, wear a smile. Remember this whether you're seen, heard, or neither. These facial expressions influence your communication style even when texting or emailing. The same is true in the opposite direction. If you don't want to come off angry, for example, monitor your facial muscles. Typical signs of anger or frustration include clenched jaw muscles, furrowed brow lines, squinted eyes, or a scrunched nose; so do your best to relax these if you want the conversation to be less tense.

Remember the Small Stuff Very little of communication relies on the contents of our messages. Much more of it stems from the nuances of tone, volume, cadence, and body language. You could utter the exact same words in a variety of ways, and it would relay a totally different meaning each time. Think about the different ways you could say "Hey, you." It could come off loving, friendly, professional, or angry, depending on the way you deliver the message.

For pure auditory communication, when facial expressions and body language aren't seen, interpretation will rely more heavily on tone, volume, and cadence. For written communication, when only content is available, a receiver will fill in the gaps with their own assumptions of a sender's tone and emotional state, which rely heavily on the context and the dynamics of your relationship. Imagine writing "Hey, you" to someone. The context and relationship alter whether it's interpreted as abrupt, rude, or jovial.

In any medium, for our intended message to be received most accurately, we need to monitor our tone, cadence, volume, facial expression, body language, and physical positioning, whichever are at play, and all within the context of the situation and relationship.

This all being said, considering all of the little, nuanced processes and mechanisms involved in communication, it would be too heavy a cognitive load to stay aware of each and every element involved at all times. In fact, doing so could lead to neuroticism and hyper-reflection—a phenomenon known as *self-monitoring overload* or *metacognitive interference*. In other words, if you think too much about what exactly you're saying and how you're saying it, you're likely to stumble and be less effective at communicating. So, although self-awareness about how we are communicating should level up when we'd like to resolve a conflict and improve a relationship, especially when the stakes are high, I suggest focusing on just one or two elements at a time (e.g., tone and/or body language). Experiment with them. See how they feel and if they enhance your ability to communicate more effectively, with special attention on how conversations around contentious issues go. Are they seeming to go more smoothly, getting to solutions more quickly, and building trust more evidently as a result of greater self-awareness?

At the least, if you were to focus on only one element when sending a message, bring it back to your intention. When you are extremely clear and purposeful about what and how you'd like to communicate, your brain will likely figure out the rest. It will steer your tone, body language, and decision-making about context, word choice, and channel in a way that has the best chance of landing your intended message.

Choosing the Channel

As stated, one of the decisions you have to make as someone initiating a conversation is the best delivery system or medium of communication. Ask yourself these questions:

- "Will it be best with verbal language or communicated some other way (e.g., facial expressions or physical gestures)?"
- "Will the language be sent verbally or written?" (I highly recommend any emotionally charged conversation take place via phone, video, or in person—not written, as there is too much room for misinterpretation of tone and intention.)
- "If verbally, will it be sent via audio channels only? Will that afford me the ability to most appropriately land my message? Would having visual cues be more effective, such as on video or in person?"
- "What's the likelihood of misinterpretation in my chosen channel?" Text strips away tone, audio strips away facial cues, video restores both but can add pressure.
- "What level of richness does the message require? Does it need immediate feedback, emotional nuance, or nonverbal cues?"
- "How permanent should the message be? Do I want it documented in writing, or is this better as a transient, spoken exchange?"
- "What level of privacy is required? Is the medium secure and confidential enough for the sensitivity of the message?"
- "What accessibility factors matter? Does the recipient have hearing, language, cultural, or technological needs that make one channel more effective?"
- "What is their communication preference? Do they feel more comfortable processing ideas in writing first, or do they thrive in dialogue?"
- "How much control do I need over pacing?" Asynchronous channels like email allow thought-out responses; synchronous channels like calls allow immediate feedback and room for clarification.

Communication scholars have devised *media richness theory*, which suggests that richer channels like face-to-face and video—those that provide immediate feedback, multiple cues (verbal, nonverbal, emotional tone), and personalization—are most effective when the message is ambiguous, sensitive, or emotionally charged. Leaner channels like email or text, which strip away many of these cues, are better suited for straightforward, low-ambiguity information such as driving directions or scheduling logistics. Keeping this in mind can help ensure we match the right message with the right channel, reducing the risk of unnecessary conflict or misinterpretation. Let's be more mindful of our channel choice and the opportunities and limitations each channel affords.

Communicating as a Receiver   To communicate effectively, we also need to be an effective receiver, and that means receiving sense data with the right kind of brain. Indeed, listening or reading to receive is just as, if not more, important as sending a message. The way we interpret someone's messages will influence how we respond, which influences the interaction from that point forward. The key is to do our best to infer meaning with the least amount of distortion, including from our own filters and predictions. Of course, we can't know for sure what someone's intentions are, even though we automatically and unconsciously attribute their intentions to the behaviors we witness. But being aware of our automatic attributions and limiting them in a reasonable way can be helpful in being an effective receiver. Here are a few tools to consider.

Pause Before Responding   Most of us are habituated to respond quickly when people speak to us. We're used to having easy, back-and-forth conversations in everyday interactions. Some of us are also accustomed to responding swiftly and perhaps aggressively when in a difficult conversation and our defense systems bolster; others may shut down and go quiet. To be effective receivers during conflict, preparing for an appropriate response, we ought to stay engaged and learn to respond strategically. This often requires reconditioning and practice.

Every situation is different. Some interactions will call for more intense responses, while others require more empathy and caretaking. The best thing you can do as an effective receiver who is prone to respond in the most appropriate way for the goals of the particular interaction is to simply pause before responding. This doesn't mean disengage or shutdown. Rather, just give yourself a moment to really let the message sink in before formulating a response. Take time to consider what your goals are in the situation and with the relationship. What would you like to see happen? How best to make sure the sender feels heard, like their needs are being considered, and also to advocate for your own needs? What would be the most appropriate response considering this relationship and where you'd like it to be?

You might even let the sender know that you are purposefully pausing so they don't assume you are disengaging. For example, you might say, "Thank you for letting me know. Give me just a minute to process that. I want to make sure I really consider what you're saying."

Pausing before responding can make an incredible difference in the trajectory of that conversation. And every conversation has a real impact on the trajectory of your relationship. Remember, it's all the little moments, combined over time, that count.

Separate Sensory Processing from ToS   The next important element of being an effective receiver is to receive in the cleanest way possible. Remember all the filters that sense data goes through when being processed by our sensory systems: from receptors through neurons to various brain areas. Remember also that signal processing requires both these neurophysiological mechanisms and our brain's top-down predictive processing, which includes interpretation of sensory data. There's nothing much we can do about the way our brains process sensory information, and we wouldn't want to. But there is potentially something we can do about the unconscious automaticity of combining both sensory and interpretative data: we can become conscious of the two elements as separate processes. I call this *separating sensory processing from ToS.*

In usual, everyday communication, we are sensing others' sounds, behaviors, and/or symbolic texts and then quickly attributing emotional, physiological, and mental states to them. This process is where we can get tricked up with miscommunication and misinterpretation and why we need to remain aware of these attributions when attempting to resolve conflict and establish trust in relationships.

Let's be clear. The stimulus of conflict—that is, the thing that makes you feel stressed or frustrated about someone else—is not the person. It's the combination of their *behavior* and how our nervous systems appraise that behavior. The extent to which we do not like what someone says or does depends on our interpretation, judgment, or evaluation. So, separating sense data from ToS can also be thought of as separating someone's behavior from our interpretation of that behavior.

Now, it might be clear that someone's behavior is, in fact, problematic in a particular setting. Every context, from a workplace to a family setting, has a set of cultural norms, rules, and expectations that are applied to language and behavior. When someone deviates from those norms, most observers in that context find the behavior problematic and potentially find themselves in conflict with the person(s) who deviated. For example, when someone level-skips at work, going around someone to their boss, such a deviation from the implicit or explicit rule is likely problematic. But notice, even when most people in a particular setting agree that a behavior is problematic, it is due to an interpretation of that behavior. Yes, the level-skipper broke the norm, and that might be an issue, but it's most emotionally triggering not because of the rule violation alone but rather because of the meaning of that behavior (e.g., "they don't respect me, so they just cut me out and went to my boss.")

In other words, conflict is not only about behavior; it's about how we interpret behavior. And in most cases of interpersonal conflict, someone's behavior is not so cut and dry. Perhaps the level-skipper didn't understand the rule or mistakenly thought going to the boss directly *was* the rule. There are potentially other explanations, intentions, or interpretations of a behavior, which it would serve to explore and clarify.

Also, some behavior might not be objectively defined as problematic. We often find ourselves in conflict with someone purely because of a subjective experience of that individual's communication or actions—what we believe they meant relative to ourselves or those we care about. Maybe everyone level skips at your workplace, and it's not necessarily a rule in your work culture. But for some reason, when that particular individual does it, the behavior bothers you because you think it means something particularly malicious or deviant. Again, a ripe place to begin separating someone's behavior from your interpretation.

There is another layer to this worth exploring as well. One might say that it's not someone's behaviors that anger me, it's their ideas or their values. However, I would challenge that claim. Someone's ideas cannot hurt you *unless* those ideas turn into actions that are in conflict with you. So, what bothers us about people's ideas is not the ideas themselves but rather the imagination of what those ideas might lead to in the real world relative to you and the people you care about. In the case of ideas, it may not be behavior in the present that feels problematic, but rather a projection of behavior, action, or events in the future.

So, we need to get extremely clear on exactly what someone's message(s) actually meant and what it means for us now and, potentially, in the future. And, if we feel deeply stressed or angry, we should do some digging beneath the surface of our thoughts to discover our deeper interpretative stories. If we do not separate these out and gain clarity from the individual or group about their intentions and plans, we are likely to spiral into story land, assuming the worst, and seeing them in an increasingly cynical way all the while our stress response becomes more activated.

The point is that we want to interrupt our automatic judgment of someone during communication. For instance, if you were to take someone's message and place it in the mouth of a complete stranger or even a robot, what do you think it would mean? If you were take yourself out of the equation, imagining the message was not sent to you but rather to someone else, would it mean the same thing? To practice in real time, we'll simplify. We're going to separate the sender's behavior from our own interpretation of the behavior.

Think of your upcoming or recent conversation—when someone in particular did or said something that really bothered you or made you feel stressed or insecure. Picture it in your mind. Have it? Okay, now let's separate out what they did or said from your interpretation of it. What did it mean to you? What do you believe they intended, and what negative outcomes might arise from such intentions? What were you concerned about? Let's call your someone Sam.

You might have heard Sam say, "I guess you won't be at the meeting." And the way you interpreted that was: *Sam is angry that I'm not coming to the meeting.* And what that interpretation means for you now or in the future is that *Sam's unhappy with me, and this could hurt my professional standing here.* At this point, I want you to dig even deeper, underneath the surface-level interpretation. Let's get to the core of the story. Ask yourself *what's scary about that?* But don't ask your rational brain. Ask your irrational brain—the part that is connected to your threat perception network. For instance, your digging might look like this:

> *If Sam's unhappy and it hurts my standing, what's scary about that?*
> **Well, I might lose my job.**
> *Okay, what's scary about that?*
> **I might not find another one. And I won't have money to support my family or pay my bills?**
> *What's scary about that?*
> **My family will be ashamed of me.**
> *What's scary about that?*
> **They will leave me. I will be alone. And I will feel ashamed.**

This is often the conversation I have in private conflict coaching sessions. I want to know the deep, irrational fears operating under the surface-level interpretation of another's behaviors. Most people, when they turn on their intellectual brain again, realize *that will never happen. I'll find another job. My family won't leave me. We'll be fine.* But, their reactive, threat-detection network—even if it produces just a distant echo in the subconscious—is still active and pulling some of the levers of their nervous system, thereby perpetuating a conflict at a level that is most likely unnecessary.

By digging underneath to the deeper story—the true underlying stimulus of the conflict—we might dispel some of its power and thereby dispel some of the energy in this conflict. We identify the irrational story, interrupt with the rational, and take off some of the heat. When a story lurks in the deep background, it has power. When we surface it and deal with it in the light, we dissolve its energy.

At this point, ideally we realize that at least part of the conflict isn't the individual's behavior, it's our stories about what their behavior means. Sometimes, it's a deep, dark, and scary story. Notice also by doing this, we take Sam out of the power position. Because no matter what happens, even in the worst case scenarios (e.g., we lose a job), we've come to the rational realization that we will actually be okay. That Sam's behavior and attitude toward us, even if did lead to so much conflict that we lost our job, doesn't mean our ultimate destruction.

After dispelling some of the deeper fear story, we're likely to be in a better mental state with a calmer nervous system to actually have a conversation with Sam about his behavior and get clear on what he intended and what our concerns are. We can illuminate for Sam how his words or actions were interpreted, ask him to confirm our interpretations or clarify what he actually intended, and voice our concerns in the spirit of collaborative resolution.

You might say to him, "Sam, when you said . . . , the way I interpreted that was . . . ."

You could also use the following interpretive sentences: "Sam, when you said . . . ,"

- "The story I told my self was . . . ."
- "The way that landed with me was . . . ."
- "What I thought you meant was . . . ."

And then, it's important to open up the conversation to allow Sam space to clarify his intentions.

- "Is that what you meant?"
- "Do I have that wrong?"
- "Did I interpret that incorrectly?"

This type of communication not only helps you gain clarity and express concerns but also allows the other person to get clear on how their behavior is landing with you. Many times, people aren't aware of the interpretations or the psychological impact of their behavior. In fact, most of us believe that our language and actions are interpreted in the way we intended. However, both common sense and research show that we humans are way less accurate than we'd expect when it comes to aligning our intentions with others' interpretations. Miscommunications are indeed frequent, so give someone a chance to recommunicate and reinterpret.

Always recognize the difference between someone's behavior and your interpretation. Yes, your interpretation matters, and someone should understand the impact of their words or behaviors. But give them a chance to correct the interpretation or behavior. Before we make an assumption about their character, we should help people get clearer with their messaging by letting them know what their behavior or language seems to mean to us.

Each of us—yes, you included—have all sorts of filters and perceptions that color our understanding of the world and all the people in it. To be effective receivers in communication, we need to be aware of our filters, interpretations, and theories of others' systems. It's fair to let someone know the impact of their behavior on you, and to remind them in the future when it happens again; but it's not fair to assume they always know how their behavior makes an impact and/or that they are purposely or intentionally aiming for that impact. Separating our interpretation or ToS from others' behaviors and language is a critical practice in conflict resolution.

Moving Forward

Communication is absolutely the currency of conflict resolution, the medium across which all relational peace is built. Maybe that's obvious. What's less obvious, however—what we hardly ever think about—are the incredibly minute, nuanced elements of communication that we typically take for granted. Most of us hardly ever slow down to take in just how incredible our ability to communicate really is. It is a conglomerate of thousands of little movements and processes all working together to create what seems like a seamless interactive experience. But the magic lies in the nuance, the mundane, the tiny, instantaneous moments we often take for granted. It's in these moments that the secret to effective communication exists. It's here where we can use tiny actions and insert minute processes to enhance peace-oriented, relationally focused conflict resolution efforts.

With so many tiny elements that can influence someone else's thoughts, emotions, and behaviors, it can feel overwhelming to be hyperaware of how exactly we're communicating during tense conversations or negotiations. But don't fret. Your simple awareness alone of these elements will bring a newfound self-awareness to your communication and conflict resolution abilities. You don't have to get neurotic about it. In fact, please don't! Just take it slow, take the pressure off, and start small. With little, consistent movements toward resolution, time will help us find lasting peace.

We've discussed important elements about how we communicate during conflict, including how to be effective senders and receivers. Now the question is, *what* do we communicate? What exactly are we trying to get across if we're interested in resolving conflict, especially when we're looking to transform a relationship? If we hope to make real progress, the foundation of our messaging should aim to build trust and communicate care.

5 | Resolution Requires Care, Transformation Requires Trust

As effective communicators, we should be able to clearly articulate our messages, send them via appropriate channels, and receive messages with some awareness of our own interpretative-predictive processing. This will certainly help in all of our interactions. But when our goals are to resolve conflict and possibly even transform a conflicted relationship, *what* exactly should we be trying to communicate? What messages, sent in which ways, are most likely to help us achieve sustainable solutions and better relationships? Solutions require care. Relationships requires trust.

Without trust, there can be no real relationship, at least not in the long-term or meaningful sense. For any relationship in which trust has been broken or had never been established, conflict is not only inevitable, it is already there. In a relationship without trust, conflict is always lurking just below the surface, waiting to emerge at the first sign of tension—any small disagreement or misunderstanding will cause a rupture. In short time, parties will either separate to avoid each other or attempt to coerce one another by a variety of means including intimidation and aggression. Trust is absolutely the foundation of peace. Without it, we're just managing conflict, keeping it from erupting or dissolving the relationship.

Here's the inconvenient fact about trust: You can't force it. Trust comes only with time, over many experiences and perceptions of small behaviors from someone who consistently acts in a predictable manner, maintains a safe or nonthreatening dynamic, hasn't withdrawn or been perceived as rejecting or abandoning us, hasn't escalated or been perceived as aggressive or intimidating, hasn't behaved in a way that was perceived as manipulative, and hasn't said or done things that indicated they were judging us. In general, they haven't threatened or impeded our basic psychological needs. Maybe it's a lot to expect from someone. That's why there's likely few people that we absolutely trust. And why transforming a relationship from non-trusting to trusting requires time and consistency.

When it comes to resolving conflict, however, we don't necessarily need trust. At least, not immediately. Yes, we need to give each other the benefit of the doubt that whatever solutions we come up with will be upheld. But solving a complex or emotionally charged issue in the moment doesn't necessarily require the parties trust each other. If it did, we'd be doomed; there'd be no point to conflict resolution prior to rebuilding trust, which could take months or years.

On the contrary, many conflicts, large and small, are resolved by parties who don't trust each other much if at all. To resolve a conflict, we simply need to exhibit care. Care is the conflict lifesaver. It doesn't require time or consistency, and it can be deliberately, consciously implemented at any time regardless of the nature of the relationship. People can feel caring and cared for, with or without trust. Indeed, care and trust are two distinct psychological constructs that emerge from different neural networks, which can help explain why care is the foundation of conflict resolution and trust is the foundation of relational transformation.

The Care and Trust Systems

When people ask me why I got into the field of conflict resolution, I often recall my first professional mediation. The short dialogue was so impactful, it changed my experience and thus my predictions about what conflict resolution could achieve. It's one of the main reasons I stuck with this career and was inspired to grow Pollack Peacebuilding Systems. I saw, in a brief period of time, how guided, constructive dialogue could positively affect people's minds, hearts, and nervous systems.

I was hired to mediate a conflict between Kate, the CEO of a company, and Emery, the chief marketing officer. The two had been working together for many years and started off as friends and allies. Kate had been there longer than Emery, and both had worked together as C-level executives before Kate was promoted to CEO. Even after the promotion, they maintained a good relationship, continuing to meet for coffee, have friendly banter, and collaborate productively. They even got together with their spouses for couple's dinners occasionally. Slowly, however, the dynamic began to change, possibly due to Kate becoming Emery's boss. There was a disagreement here, some tension in a meeting there—over time, many small instances of friction led to fewer positive interactions, increasingly infrequent social engagements, and progressively skewed perceptions of one another. By the time I arrived at the situation, Kate and Emery were hardly talking outside of strict logistical and operational tasks, and even those conversations regularly caused friction.

When I met with each of them individually, I could tell they had both developed strong defensive armor against the other. They were matter-of-fact, almost hardened. They also had virtually the same story (which is often the case in conflict). The stories from both went something like the following:

"She doesn't think I'm doing a good job."
"She doesn't appreciate me."
"She doesn't respect my contribution or ideas."
"We used to be close, but now she doesn't like me."
"No matter what I do, I can't seem to do anything right."

Each spoke at great lengths about what the other person was doing or not doing, and how the other's attitude was negatively affecting the dynamic. But I wanted to know how each of them felt about the other, not just what they perceived the other to feel about them. So, I asked each during our private meetings, "Do you value her? Do you respect her ideas? Do you think she's doing a good job? Do you care about her?" And the fascinating thing was that they both affirmed all of it. Each of them truly respected, appreciated, valued, and cared about the other. They just never told each other, at least not in a way that got through the armor.

Now, I will acknowledge that this is not always the case. Many conflicts I have mediated involve at least one of, if not both or all, the parties truly not seeing the value the other person brings. But in just about every case, regardless of whether someone sees value in the other person, they always report caring about the person, even at a basic human level. And with a sense of human-to-human care, we can help them find what they *can* value or appreciate about the other. Or, in some cases, we can help them find a peaceful and caring way to separate. But in the case of Kate and Emery, I was lucky. *They* were lucky. Because when conflict begins with a foundation of mutual appreciation and respect, it's easier to get the parties to embody care during a dialogue. Privately discussing what Kate and Emery each valued about the other led to an interesting sequence during their dialogue—one that emerged naturally but which I would then deliberately employ in mediations for years to come.

Typically, when bringing parties together to discuss their issues, each naturally launches into all the things they find wrong. But this time, because we spoke quite a bit in private about what each values about the other, the mediation went differently. When Kate began speaking during the dialogue, she started with all the things she appreciated about Emery. This wasn't planned, and it wasn't a bunch of surface-level jargon you might hear in a performance evaluation. Kate was speaking from the heart. She told Emery how much she respected what she did, how she was the best marketing strategist she's ever worked with, how lucky the company was to have her, how lucky she personally was to have her on her team, and that she missed how they used to be together. She missed their relationship, and she wanted it back. What happened next was profound and totally unexpected.

Emery's face softened for the first time since I'd met her. She took on a totally different energy. She looked down to the ground, as if lost for a response, which I had not seen from her. After a few seconds of processing what she heard, Emery began to cry. Not hard or loud, but lightly. This previously hardened, powerful executive was softening. Through her tears, Emery muddled, "I didn't know you felt that about me . . . I miss you, too."

I looked then at Kate, and tears welled in her eyes. The armor had suddenly faded. Both took a moment to wipe their tears. The room was silent except for sniffles.

I realized what was happening. For a long time prior to their tension, they had felt cared for by one another. And then at some point, that ended; they stopped feeling cared for or exhibiting care. But now, in this moment, here it was again: *Care* reentered the picture. The thought: "She actually cares about me" was running through both of their minds, reconditioning their systems, altering their working models of the other, and it swiftly melted away their hardened defenses.

From that point forward, the dialogue ran rather easily. They talked about operational challenges and solutions they could both enact; there was no personal judgment or character attacks. In fact, the solutions-building portion of the conversation seemed almost like an afterthought. The real healing took place in the sharing of mutual care and recognition.

Several months after their dialogue, Kate and Emery had become close again, working together like they might have in the early years. The dynamic didn't all change, however, from one dialogue. That was just the catalyst. It took repeated, consistent experiences of care, validation, and appreciation to rebuild their relationship. But the reason they were able to be consistent and put in the effort to rebuild was because they both cared enough to do so. Now, several years later, I still occasionally check in with Kate. Emery has since moved on to another company, but they never regressed back into conflict.

This experience showed me what was possible when people get together and speak not just *from* their heart but with the other's heart in mind as well. It was clear that Kate and Emery both cared about the relationship, about the working dynamic, and about each other as human beings. The job of a peacebuilder, I realized, was to help parties express and hear care from one another. Sharing mutual value and care *before* getting to the problems and solutions is a practice I would employ in all future mediations, whenever possible and appropriate.

I also realized a core conflict resolution sequence that I still hold and teach to this day. *All relational conflict resolution requires two distinct parts: mutual care and collaborative solution building.* Without care first, getting to solutions will likely not solve the deeper issues. And *all relational conflict transformation (i.e., improving the relationship dynamic) requires repeated, consistent instances of care and collaboration, which eventually lead to trust.* Hopefully, this seems logical, though it also helps to examine how this makes sense neurobiologically and psychologically. Understanding the ways care and trust operate in our brains can help illuminate their distinct influences on peacebuilding, and why they're so important.

Care Versus Trust: Neural Networks

Care and trust, though often intertwined in our everyday language, actually emerge from distinct neurobiological systems, which helps explain why care is the foundation of conflict resolution in the moment and why trust is the foundation for long-term relationships.

Care operates on more immediate neural pathways than does trust. The caregiving system involves structures like the anterior insula, ventromedial prefrontal cortex, and periaqueductal gray, which underpin empathy, compassion, and prosocial motivation. The anterior insula, in particular, is less about caregiving behavior directly and more about interoceptive awareness and empathic attunement; it helps us register our own bodily states and connect those sensations to social and emotional awareness. This bridging function makes it critical for experiencing and expressing empathy, which often underlies caring responses. Ventral striatum (nucleus accumbens) activation also reinforces caregiving behaviors, and endogenous opioids, such as endorphins, support social bonding and are involved in the warm, calming sensations of closeness. These systems can be activated rapidly, even toward people we don't know or don't yet trust. Oxytocin and dopamine release further promote affiliative behavior, enabling individuals to express and feel care on demand. Unlike trust, care doesn't require a history of consistent interactions. Instead, it can be consciously chosen and enacted in the present moment.

Receiving care activates overlapping but distinct systems. Oxytocin is released when we feel safe and connected, whether through eye contact, touch, or compassionate presence, reducing vigilance and calming the autonomic nervous system. Vasopressin release plays a role in pair bonding and social recognition, particularly in attachment relationships. Endorphins and dopamine activation reinforce the pleasurable experience of being nurtured or supported, strengthening relational bonds through reward circuits. Social support consistently lowers hypothalamic-pituitary-adrenal (HPA) axis activation and reduces cortisol release, which is why feeling cared for can lower feelings of distress.

Psychologically and physiologically, feeling cared for shifts the nervous system into a state of safety and regulation. It increases vagal tone via the vagus nerve, leading to slower heart rate, deeper breathing, and reduced blood pressure; it also decreases threat reactivity via downregulation of the amygdala and related circuits, making us less defensive and more open to connection.

Trust, however, depends on the brain's capacity to learn from repeated patterns and build reliable predictions about others. Regions like the hippocampus and medial prefrontal cortex consolidate past experiences into working models of how someone is likely to behave. When behavior is consistent, predictable, and nonthreatening, the brain gradually encodes this as safety. By contrast, when someone behaves aggressively, unpredictably, or manipulatively, the amygdala and anterior cingulate cortex flag these as violations, leading to vigilance or withdrawal. In short, trust takes time, repetition, and the accumulation of safe experiences for these neural systems to settle into a reliable expectation.

Another important factor here is cortisol, the primary stress hormone released by the HPA axis, which is exactly what happens when trust is broken and threat detection is heightened. Elevated cortisol not only amplifies vigilance and defensive responses but also strengthens the encoding of emotional memories in the hippocampus and amygdala. This helps explain why breaches of trust often feel especially vivid and difficult to forget. Stress hormones make those experiences more salient and enduring.

Oxytocin also plays a powerful role in trust, as it can dampen threat detection in the amygdala and boost the brain's reward responses to positive social cues, thereby facilitating trust. It's worth noting, however, that oxytocin's effects are context-dependent. While it can reduce vigilance and support affiliative bonds, research also shows that oxytocin can heighten ingroup favoritism and even increase distrust or defensive behavior toward outgroups. In other words, oxytocin is not universally pro-trust but rather amplifies social salience, making positive cues feel safer and negative cues feel more threatening depending on the relationship and context.

While activating some overlapping structures, neurotransmitters, and hormones, the distinct neural networks between care and trust matter for peacebuilding. The neural underpinnings of these systems manifest in distinct psychological and emotional experiences, lending themselves to particular forms of conflict processes.

Care Versus Trust: Psychological Constructs

Care can be described as a psychological state of concern for another's well-being, often expressed through empathy, warmth, and prosocial motivation. Emotionally, it blends compassion, responsibility, and nonthreatening presence. Care also reflects a motivational state to reduce another's suffering or promote their thriving. And remember, care is also a verb, which means it's a behavior. In conflict resolution, the act of caring for someone cannot simply be the psychological and emotional state but rather must be the *behavioral* state. In fact, for purposes of peacebuilding, the emotional state is helpful but not as necessary as the behavior. That's because no one else can know or feel our internal states; they only know what they see and hear from us. So, we must outwardly communicate care.

What is the behavior of care? It is the act of undivided attention. To truly care for someone in the moment, we drop everything we're doing, including our agendas and defenses, and simply listen to someone, express support, and attend to their needs. This can be done instantly with a simple choice and then can be adjusted or taken away just as easily.

Caring for someone doesn't obligate or trap us in a state of everlasting care. Rather, caring is done from a place of agency and choice, and we decide when it's appropriate to dial it up, down, or withdraw it completely depending on the circumstances. In fact, it's absolutely necessary to turn care up in appropriate circumstances for short periods of time, and then take it back down. High levels of care require that we put our own agendas, needs, and goals aside for a moment to attend to someone else's. This is effective during times of distress, but becomes unhealthy if that level of care lasts for too long. Persistently high care, where one's own needs and goals are put aside, is called *codependence*. This is an unhealthy relational dynamic where one person is always the caretaker, depleting their own needs in the service of the other, while the other becomes dependent on the caretaker. It creates resentment, deteriorates healthy boundaries, and stifles growth for both people. Exhibiting a high level of care during conflict is like an extremely temporary state of codependence; the difference is that we dial it back down as appropriate so we can attend to and advocate for our own needs in the dynamic.

Being on the receiving end of temporary, high care usually produces a profound feeling. When we truly feel cared for—that is, when we sense that we have someone's undivided attention, that they really hear and see us, that they are present for us, ready to attend to our needs and support us—it's intoxicating. And it's rare. This level of undivided attention may emerge, for example, at extremely intimate moments in romantic relationships or parent-child relationships, and sometimes in close friendships. However, it's especially important during moments of distress and pain, including when involved in difficult conversations and high conflict.

When we are in distress, and we feel that someone has no other agenda but to pay attention to our distress and support us in getting our needs met, it's like taking a deep breath of relief. We feel safe. We can drop our guards, allow ourselves to become more vulnerable, and we become more open to receiving care. Receiving care from anyone can be helpful in moments of distress, but it's particularly helpful in resolving conflicts when the caring person is the one with whom we are in conflict. It tells us that they care enough to listen, support, and learn how they can reduce any perceived threats to our needs or goals.

Care comes in both passive and active forms. The major difference is caring *about* someone versus caring *for* them—the mental-emotional state versus the behavior. When you care about someone, you keep them in mind, wishing the best for them, hoping they are okay. When you are actively caring for them, you take action to support them. While caring about someone passively can certainly be helpful from a motivational perspective during conflict, what's important for resolution is actively caring for someone. These two forms are operationally distinct: one can exist without the other. We often care about people but do not do much to care for them. And you could choose to care for someone in the moment whom you've never previously met and will never be around again, in which case you've never thought about them prior and likely won't pay them much more than a passing thought in the future. In conflict resolution, the active form of care is the one that counts; it's the care the moves the needle toward peace.

Let's move now to the psychology of trust, which is often described as a feeling or intuition. Nevertheless, that feeling stems from cognitive predictions about the behavioral consistency of the individual(s). And that prediction, as we know, arises from memories encoded from experiences with or about the person, our relationship with them, and the context or situation.

Psychologically, trust is a bit more complex than care, or at least not as straightforward. That's because trust is a multidimensional construct involving various forms of confidence. We might, for example, trust someone to perform well at a job or task, which has been referred to as *performance, ability, or competence trust.* We might also trust that someone will take responsibility for their actions, follow through on commitments, and live up to agreed-on expectations, including shared cultural norms, which is called *accountability, benevolence, or integrity trust.* We also trust some people to act in a consistent, predictable, and constructive manner, which we call *behavioral or knowledge-based trust.* And we can trust someone not to abuse their positions of power, status, or authority, which is called *power, authority, or role-based trust.* These are each distinct forms of trust, activating somewhat different neural and psychological networks. We might trust someone in one or multiple of these dimensions but not in others.

In any of these dimensions, trust grows from a combination of (1) the way we experience and interpret the person's behaviors; (2) any assumptions, presuppositions, and stereotypes we hold, consciously or unconsciously, about the groups they represent, referred to as *identification-based trust*; and (3) our own unique capacities and tendencies, shaped by early attachment and temperament, to trust or distrust others in general, referred to as *dispositional trust.* Dispositionally, our internal working models of the world developed most significantly from early to late childhood, creating predictions about how trustworthy people generally are, based on the extent to which we experienced safety, inclusion, loyalty, and consistency versus abandonment, rejection, betrayal, or injury from our primary caregivers and then early childhood friends. This is essentially what attachment theory describes: Secure, anxious, and avoidant attachment styles reflect patterns of early caregiving that shape how readily we extend or withhold trust in adulthood. People with a secure attachment style generally find it easier to both trust and repair trust, while those with anxious or avoidant styles may be more sensitive to breaches or more reluctant to depend on others. This is all to say that there are many ways we might trust or distrust others and for many reasons, making trust quite a fascinating and complex psychological state.

Another interesting aspect of trust is that while it takes repeated interactions to truly trust someone, it only takes one negative experience to break trust, sometimes permanently. That's why trust is such an incredibly valuable commodity that should not be taken for granted. It takes commitment, effort, and consistency to build it, but it can shatter in a moment. Such a moment is often the catalyst for an escalated and/or protracted conflict. In complex conflicts, the types of trust that have been broken are key to analyze and understand so that we might establish new behaviors, practices, and structures that support repair moving forward.

Care Versus Trust in Conflict: Resolution, Management, and Transformation

In the peace and conflict field, there are three high-level peacebuilding models: conflict resolution, conflict management, and conflict transformation. Each model is applicable based on the relationship of the parties involved and their goals, and each requires care and trust in distinct ways.

Conflict resolution is an appropriate approach when the conflicts are, well, solvable. That is, when the parties involved can identify what the issues are, usually with the help of a skilled conflict specialist or mediator, and are willing to collaborate and get creative in developing solutions. In my experience, robust and sustainable solutions require us to uncover and solve for problems at each of the three levels of conflict discussed in the Preface to this book: the internal (i.e., the mind and nervous system of each person involved), the interpersonal (i.e., the way each person behaves toward each other), and the structural or systemic (i.e., the systems, processes, policies, and cultural elements that contribute to the conflict). When we can build at least one actionable solution for the parties to work on at each level of conflict—solutions that the parties are willing and able to enact—then the conflict becomes solvable.

For a simple example, Elliott became upset that Sam frequently arrived late to their scheduled meetings, leading him to feel that Sam simply doesn't respect him or his time. As a result, Elliott now feels stressed and angry anytime he's around Sam, and often speaks to Sam rudely as a result, regardless of whether Sam shows up on time. If we were to resolve this issue, we'd have to help Elliott recondition his internal reaction to Sam (i.e., from a stress response to a calm or benign response), we'd have to figure out how to change Sam's behavior about punctuality and Elliott's behavior about expressions of anger, and we'd have to look at any structural or systemic issues affecting the dynamic, including the level of workload on Sam's plate, making it difficult for him to organize his time effectively. Once solutions are agreed on, resolving the conflict then becomes a matter of will and accountability.

On the trust dimension, what's needed first on Elliott's part is accountability trust; and Sam needs to develop behavioral trust in Elliott. Both of these will only develop over repeated instances of living up to their agreements. So, we start from a place of little trust, with the hope of building it as quickly as possible.

For conflict resolution, we also must start from a place of high care; otherwise, none of this will make a difference. Remember the two primary steps to all conflict resolution: care and then solution. For any solution-building to take place at all, it requires that each party cares about the needs, goals, and values of the other. If we jump straight to solutions, without first implementing caring behavior (e.g., listening with authentic, undivided attention), any solution is unlikely to solve the deeper issues. Additionally, the sort of processes required for conflict resolution, including various meetings with each party to help uncover their deeper conflicts and build solutions that they buy into, takes time and effort. If either party, like Elliott or Sam, senses that the other doesn't really care about the issues, the process will quickly deteriorate.

We absolutely must communicate care if we hope to resolve a relational or emotionally charged conflict. Without the sense that there is mutual care about one another's problems and about finding solutions, resolution is unachievable. In those cases—and, yes, there are many where both care and trust are absent—peace requires that we instead *manage* the conflict.

Conflict management is applicable when conflicts are virtually unsolvable, at least in the near future. When at least one of the parties does not care about the other's needs, goals, or values, the hope for effective, sustainable solutions dissolves. Sometimes one person or party is not good at articulating that they actually do care, and so care doesn't land effectively with the other party. Or, one person or party is unable to receive and register care no matter what the other does, often because too much trust has been broken or because dispositionally they have trouble accepting care from anyone. In any case, when mutual care is not given or felt, resolution is almost impossible. To manage the conflict, then, we would stop trying to solve the issues and instead look to manage them.

To manage conflict, we first clarify the current or potential negative outcomes of the conflict. We ask, what are some of the side effects, consequences, and results, including the worst possible outcomes, of this conflict continuing? Then, we implement structures, policies, rules, and/or processes that directly aim to counteract or limit these effects. While we're not trying to solve the actual conflicts, we're trying to manage and constrain their consequences.

For example, if Sam experienced too much repeated anger from Elliott and now did not care enough to show up on time to meetings or about how Eliott felt, the resolution process would halt. In which case, we might have to involve human resources or a senior leader to set a policy about meeting punctuality (on Sam's part) and interpersonal conduct (on Elliott's part) and impose consequences for violating the policy.

Conflict management typically requires a third-party manager who can keep the parties accountable and implement consequences for breaking the rules. Getting agreement from the parties to adhere to these rules is ideal but not always necessary. That's because an effective conflict manager is typically a third party who has some authority over the situation and the parties. This might be a parent over children, a legal agreement (i.e., courts) over business partners, a boss over employees, or a powerful country or alliance of countries over disputing nations. When conflicts are only managed, care and trust between the parties are not required. The parties would only need to care about the potential consequences of breaking the imposed rules and trust that they would be held accountable should they break them.

Sometimes, parts of the conflicts can be resolved while other parts need to be managed. People can be perceived to care about certain challenges enough to solve them, but not other challenges. Former romantic partners and now co-parents Joe and Amanda don't have a great relationship, and neither thinks the other cares about that, which has eroded trust. So, the way they talk to and behave toward each other has to be managed through legally established rules and consequences mandated by a court. However, they both care about their children, so they are able to agree to various logistical matters and creative custody options for the sake of the kids. When a seemingly larger, unsolvable conflict can be broken down into distinct elements, those elements that are more logistical are more likely to be resolved while the relational elements are more likely to be managed. If there is hope to transform the relationship, however, we merge into the realm of conflict transformation.

Conflict transformation can contain both conflict resolution and conflict management. Transformation is not a short-term process but rather a long-term, complex series of processes that may require resolution or management of various parts of the overall conflict at different times and in different ways. The fundamental goal of transformation is to change the way the parties perceive and relate to each other—not only to care about and feel cared for by the other but also to build trust over many instances of small wins, positive contacts, care-based interactions, and solution-focused collaborations. To transform conflict is to transform relationships. Whether it takes 1 year or 10 years, the parties manage what they can, solve what they can, and all the while keep optimistic that with enough mutual care, collaboration, and shared goals over time, they will eventually begin to trust each other.

Transformation requires that each party truly sees the benefit of a renewed relationship. Whether self-guided or led by a mediator or counselor, the guiding entity must continuously help each party recognize how a new relationship, built on trust and care, would serve each of their needs and goals, how it would positively affect their nervous systems and levels of stress, and how it would benefit the people around them whom they already care about and trust, such as family members, coworkers, or community members.

Recap: The Care and Trust Systems

Trust is essential for building and transforming relationships over the long haul. We don't have to build confidence in every dimension of trust, just one or two may suffice for a deeper, more fulfilling and peaceful relationship. Time, consistency, authenticity, and some level of optimism can reestablish trust and rebuild historically conflicted relationships.

But in the heat of conflict, waiting for trust to rebuild would make deescalation and resolution nearly impossible. Instead, care becomes the lifeline.

By communicating care, parties can create enough psychological safety to solve immediate problems, even in the absence of trust. Over time, if care continues to be expressed consistently, trust may follow.

Tools to Exhibit Care and Build Trust

How do we effectively communicate care for purposes of resolving conflict? And how can we build trust and ultimately transform relationships from conflict-dense to collaborative and peace-oriented? Let's discuss some practical tools.

Exhibiting Care

Most of us intuitively know what it feels like to care about others and to be cared for by someone. But let's make sure we're aware of our own behaviors so that we can choose to communicate care when trying to resolve conflicts. Here are a few ideas.

Adjust the Care Knob   Imagine you have a care knob that you can turn from 0 to 10 at any time when interacting with someone. At 0, you don't show any care at all. You pay no attention to the person, essentially ignoring them. Your knob is turned to 0, for example, when you pass a stranger on the street and do not acknowledge them. When you smile at the stranger, you turn your care knob up to 1, and when you say hello, you're dialed up to 2. Then, you move along the sidewalk and it's back to 0 again. In everyday conversations with friends, family, and coworkers, you've likely turned up your care knob anywhere from 4 to 6, depending on how engaged you are in the conversation, the dynamic of your relationship, how much energy or bandwidth you have at the time, and how much attention you sense the person needs. Okay, get the picture?

Now, the goal is to be highly deliberate about turning your knob up and down. You probably didn't realize you have conscious control of the care knob. You just go about your everyday conversations and interactions, unconsciously turning it up or down. But now, I want you to practice being deliberate about it. Especially during conflict.

In escalated conflict, if your goal is to de-escalate someone, you can turn that care knob up to level 10. That means complete, undivided attention, nothing else matters in this moment, it's all about them and their needs. It's the same as you might apply in an emergency, life-or-death situation. A person in high escalation is experiencing a nervous system that is in survival mode, whether or not that mode is responding appropriately to the situation. Then, as the individual calms in response to your attention and support, you can start turning down your dial gradually as you see fit. You're attuning to them—co-regulating by helping to regulate their nervous system through your behavior.

Once they calm and you reach baseline conflict, perhaps you stay at a level 5 or 6 until the conflict is resolved. Level 5 or 6 can also be applicable when you are in a negotiation with someone and tensions are a bit high. The mission here is to consciously control your level of behavioral care. You have the power to dial it up or down. Once you dial it up, you're not trapped there; you can turn the knob whenever you need to.

Try this technique the next time you interact with someone, no matter the circumstances. Try it with a friend during your next conversation. Dial it up and turn it back down. See how it feels to care and pay attention at different levels dynamically. Remember, behaving in a caring way is a choice, and you have control of the dial.

Listen and Repeat   This technique, commonly called *reflective listening*, is a form of active or focused listening paired with repeating back what you hear from the other person. You will notice that well-trained customer service teams always repeat back your issue before jumping to the solution. That's because human beings naturally want to feel heard and understood before we are ready to receive advice or hear solutions. When engaged in active listening, we focus in and cut out all other noise in the world. We're listening not just to someone's surface-level story but also for how their underlying needs, goals, and feelings are affected.

Then, we repeat back some of the main or most significant components they expressed. When you repeat someone's words back to them, it is a form of mirroring and validation, indicating that you're truly there with them, hearing what they are going through and understanding what they're experiencing. Repeating could come in the form of paraphrasing their story, echoing back an important sentence you heard, or simply reiterating verbatim a few key words they said.

Make this paraphrasing sound natural. Avoid starting with phrases such as, "What I hear you saying is . . ." because it can sound condescending and formulaic, as though you're just trying some communication technique you learned. Instead, just repeat back naturally. For example, "Okay, so you're wanting time off to be with your family. Understood." You could even ask for permission to repeat back first, which can also dampen the sense that you're being formulaic. For instance, you could first say: "Okay, that's a lot of information. Would you mind if I just repeated back what I heard so I can make sure I'm understanding?"

Repeating back someone's words to them not only helps them feel heard but it also helps us get clear on what they said. For example, we might repeat back, "Okay, so you're wanting time off to be with your family." And they might reply, "No, that's not what I'm saying. I'm just asking if I can work remotely for a week." Perhaps we didn't hear them correctly, and this was a great opportunity to clarify our understanding. Or perhaps we're just interpreting their side differently than they are. Either way, this feedback loop opens a space for greater clarity.

An especially powerful enhancement to reflective listening is *steelmanning*. Remember, this is when you don't just repeat what you heard but also attempt to articulate the other person's arguments. Steelmanning can help someone feel both listened to and more deeply understood. You're essentially letting them know that you both hear their side of things and understand where they're coming from and why they might hold that perspective. When it comes to reflective listening and steelmanning, use your discretion as to what's applicable and appropriate for the situation. This technique, like any tool, is not the right one to use in every situation.

Use Empathic Expression and Tone   Communicating that we care about someone and their experience requires that we actually show them. Don't listen with a completely neutral face or repeat what you hear with a robotic, flat vocal tone. Empathy is not just a feeling or internal state for you to take someone's perspective; it is a behavior, or at least it can be.

Use your facial expressions and vocal tone to show someone you are listening, you are understanding their experience, and you are even feeling some of their emotions. Raise your eyebrows when you hear something surprising. Shake your head when you hear something disappointing.

You can also vocally express your alignment through verbal interjections such as *ugh, oy, wow,* or short alignment statements like "That's unbelievable" or "I've never heard of such a thing."

If they are elevated and animated, you should mirror this to some extent by also being animated. You do not have to be as intense as they are—in fact, that could come off as inauthentic or condescending. But some animation in your expression and tone is warranted to let them know you really are in the story with them, not just observing from the outside. Then calm back down to normalize the fluctuation of emotion and to help them attune or co-regulate with you as you lower your intensity.

Don't fake empathy. Actually try to feel what they're feeling, and react naturally. If facial or vocal animation is unnatural to you, just do your best to take it up a slight notch. Even small empathic behaviors can help someone feel heard and cared for.

Quick Tools for Caring   Here are a few quick techniques you can employ during difficult conversations to communicate care and attention:

- **Nod while listening.** Nodding signals attention and empathy. Use small, steady nods to encourage openness.
- **Mirror subtly.** Lightly matching posture or speech rhythm builds rapport. Mirror only small elements. Keep it natural.
- **Lower your volume first.** People unconsciously adjust their volume to yours. If voices rise, deliberately lower yours to invite calm.
- **Soften eye contact.** Too much intensity can feel threatening. Hold eye contact 60–70 percent of the time, and take natural breaks.
- **Lean forward at key moments.** Slight leaning forward shows interest and care. Lean in especially when validating, then return to neutral posture.
- **Self-touch for sincerity.** Gestures like hand-on-chest signal authenticity. Use this mindfully during validation or apologies.

Remember, to resolve conflicts, people need to know we care. And moments of caring behavior are the first steps toward rebuilding trust when relational transformation is the goal.

Building Trust

We have limited control over whether someone trusts us or not. We might be doing everything right, and for one reason or another, someone still can't trust us. The thing we do have control over at all times, regardless of how we are perceived, is the choice to be trustworthy. We always have agency in deciding to stick to our word, live up to our commitments, and be appropriately honest. In that respect, there are several practices that we might implement to rebuild trust with someone. Determine which of the following might be appropriate for each relationship, and practice them repeatedly as applicable. Remember, trust takes time to build new experiences, memories, and predictions about behavior.

Analyze and Commit   Sit down with anyone you'd like to build trust with, and ask them to help you fill out a rating scale. For each dimension of trust, ask them to give you an honest rating of the level at which they trust you, with 1 being "not at all" and 5 being "absolutely." The trust dimensions are as follows:

- **Competence:** to perform well at a job or task
- **Accountability:** to take responsibility for actions, follow through on commitments, and live up to agreed-on expectations, including shared cultural norms or social agreements
- **Behavioral:** to act in a consistent, predictable, and constructive manner
- **Power:** to not abuse positions of power, status, or authority

Again, ask them to be brutally honest with you because you'd like to improve. If they're all 5s, that is rare. For any rating less than 5, ask them, "What would you need to know, see, hear, or experience from me for that rating to move up by 1 point?"

Once you get the answer, determine how to make it actionable and reasonable for you to enact. If you can find a way to give this individual what they need to build more trust in you, let them know your plan and verbally commit to it. Then, it's up to you to stick to your commitment.

Repeated Positive Interactions   Trust grows through consistency, not one-time gestures. Each positive interaction, whether it's showing up on time, keeping a promise, or offering encouragement, strengthens the brain's predictive model that this person is reliable and safe. The next time you see the individual with whom you'd like to build trust, be friendly, smile authentically, ask how their day is going, ask if they could use any help, or do anything else you feel would be in the right spirit. Perhaps stop bringing up the issues or challenges for a bit, at least until you can get back to a cordial dynamic and build a little rapport.

Make positive interactions a conscious practice. You might even schedule it into your calendar or task list if necessary. Over time, these small experiences accumulate into a powerful sense of stability.

Be Calm When Receiving Hard Feedback   One of the most powerful ways to build trust is to ask someone for feedback that might be hard for you to hear, and then to stay calm and receptive when hearing it. Staying calm communicates that you care enough to listen without defending or exploding, and that you're interested in the other's experience. In other words, that you're a psychologically safe person. Remaining composed reduces threat signals in the other person's brain, making them more willing to speak truthfully in the future.

The next time you receive challenging feedback, use your self-regulation techniques. Stay calm, listen, and whatever happens, do not get defensive. If you feel overwhelmed and need time to process before responding, that's totally reasonable. Just let them know you'd like to think about what they said, and ask if it would be okay to follow up at a specific time and day.

Be Behaviorally and Emotionally Consistent   If someone doesn't know which version of you they're going to get at any moment (e.g., the happy one or the angry one), it makes trusting you incredibly difficult. Unpredictability makes others hypervigilant, while consistency lets others relax. When people know what to expect from your moods, tone, and actions, their sympathetic nervous system can downregulate. This predictability allows trust networks in the brain, particularly memory and reward systems, to code you as "safe." Inconsistency, even without malice, undermines trust because it forces others into constant uncertainty.

Interestingly, a lot of people have a negative connotation about being predictable. But the truth is that the more predictable you are, the more people know what to expect and how to prepare to interact with you. If you're predictably miserable, they may try to avoid you, they may react emotionally to you, or they may learn to not react to you. But if you're predictably positive, pleasant, optimistic, supportive, or even simply stoic, you will be significantly helpful in regulating others' nervous systems.

So, it's important to ask yourself these questions: How predictable is my behavior or mood? Am I predictably negative/disruptive or positive/supportive? The more often you show up consistently positive and supportive, the more their brains will know what to predict about you, which means less upregulation of the sympathetic system preparing to expend metabolic energy to manage their interaction with you.

Moments of Personal Curiosity   Showing genuine curiosity about others communicates care and validation. Even a simple, "How was your weekend?" or "How are your kids doing? Did they start school yet?" can let someone know you're interested in their life and not just their utility to you. These micro-moments of curiosity activate reward circuits in the brain, making the relationship feel more rewarding and meaningful. Asking questions with curiosity is not an interrogation. It's an invitation into connection.

Ask for Help or Advice   When you request help or support from someone, it reminds them that you're human and you don't have all the answers. Especially if you're in a position of power or authority over someone who has lost trust in you, going to them for advice can be incredibly helpful, as it flips the power dynamic and demonstrates humility.

Find something you know they are good at or have experience with. It could be something work-related or personal. For example, you could acknowledge someone's competence in report analysis and ask them for a tutorial. Or you could go to a direct report who has three kids and ask them for parenting advice. Whatever support you ask for signals that you value the other person's expertise or perspective, which affirms their competence and importance. Ironically, asking for help often strengthens trust more than offering help does.

Be Transparent When people perceive themselves to be in the dark about something, it breeds frustration and mistrust. Do some reflection: Where have you not been totally transparent with someone? Is there anything you could more clearly communicate or reveal that would help them trust you more? If you were in their shoes, is there any topic or situation that might seem unclear, strange, or shady? If so, how could you make it less so? What would you tell or show them to foster transparency? People may not always like what they hear, but honesty earns more trust than polished spin.

Don't Level Skip Remember, level skipping is the act of going around someone or skirting the chain of command to get what you want. This could be done at work when someone bypasses a manager to go to their manager's boss for an answer or decision. It could also be done at home by going around your brother to get an answer from his wife because you know your brother won't give you the answer you want. In any case, this is incredibly frustrating and trust breaking. Not only does bypassing someone's role or authority show disregard but it also threatens that individual's status or importance and signals that you don't trust them.

The next time you're inclined to level skip in order to get what you want, take a pause. Ask yourself, is getting what you want in this way worth breaking that person's trust? If not, then take a different approach. Involve the individual in the process of getting other perspectives or answers. If your boss says no, then ask if they would be open to bringing in another perspective, and offer the name(s) of those you'd like to bring into the conversation. If your boss says they are not open to this, and you feel it is important enough to push for another perspective, then simply be transparent. Let them know what you intend to do. Being transparent about level skipping is, at the least, better than the individual finding out on their own. They may not like your behavior, but they can at least trust you won't go behind their back.

Include People in Decisions That Affect Them   Few things build trust faster than giving people agency. This is especially important when decisions have to be made that are going to affect them. Whether at work or at home, do your best to give people a voice in such decisions.

Sometimes it's not appropriate or efficient to get everyone's input on a decision. In these cases, you might make a decision and then create a forum or space for feedback. Getting people's feedback helps ensure it is carried out in a way that makes sense for everyone and gives them at least some input in the process.

In some cases, not even feedback would be pragmatic. However, you can choose to be transparent by communicating what the decision is, why it was made, what information and choices you weighed in making the final decision, and other details as appropriate. When people feel they have no control over major decisions that affect them, it erodes trust quickly, but even more so when they feel totally in the dark about the process. Put yourself in their shoes; remember what it feels like to have no control over something that affects you. Do whatever is in your power to make sure others don't have that sort of experience.

Build Trust in Others

So far, we've focused on how to help others trust you. Now, let's flip the script. If we hope to be trusted, we also have to trust. Here are two practices to help you foster trust in someone.

Analyze and Ask for Commitment   Remember the ratings we helped someone else fill out? Now it's your turn. Choose someone you'd like to trust more, and give an honest rating of the level at which you trust them along each dimension, with 1 being "not at all" and 5 being "absolutely." Recall, the trust dimensions are the following:

- Competence
- Accountability
- Behavioral
- Power

For any rating less than 5, ask yourself, "What would I need to know, see, hear, or experience from them for that rating to move up by 1 point?"

Once you're clear, ask the individual if they'd be open to an authentic conversation about improving your relationship. If they're not, then at least you've gotten a bit of clarity for yourself. But if they are willing, then help them fill out the rating scale as it relates to you, share your ratings and answers with each other, and collaborate on actionable ways to build trust based on what you both learned.

Give the Benefit of the Doubt A final important piece to trusting someone again is giving them the benefit of the doubt when they are attempting to improve the dynamic. If someone wants to improve your relationship and gain your trust, and if you're interested in the same, then it's your job to (1) acknowledge their positive efforts, even if small, and (2) stop jumping to assumptions or worst-case scenarios.

Put yourself in their shoes, as if you were trying to rebuild trust, but no matter what you did, you couldn't seem to move the needle. Imagine if the other person just kept assuming the worst and not giving you any room to improve. That feels like an ongoing punishment rather than a relationship under constructive repair. If someone is genuinely trying, stop punishing them. Either decide to leave the relationship or start opening to the idea of a better, more trusting connection, especially if they've owned their part in the situation.

There's no rush. You don't have to totally trust them overnight. Give yourself space and time to build new experiences, memories, and predictions of this person. As challenges arise—and they always do in relationships—give feedback swiftly in order to help you both course correct.

Ultimately, if they're trying to rebuild trust, and you want to trust them again, then it's worth taking a risk with trust, even if in small increments. Let it build over time. But at least let it build.

Moving Forward A relationship is like a house. All relationships, like all houses, need a strong foundation in order to stay standing upright in one piece. If we don't have a strong foundation or if the foundation is cracked or there's no foundation laid at all, then our house is unstable, and it is essentially a house of cards. In this case, any type of tension, any little tremor or mini earthquake or wind storm, is likely to damage the house if not completely destroy it. And the bigger the storm or quake, the more severe and long-lasting the damage will be. That's why it's so important that all of our houses have strong foundations, that we maintain those foundations, and that we repair them as necessary, as they get wear and tear from the natural, normal tensions that arise in our dynamic environments.

Similarly, all of our relationships need strong foundations in order not to crumble at the first sign of conflict or tension. When it comes to relationships, the foundation, which protects our relationships from becoming severely and permanently damaged due to tension or conflict, is concrete made of care and trust. The level and intensity of care and trust will depend, of course, on the particular type of relationship. I'm going to care for and trust my spouse a lot more deeply and differently than I do others. Nonetheless, in order for any sort of tension or conflict with someone to not completely erupt into chaos, I need to feel some level care for that person, even if it's just a fundamental human-to-human level of care.

When conflict arises in a relationship, the likelihood of you destroying that relationship—wanting to simply be done with it, avoid the person, fire them, get rid of them, leave the department or the company or the relationship altogether—becomes higher when there is no foundation of care or trust. On the contrary, think about a time when you got into an argument with someone whom you did or do deeply care about and trust. A family member, a friend, a loved one. You probably felt extreme uneasiness, distress, maybe even sensations of sickness or nausea. Not just because of the tension itself, but because you don't want to be in this sort of conflict with someone that you care about and want to trust. This type of interpersonal conflict creates a massive neuropsychological conflict in you. Here you are, angry or hurt by someone whom you simultaneously care about and desperately want to trust. This creates a real cognitive dissonance that leads to high stress.

Your foundation of care and the resulting internal conflict ideally, then, highly motivates you to resolve the conflict as quickly as you can. Both because you want to relieve the tension of this internal, psychological stress and because you want to get back to fulfilling that deep desire you have for mutual care and trust with that individual. We all have a deep desire to be cared about and trusted by the people around us, especially those whom we actually trust and care about. This is why it's so important to have a strong foundation in relationships.

When conflicts arise, if you don't focus on care and trust, you probably go straight into defensiveness, dismissing the other person's perspective, wanting to prove that you're right and they're wrong, and so on. But what if instead, in the moment you feel conflict or tension with someone, you immediately remind yourself, "Wait a minute, I really care about this person. They're someone I can trust." Or "Wait a minute, let me just feel caring toward this person for a moment before I jump all over them." If you focus on that foundation, it's much more likely you will show up in a productive way to solve the conflict.

Now, I'm not suggesting that all your conflicts will disappear with just a simple choice of feeling care and focusing on trust. But the *way* you show up in this dynamic, the space from which you think about solutions, the style in which you talk to this individual while trying to resolve some of the tension, will completely shift if you come from a place of care and a focus on trust—if you reinforce the foundation under the house of this relationship. Keep this in mind moving forward.

Up to this point, we've learned the importance of de-escalating tension prior to attempting conflict resolution, keeping an opportunistic mindset, understanding the limits of our perception and certainty, and communicating with care. Again, care is the first step in all conflict resolution. So, we have arrived at the second step: solution-building. Any effective and sustainable solution requires buy-in from all sides, and buy-in requires that we collaborate when building solutions.

What are the critical elements of collaboration? And how can we ensure our collaborations are fulfilling and successful? Let's dive in.

6

We're Built to Collaborate

Human beings are what anthropologists and evolutionary biologists call *ultrasocial*. This term describes species that go beyond basic group living to exhibit complex, large-scale cooperation, often involving divisions of labor, collective defense, shared child-rearing, and sometimes even self-sacrifice for the group. Only a handful of other species can claim such a status, and they are all insects. Bees, ants, wasps, and termites are also considered ultrasocial. Some people argue the naked mole rats and some bird species are ultrasocial, but those are debated subjects. In any case, we humans are unlike any other ultrasocial species; since we don't all consider ourselves to be part of the same "family" or superorganism, we are not born with innate, unchangeable social roles; and we, of course, are self-aware. Therefore, we can deliberately choose to behave in a variety of ways (assuming we believe in free will) rather than simply behaving or reacting instinctually as do the other ultrasocial species.

How do we choose to behave most of the time? Cooperatively. In fact, most normally functioning human brains don't *choose* anything other than cooperation. Sociopaths and psychopaths aside, the vast majority of human beings on the planet desire and attempt to live peaceful lives. When we find ourselves in escalated conflict, we're behaving via unconscious autonomic processes that are designed for protection and survival. Indeed, the majority of our interactions are spent in cooperation and collaboration, not in conflict.

> **NOTE:** *I realize some of you who are experiencing or witnessing intense conflict may not feel like that. But take a moment to recognize the cooperation you are, in fact, experiencing. Every benign, pleasant, or supportive interaction you have with others—in the elevator, on the phone, on the street, and so on—is a moment of cooperation.*

We're so cooperative, in fact, that we're actually quite weird among the animal kingdom. No other vertebrate (that has not been socially engineered by humans) can pass by or stand next to strangers and simply ignore them. That would typically lead to hasty avoidance or violent conflict among animals. But most of us humans do this peacefully, and every time we do, that's all of us cooperating. Of course, this ability is supported not just by our biology but also by cultural norms, institutions, and systems of enforcement that make such peaceful coexistence possible. In many other societies or historical contexts, close proximity to strangers without acknowledgment could be interpreted as threatening. But that is culturally conditioned behavior. Our natural state is cooperative. Yes, productive cooperation also requires some level of conditioning, but it is more natural to us than conflict.

Cooperation is a natural part of our evolved human brains, and just like every other animate species, social or nonsocial, we have conflicts. The fact that we expose ourselves to so many social interactions, with strangers and non-strangers every day, and only few of them result in escalated or emotionally heated conflict supports the notion that we are more prone to cooperation and collaboration than we are to conflict.

The terms *cooperation* and *collaboration* are often used interchangeably, but in the evolutionary biology and psychology disciplines, they are not quite the same. *Cooperation* is when people work alongside one another toward a shared objective, typically dividing tasks and minimizing conflict. This shared objective could be as simple as "keep the peace" as strangers pass each other without incident on the street. Neurobiologically, cooperation relies on trust and fairness circuits in the brain and reward pathways in the striatum. *Collaboration*, however, is deeper and more integrative: it involves merging ideas and cocreating something new that none of the individuals could have produced alone. This requires additional engagement of the brain's social network. While cooperation allows us to coexist, collaboration enables us to build and transform. In the context of conflict resolution, the goal is rarely just cooperation. It's genuine collaboration, where renewed relationships are created and innovative, win-win solutions can emerge.

The Collaboration System

Melanie was the visionary CEO of a small but growing software company, which she founded with her husband, Mark, the chief operating officer. They also had a major investor, Daniel, who was positioned as chairman of the board. Melanie's style was soft and meticulous; she took her time to think things through, processed information carefully and slowly, and was not always adept at making clear, efficient decisions. Daniel was the opposite. He was fast-talking, a bit brash, decisive, and gave and expected answers quickly. The dynamic between Daniel and Melanie was a classic communication styles difference that I have witnessed many times become a catalyst for conflict.

When I was brought in to mediate an increasingly tense situation, Daniel and Melanie were no longer directly communicating. They each triggered one another's stress responses too intensely. When Melanie was slow to respond or not give clear, direct answers to his questions, Daniel felt she was ignoring, dismissing, avoiding, and disrespecting him. And when Daniel spoke loudly or quickly, demanding answers and decisions before she was ready to make them, Melanie felt he was trying to intimidate, bully, and manipulate her. Now, since they were no longer able to directly communicate, they made Mark the go-between. This was incredibly frustrating and exhausting for Mark; and it put additional stress on Mark and Melanie's marriage, which was already under the pressure of running a business together. Both Melanie and Daniel recognized what it was doing to Mark but didn't know what else to do. Mark was ready to quit. Daniel was about ready to leave the board and withdraw his funding. And Melanie was ready to start something new without either of them. Bringing me in was a last-ditch effort at holding the ship together.

The good news was that each of them highly valued one another. Melanie and Mark greatly respected Daniel for his business acumen and felt it would be incredibly difficult to grow the business without his guidance. Daniel and Melanie felt they needed Mark to keep the company steady and operationally on track. And everyone knew that Melanie was the visionary; without her, there was no company. Suffice it to say, splitting apart was not ideal. Staying together, in a healthier, more productive way, would be incredibly valuable—for the company, for Mark and Melanie's marriage, and for everyone's nervous systems.

Here's the thing: when people get lost in the stress of ongoing conflict, they lose sight of what they're trying to build together. Work relationships and marriages are all about creating something mutually beneficial and doing so interdependently. The most fulfilling business and personal partnerships keep their eye on the North Star—the vision, goal, life, culture, family, community, and/or value they are building together. And they recognize they need each other to build it. Heightened sympathetic nervous systems, hypervigilant thoughts, and defensive behaviors and communication only muddle the vision. So, I saw it as my job to help Melanie, Mark, and Daniel clear away the mud and refocus on their North Star.

Meeting privately with each, I asked a series of simple questions. Each question opened a conversation, where I dug a little deeper, asked clarifying questions, and helped them articulate their answers. At a high level, my questions to Melanie went like this:

"What are you trying to build with Daniel?"

"What do you get from achieving this goal? What's the dream?"

"What does he get? What's his dream?"

"Do you want that for him?"

"How do you see Daniel's role in this? How do you see him contributing to the vision?"

"If you're being honest, how are you currently making it more difficult for Daniel to do his part?"

"What could you do to make it easier for him to do his part?"

"What would you ask of him to make it easier for you to do your part?"

"Would you be willing to meet with him and me, so you can tell him all of this and so he can tell you his answers to these questions?"

This inquiry took almost an hour of discussion to clearly answer, but we came to some important conclusions that I felt were important for Melanie's investor/board chair to hear. Then, I met with Daniel and Mark individually as well. First, I wanted to make sure they were all aligned on the North Star. Did they all share the same, mutually beneficial goal(s)? Were they all clear on the vision? Once we established that, we could clarify what each of them needed from one another to successfully build this company together.

Some important events happened when we finally got Daniel and Melanie together for a meeting. First, we took time to establish mutual care and appreciation, the first step in conflict resolution processes. Then, they made space to listen to one another, without Daniel rushing or speaking loudly and without Melanie disengaging or withdrawing. They made room for mutual input on their goals and needs, which is crucial in collaborative solution building. Finally, they recognized and re-energized their focus on the shared goal—the North Star. This shared goal set the stage for a productive conversation about how they perceived one another's behavior, how they would each like to interact going forward, and how they could make each other's roles easier as they continue to cocreate a company.

The three of us met several more times. During our meetings, Melanie and Daniel practiced self-regulation around one another, worked on reconditioning their nervous systems and perceptions of the other, reestablished a foundation of mutual care and trust, refocused on how they needed each other to build the company and reach their common goals, and collaborated on devising actionable steps each of them could take toward those goals.

After several meetings, it became clear to all that it was time to stop making all of this so hard. They just wanted their relationships and their co-endeavors to be easier. Even though an acute stress response is virtually unconscious and fairly easy to slip into, it's not easy to experience. On the contrary, cooperation, co-regulation, and collaboration are much easier on the body, mind, and relationships. And of course, it's better on the culture and work product. So, we had to continuously ask these questions: What are we trying to build together? How are we making it harder to do so? How can we make it easier? What's more important: proving the other person wrong/bad or creating something amazing together? What can each of us do to help one another build this company?

Simple, right? Of course, not. Reconditioning, refocusing, rebuilding— all of this takes time, motivation, energy, effort, and practice. That said, we typically forget a simple fact about life: that cooperation and collaboration are much easier and more natural than conflict. Conflict is, in fact, much less common or natural, even if it doesn't always seem as such. In other words, we were built to collaborate more than we were to fight. And the proof is in the ways our nervous systems work.

Collaboration Is More Natural Than Conflict

It's not just some romantic notion that humans are "better together." From both neurobiological and psychological perspectives, our brains and nervous systems appear to have evolved precisely for cooperation as an operating system that has enabled us to survive and thrive over evolutionary history.

Our nervous systems are inherently prosocial, meaning we are attracted to and thus attempt to foster cooperation and collaboration far more than conflict. One of the strongest pieces of evidence for this is evolutionary psychologist Robin Dunbar's social brain hypothesis, which suggests the human neocortex grew disproportionately large in order to manage the complex relationships of group living. Unlike solitary creatures or species that live in smaller groups, we need cortical regions big and dense enough to track alliances and coordinate large-group behavior. In fact, in studies across primate species, brain size is closely correlated with the size and stability of social groups. That's because successful collaboration requires us to understand what others are thinking and feeling. This is handled by the social brain network, which includes structures like the medial prefrontal cortex, temporoparietal junction, superior temporal sulcus, and amygdala. Together, these regions enable us to model the minds of others, anticipate their reactions, and coordinate our behavior accordingly.

Inside that big brain, we also find circuitry designed for connection. Mirror neurons, first identified in monkeys and later confirmed in humans, enable us to simulate the actions and emotions of others. The mirror neuron system, located in premotor and parietal cortices among other regions, activates when we watch others act or express emotions. This system helps us *resonate* with teammates and group members. We can essentially feel their frustration, excitement, or determination, which keeps us in sync. Mirror neurons are thought to support our capacities for empathy and imitation and our ability to anticipate others' needs, all of which are critical for collaboration.

Inherent in the architecture of a prosocial brain is also, of course, neural capacities for prediction and defense against social threats, such as aggression, exclusion, rejection, humiliation, and abandonment. Although this defensive architecture is critical for navigating social environments, it is not what human beings naturally strive toward. On the contrary, our neurochemistry clearly indicates that brains reward collaboration, not conflict. For instance, oxytocin release during positive social interactions lowers amygdala reactivity to threat, making others seem safer and more reliable. At the same time, collaboration can activate the mesolimbic dopamine pathway, especially the ventral striatum and nucleus accumbens, which are key reward centers providing a motivational kick that reinforces collaborative behavior. Also, endorphins, produced primarily in the pituitary gland and the hypothalamus during collaborative activities, are released throughout the central nervous system where they bind to opioid receptors in brain regions such as the limbic system, brain stem, and spinal cord to reduce pain and generate feelings of well-being. This neurochemical cocktail during collaboration reduces stress and pain while boosting pleasure, trust, and social bonding, creating a sense of safety and connection that strengthens collaboration.

Polyvagal theory supports this by suggesting that our vagus nerve (via the parasympathetic system) evolved to bring the body into a calm, socially engaged state during safe social contact. The theory suggests that working together can move the nervous system from a defensive mode into a state of openness and creativity. In other words, we are wired to calm down when we sense others' trust and goodwill (i.e., cooperation) and to become positively stimulated when working with each other to build something (i.e., collaboration).

Understanding that our nervous systems are built for collaboration also helps explain why conflict feels so disruptive. When cooperation breaks down, our brains interpret it as a survival threat. Disagreements, exclusion, abandonment, rejection, or betrayal can activate the same circuitry involved in physical danger, like the amygdala region and the anterior cingulate cortex, pulling us into defensive states of fight, flight, or shutdown. All of this points to the fact that collaboration quite literally feels good, cooperation feels calming, and conflict can activate brain regions associated with physical pain.

In other words, we are already wired for peace. Peace feels calming, rewarding, and stimulating. We are only wired for conflict in that we have neural mechanisms available for defending against threats. When threats don't exist, or at least are perceived to be absent, our natural state is cooperative and our thriving state is collaborative.

Now, some people appear to thrive on or seek out conflict. It almost seems like a natural state for them. But conflict-prone personalities are not natural; they are learned through conditioning. No nervous system comes into the world seeking tension and stress. On the contrary, our nervous systems are naturally seeking regulation and homeostasis. Those who seem to enjoy conflict have been conditioned to view it as a way of establishing status or control, serving multiple underlying needs that were likely threatened and depleted throughout their childhoods, including safety, affiliation, positive identity, independence, and/or stimulation. If conflict served those needs in any way during their youth or young adulthood, such as leading to successful outcomes, then such behavior became reinforced as a way to self-protect and satisfy their basic needs. In this way, their brains learned that nervous system regulation was available mostly through domination and aggression.

Others who seem to always be in conflict but not to necessarily enjoy it have been conditioned to be hypervigilant, perceiving threats everywhere and regularly, leading to habitual self-preservation behavior and communication. These individuals are usually more driven to find ways of unlearning the habit, since they are not enjoying or finding successful outcomes from conflict. Whether a conflict-prone person seems to enjoy conflict or not, if that individual were interested in living a more harmonious life with a calmer nervous system and more stable relationships, they would have to recondition their system and return to a more natural, collaborative state. This is a difficult change for deeply conditioned systems to achieve, but not impossible for those who are highly motivated.

Critical Elements for Effective Collaboration During Conflict

If you're reading this material, ideally you are motivated to live a more peaceful, collaborative life. Implementing collaboration during conflict resolution doesn't just help resolve the problem, it regulates the nervous system and establishes a new interpersonal connection. Acts of listening, validating, and cocreating calm defensive circuits, release bonding chemicals, and rebuild trust networks. In this way, conflict resolution is less about winning arguments and more about returning people to their natural state: connected and collaborative. Let's discuss the important components of collaborative solution-building during peace processes.

It's All About Agency   The critical, primary element of collaboration during conflict resolution is to give each participant a seat at the table and a voice in the process. So often during conflict, people do not feel listened to or understood. That's why we start peace processes with mutual care and validation practices, and also why our solution-focused portion must be centered on giving each participant agency. This serves the psychological need for control or independence. Each person involved in building solutions should be able to play a role and contribute to both the ultimate goal or vision for the relationship and the proposed actions to reach the goal and achieve the vision.

Creating buy-in on the solutions or actions proposed also requires agency. When people feel they have a hand in building those solutions, or at the least a chance to voice concerns and get them addressed, they are far more likely to believe in and adhere to the solutions agreed to. Afterall, the solutions were partly their idea.

Giving someone agency can be done formally during a conflict resolution or mediation process by ensuring everyone has an equal opportunity to speak and contribute. It can also be done informally and naturally during a one-on-one difficult conversation. Simply keeping in mind that each person should have a chance to get their ideas heard and considered is the critical core of collaboration. When working together to create something new, whether that's a renewed vision for the relationship or a creative way of getting each person's needs met, all collaborative processes must be built on a foundation of multiparty agency.

It Comes with Humility   When it comes to resolving conflicts, humility is one of the most powerful practices and cognitive states one can embody. As discussed previously, humility is highly correlated with curiosity in that true curiosity both drives and can be driven by humility. Remaining humble is also incredibly important for productive collaboration. It is the engine that drives our ability to offer others a seat at the table and a voice in the process. Humility counteracts defensiveness and the desire to be right, and opens us to learning from and building on the ideas of others, even when we don't totally agree.

Similar to care, humility does not require practice or time. It simply requires us to make a choice: to let go of the notion that "my way is the right way," to listen and learn from others, and to engage with others to bring a new idea, product, relationship, or structure into existence. Research also indicates that intellectual humility is highly correlated with open-mindedness and willingness to collaborate. In fact, it's hard to imagine a successful collaboration without some level of humility at play. Choosing to enter a state of humility immediately propels more collaborative potential.

It's Driven by Shared Goals   Another critical element of collaboration during conflict resolution is a focus on shared goals. Before parties in conflict negotiate potential solutions, it's important they clarify what each person's goals are and find a way to align their goals. In some cases, it's obvious that all have the same goals but perhaps different methods of reaching them or communication style tensions along the way. In these cases, helping parties refocus on their North Stars can help cut away the noise of conflict. Beneath the stories about who did what wrong, their shared goals can reunite parties toward a common vision, which is often powerful enough for them to put aside their stories and collaborate on productive ways to move forward.

In other cases, common goals are not as clear. When this is the case, the parties will have to dig under their surface-level positions to find alignment on underlying, core needs, goals, and/or values. Somehow or another, they will need to find alignment in order to collaborate on a solution. For example, if one party says "Fewer guns" and the other says "More guns," the digging inquiry should ask, "What do fewer guns/more guns get you?" Under the surface, we'll arrive undoubtedly at a basic need for safety, which both people want and need—the common goal. They simply hold opposing views on how to achieve it. But, if they can find alignment on a shared need, goal, or value, they can tackle the surface-level problem (e.g., whether to have fewer or more guns) as a partnership addressing the underlying need (e.g., safety) together, rather than viewing the other person or their ideas as the true problem.

In any conflict, the most basic but important goal is solving the conflict. In other words, the problem is not a person but rather a third thing to solve together. If we can agree on viewing the problem as something separate from each of the parties involved, then we can tackle it together as a team.

The focus on a shared goal motivates the collaborative endeavor: to work together to create new, innovative ways of solving our collective problems and satisfying everyone's underlying needs. Your problems become my problems; your goals become my goals; your needs are the same as my needs. We're in this together. This is the spirit of collaboration.

It's Enhanced by Interdependence We can modulate the power of common goals by recognizing how we are interdependent relative to those goals. In order to realize the vision we're building and achieve our goals, we'll each have a role, and we won't get there without everyone doing their parts. Clearly identifying our shared goals and determining how those goals require all of us to do our parts should help motivate each party to make it easier for the other to do their part. If the goal is authentic (i.e., if I actually believe in and desire the vision) and I believe we need each other to achieve it, why wouldn't I try to make it as easy for you as possible? To reach my goal (i.e., our shared goal), it would only serve me to support you in any way I can.

If you'll remember, interdependence toward a shared goal was one of Allport's suggested conditions for resolving conflict between groups (see "Conflict Resolution with Communication" in Principle 4). Plenty of research has since supported the idea that while this isn't an absolute requisite, it certainly enhances our ability to resolve conflicts collaboratively. The more we focus on shared, interdependent goals, the more likely we are to change perceptions of those with whom we've experienced conflict and build solutions that make sense for all parties.

Recap: The Collaboration System

Want to find effective solutions to a conflict? Give everyone a voice, remain humble throughout, establish shared goals, and focus on how we need each other to achieve those goals. While communicating care and establishing trust set the foundation for successful peace processes, truly sustainable and transformative solutions are built by humans collaborating in spirit, in thought, and in action. In fact, research shows that the best predictor of innovation and collaboration is the level of trust one has in their collaboration partners and leaders. So, the more care and trust we can build first (see Principle 5), the easier collaboration should be. Once we've implemented tools to build care and trust during conflict, we can begin collaborating on solutions. Let's go over two practical sequences to collaboratively reach solutions.

Tools to Do What We Were Built to Do: Collaborate

To collaborate effectively, we'll need to think of our conflict counterpart not as an opposing force but rather as a collaborative, problem-solving partner.

After establishing a level of care for the other, we can move into collaborative solution building. Remember to first make sure everyone feels they have a seat at the table and a voice in the process. This requires that you foster and maintain humility. Then, it's time to find or reestablish common goals. The following two sequences are designed to help you find shared needs or goals and then work collaboratively on satisfying them with your problem-solving partner.

You might first want to practice these techniques with a partner you're not in conflict with or someone with whom you have only a minor conflict. See what parts of the techniques work and what needs modification. Refine and practice your collaborative approach so that you're prepared to resolve more intense or complex conflicts.

Realigning on Shared Goals: When a Partnership Has Been Established

Sometimes we find ourselves in conflict with someone who obviously shares some of our goals, at least in theory. Whether it's a coworker, business partner, spouse, or co-parent, there has been some implicit or explicit establishment of a personal or strategic partnership. In these cases, it's time to clear the cobwebs of conflict to refocus on our shared goals. From that point, we can collaborate on ways to achieve them.

Here's the protocol:

1. Invite them to a conversation using agency giving and humility. For example, "I'd really like to work together more collaboratively. I have an exercise that can help us do that. Would you be up for trying it?" If they agree, you can start right away or schedule a time and day that works for both of you.

2. To start the conversation, give agency with humility. For example, "Thank you for doing this with me. I don't believe I can achieve [shared goal] without your partnership. So, your input here is incredibly important."

3. Explain the sequence. You might read this verbatim, and just let your partner know you will be reading through the instructions: "The following is a sequence of questions we will both answer. We'll each read them and write down our answers privately. We should write what feels honest and authentic, but let's also be constructive and respectful. There is a way to say anything we need to say in a respectful and constructive way. Once we've written our answers, we'll hand them to each other and read each other's answers quietly. We will not judge or evaluate the answers; we'll simply read with an open mind. Then, we'll work together to create actionable steps for a more collaborative partnership. Sound good? Any questions or concerns?"

4. Here are the questions for each problem-solving partner to answer privately. Write down your answers:
   - "What do I think we are trying to build together? What's our intended shared goal(s) or vision?"
   - "What do I personally get from achieving this goal? What's the dream?"
   - "How do I see my role in this? How do I see myself contributing to the vision?"
   - "How do I see my partner's role? How do I see them contributing to the vision?"

- "What part of this do I need my partner for? What makes my partner important for achieving the goal?"
- "If I'm being honest, how am I currently making it more difficult for my partner to do their part?"
- "What could I do to make it easier for my partner to do their part?"
- "What would I ask of my partner to make it easier for me to do my part?"

5. When everyone has completed their answers, switch papers and each person read the other's answers quietly to themself. Read with an open mind. If anything feels emotionally triggering, use self-regulation techniques (Principle 1) and remember to stay humble. While reading, try to notice where you seem to be aligned: anything you wrote down that was similar to what they wrote or that you would agree with.

6. Now, we're going to realign and collaborate. You'll finish the following sentences together. Discuss each out loud, and write down the answers as you go:
   - We each highlighted our personal dream or vision. Does each of us want that for the other, even if we don't fully agree on the method or style being employed?
     - Yes, I want my partner to achieve their dream/vision.
     - No, I do not want my partner to achieve their dream/vision.
   - It looks like we both already share the following goals:
     - _______________________________
     - _______________________________
   - To achieve these goals, each of us will do the following:
     - Person A:
     - Person B:
   - We will make it easier for one another to do our parts by:
     - Person A:
     - Person B:
   - Each of us will stop:
     - Person A:
     - Person B:

7. Great job! Let's set a timeline and accountability structure.
   - We will check in on how our solutions or action items are working at [time and date].
   - We will check in regularly each [established weekly or monthly cadence].
   - If we seem to be getting off track or feel misaligned, we will . . . .
8. Now, we're going to collaborate on any areas of misalignment. Fill out the following:
   - It looks like we need to find alignment on . . . .
      - ________________________________
      - ________________________________
   - Regarding each point of misalignment, decide if it is either necessary or unnecessary to reconcile and align on in order to achieve your shared goals. Write the word *necessary* or the word *unnecessary* next to each point.
      - For those that are unnecessary, indicating you do not need to align on in order to reach your goals, can you agree to not discuss these items going forward, as they are simply distractions from your shared goals and vision?
      - For any that are necessary, try the Finding Common Ground approach in the next sequence. Start from number 4.

Finding Common Ground: When No Partnership Has Been Established

We may also find ourselves in conflict where there is no clear partnership. If we want to reduce the tension or solve a problem together, we'll have to become problem-solving partners. This requires we find common ground, which we'll use as a foundation from which to collaborate on solutions. Building solutions without recognition of common needs, goals, interests, or values is like a tree growing without roots. The first bit of wind will topple it. So, let's establish some roots and then collaborate on how the tree should grow. This process can take a couple of hours, so plan accordingly.

Here's the protocol:

1. Invite them to a conversation using agency giving and humility. For example, "It's seems like we can't find common ground, and I'd really like to. Would you be open to an interesting exercise? It's designed to help us understand each other better and discover ways of working together rather than against each other." If they agree, you can start right away or schedule a time and day that works for both of you. Again, designate at least two hours.

2. To start the conversation, give agency with humility. For example, "I really appreciate you doing this with me. I want to understand your goals more clearly and hope we can find a way to work together."

3. Explain the sequence: "The following is a sequence of questions we will both answer. First, I will read them aloud, and you'll answer. As you do, I'm going to write down your answers. Please say what feels honest and authentic, but please also try to find a way to say what you need to in a respectful and constructive way. Then, you'll do the same for me. We will not judge or evaluate the answers yet; we'll simply write them down with an open mind. Then, we'll work together to create actionable steps for a more collaborative partnership. Sound good? Any questions?"

4. Let's start with just one issue or point of contention at a time. We can run through this same protocol again for a different issue. Regarding the issue at hand, please answer the following questions:
   - "In an ideal world, what do you want to see happen?"
     [We will label the answer to this *Goal A*.]
   - "How do you plan on achieving Goal A?"
     [We'll call this *Method A1*.]
   - "Why do you think Method A1 is the best plan? Have you seen it work in other contexts, or is there evidence to support Method A1's efficacy in achieving Goal A over alternative methods?"
   - "If Goal A were achieved, what do you believe that would serve? What's the deeper reason it is important?"

- Serving that deeper reason would help satisfy your and/or others' basic psychological needs for (choose as many as apply):
  - Safety/security/stability
  - Affiliation/connection/belonging
  - Positive self-concept/identity
  - Independence/control/autonomy
  - Engagement/stimulation/intrigue
  - Noble pursuits/growth/self-actualization

  [We will label the answers to this question *Needs A*.]

5. Reader of the questions now to answer: Putting aside the goals and methods, do I want my problem-solving partner's basic needs to be satisfied?

   If yes, then *we have found common ground*. Even though we may not agree on the surface-level goals or the methods, we can agree on helping to satisfy your partner's or others' deeper needs.

6. Now, flip the script. The other person will start from the beginning of number 4 and ask the questions. You will answer, and your partner will write down your answers. Your answers will be labeled *Goal B, Method B1*, and *Needs B*, respectively. If there are more than two people, allow each person to go and label their answers accordingly (e.g., *Goal C, Method C1*, etc.).

7. After running through the questions, ideally we have now clarified one another's underlying needs and aligned on desiring mutual need satisfaction. Now, our question is, how can we get everyone's needs met, regardless of whether we use Methods A1 or B1 or achieve Goals A or B? Let's fill out the following grid. This should be a collaborative effort. Work with each other. Build off one another's ideas. Allow for all ideas to be on the table without judgment or evaluation. We can evaluate everything later.

   In the left column, list all the needs at play (could be one row or six rows). For this example, let's pretend, there were four needs identified between two partners. For each need, write down the stated goals and as many alternative goals that might also satisfy that need. Then for each goal, write down the stated methods and as many alternative methods that might also achieve that goal.

Needs	Goals (How might we satisfy this need?)	Methods (How might we achieve those wants?)
Safety/security (Needs A)	Goal A	Method A1 Method A2 (alternative)
	Goal B	Method B1 Method B2 (alternative) Method B3 (alternative)
	Goal C (alternative) Goal D (alternative)	Corresponding methods Corresponding methods
Positive self-concept (Needs A)	[Do the same as above.]	[Corresponding methods]
Independence/ control (Needs A and B)	[Do the same as above.]	[Corresponding methods]
Engagement/ stimulation (Needs B)	[Do the same as above.]	[Corresponding methods]

8. Once you've filled out the grid, you can begin determining which goals and methods seem reasonable to all parties. One way to accomplish this is by elimination followed by rank choice matching.

    (a) **Eliminate or modify.** Identify any goals or methods that clearly won't work and cross them out. Modify any goals or methods that might work but not in their current form.

    (b) **Prioritize separately.** Once you have a final list of goals and methods that *might* work, each person separately organizes the remaining items in order of their individual preference. For example, Person A might list, in order (1) switching the meeting time, (2) shortening the meeting duration, (3) making the meetings less frequent. And Person B might list (1) shortening the meeting duration, (2) making the meetings less frequent, (3) switching the meeting time.

(c) **Choose highest matching.** After prioritizing separately, reconvene and compare lists. Find the highest matching solution(s) on each list and discover if that will be acceptable to all. In the example, shortening the meeting is the highest matching solution on each list. Person A's first choice is Person B's last choice, so that's not highest matching. But Person A's second choice is Person B's first choice, so we'd try that as our best current solution option. Make any final modifications to the chosen solutions, as necessary.

(d) **Final options cost analysis.** If two final options exist, and each party prefers a different one, it can be helpful to perform a cost analysis. How difficult would each be to implement (i.e., what are the costs or barriers to each socially, structural, financially, logistically, and otherwise)? Write down the costs. The option that is easiest to implement and/or least costly may be the right one to move forward with. If Person A is open to shortening the meeting duration but would much rather prefer to switch the meeting time, then we might want to determine which would be easier and less costly to do.

9. If you can reach an agreement on acceptable goals and methods to satisfy everyone's Needs, then you can develop solution-focused action items for each person to take that build toward those goals and methods. In this case, let's set a timeline and accountability structure. Complete the following points together:

- We will check in on how our solutions are working at [time and date].
- We will check in regularly on [established weekly or monthly cadence].
- If we seem to be getting off track or feel misaligned, we will . . . .

However, if you're having trouble getting to agreed-on solutions, especially because you just can't seem to agree on any goals or methods, then it's time to get creative. Stay tuned for our final principle!

Moving Forward

Everything humans do and have ever done that is worthy of awe has been a result of collaboration. In fact, we are collaborating all the time without even realizing it. The accumulation of human knowledge is essentially a collaboration—humans learning from and building on the ideas of each other both contemporarily and across generations. We were, indeed, built for this. Not to mention, we were built *by* it. Our very lives each transpire from the collaboration of two human beings, just as life does with all sexually reproductive species. Collaboration is a gift from millions of years of genetic inheritance, the building blocks of all we are, feel, think, and do. And the cultures, norms, and systems within which our genes express themselves so diversely have and continue to be developed by the collaboration of human minds and behaviors. Epigenetics reminds us that our individual experience of life come from the collaboration of our genetics and our environments. In essence, the world and all we experience is a product of collaborative systems.

We've made it to final stretch of this expedition along the neural circuits of peace. We've tackled four of the five Cs of conflict resolution, learning to embody curiosity, communicate intentionally, implement care, and collaborate effectively. Sometimes that's enough to successfully navigate conflict. However, for more complex conflicts or those with many layers, parties, or histories, we might have to think not just underneath the surface but also outside the box when building solutions. We might have to not only build together, but also *explore* together. We'll need to get creative.

Transformative peace processes typically require creating a new vision for the relationship and collaborating on ways to achieve that vision. And the most transformative are carried out in a spirit of exploration and discovery, which are important aspects of creativity. So, here are our final questions on the journey toward peace: How can creativity contribute to peace processes? What are some structured ways of thinking outside of structures? How might we even have some fun during conflict resolution? Let's explore.

7 | New Solutions Lie Outside the Structure

Sometimes digging under the surface to find common ground isn't enough. We might recognize and even mutually value one another's psychological needs but get stuck on conflicting goals, methods, or other values. The inability to agree on a reasonable path that satisfies all parties' needs leads us to an impasse. This is when we must get creative to resolve the conflict. We not only have to go under surface-level positions but also outside the conceptual structures.

Thinking out of the box is a common creative trope referring to the figurative mental box in which we place concepts. Out-of-the-box thinking therefore is inherently creative and imaginative, in that it leads us to conceive of and explore concepts in new ways. But in the context of problem-solving, I prefer the term *structure* rather than *box* because a structure is more complex than a box. It can have multiple layers, dimensions, shapes, and meanings. And this is often the case in long-standing or complex conflicts with seemingly few or no shared goals, methods, or values. Creative solutions to complex problems require that we define the structure of the conflict so that we can step outside it.

Creativity doesn't require one to be a great artist or thinker. It just requires a small step outside the structure, which all of us have the capacity to do. This is just as true with creative problem-solving as it is with artistry. All it might take is a small step outside the conceptual structure to see the problem in a new way and generate a novel solution. Let's discuss exactly how our brains create conceptual structures, what it means to diverge from those structures, and thus what it takes to creatively problem-solve.

The Imagination and Creativity Systems

I'm going to present here an incredibly simple example of creative problem-solving. It's a solution that most people would say is not creative at all, in that it may be totally obvious to anyone reading. However, for one of the parties involved, it was clearly outside of her mental structure. And for this reason, it's an important example: it shows just how artless a creative solution can be. All it takes is a small step outside our conceptual boundaries.

I was called to mediate an intensifying dispute between Carl, the cofounder and chief operating officer of a nonprofit, and Bethany, the director of community engagement. Carl had cofounded the organization almost 20 years earlier, and Bethany had worked there for more than 10 years. She basically ran the entire public-facing team. As in many disputes I've intervened in, they were unwilling to directly communicate by the time I arrived. Without getting into the details of the conflict, suffice it to say that their issues were highly complex, layered with years of poor interactions, negative perceptions, and increasingly tense experiences. After meeting with Carl and Bethany each privately several times, building rapport and attempting to understand their levels of motivation for transforming the conflict, it became clear that the motivation was simply absent. At this point, neither had an interest in working together, communicating, or changing the relational dynamic. Both felt attacked and judged, and were worried about potential legal and financial consequences of interacting. They were walking on eggshells around each other, afraid to say or do the wrong thing for fear of retaliation. To both, all hope of transformation was lost, and so all motivation to resolve had deteriorated.

I asked each, then, how I could help and why I was there as a mediator. They were under the impression that I could advocate for them personally to get their goals met by the other. Carl wanted me to get Bethany to quit.

Bethany wanted me to get Carl to leave her alone, let her work autonomously, and maybe even consider retiring. Neither had ever communicated these goals to the other, and rightly so—they would have only made one another more defensive and the whole situation worse. So, they wanted me to do it. But of course, that's not my job. I wasn't there to get one person's needs met at the expense of the other; I was there to help get everyone's needs met, in whatever ways that was possible.

At this point, I recognized that the method of getting everyone's needs met was going to be a little different than typical transformative processes. My core mission is always to help people find peace through mutual needs satisfaction. Often that requires various behavioral and neuropsychological methods of transforming relationships. But on occasion, it simply means helping the parties peacefully separate. After getting to know Carl and Bethany, it was clear to me that separation was likely the only way to help them each find peace. They would likely never be happy working together at the same organization where they were expected to collaborate.

Now, here's the interesting part that prompted creative thinking. Bethany had never even considered quitting. Mindboggling to some of us, I realize. But for Bethany, the organization's mission was a calling for her; her position was a dream position she helped to create, her team was fantastic, and her compensation was solid. She literally couldn't imagine leaving. So, the structure around which she held the concept of "Bethany's work" did not contain the possibility of not working there. My goal then was to help her starting thinking outside her structure, to consider alternative methods of reaching her goals and getting her needs met. That would require at least the consideration of working somewhere else.

Any time we attempt to think outside of our habitual structures, especially when we are guided to do so by someone else, we must tread carefully. Doing so can feel jarring or confusing at first. Moving outside our structures challenges our existing beliefs and, sometimes, elements of our identity. So, after building trust with Bethany over several meetings filled with care and validation, I proposed the idea: "Have you ever thought of working elsewhere?" Her first reaction was defensive and immediately dismissive. She wouldn't even consider it. So, I left it there for the moment.

Later, I brought it up again and dug a little deeper. "What's scary about the idea of leaving and working somewhere else?" I asked. Bethany divulged a litany of stories: there were no other jobs like hers in the industry, no one else would let her lead a team like this, she couldn't make the same amount of money at other organizations, and so on.

After some reflective listening and validation, my next questions were, "But what if you could? What if there *were* another job you would love? What if there *were* another amazing team you could lead? What if another organization *would* pay you as much or more? Would you consider it then?"

"Well . . . ," she pondered. I could see her wheels spinning, the boundaries of her structure being tested. "I guess if that were all possible, then, yeah, maybe I'd consider it." Ah, a spark! This potential solution seemed so obvious to me, so simple; but for Bethany, this was apparently the first time in more than a decade she took a step outside the rigid structure of her work life. She considered a solution she had not before considered, at least not seriously or consciously. If Bethany found a new job that satisfied her underlying needs, then Carl's needs would also be satisfied via the separation. This would be a win-win solution.

"Would you be willing to explore if it's possible?" I asked her. Bethany was hesitant but willing. This would take courage, but she was highly motivated to find peace for herself. Over the next several weeks, I supported Bethany in a job search, which she hadn't done in many years. At first, she simply committed to perusing the job boards. Then, after a week or so, she committed to sending out a few résumés. After that, she committed to asking her friends and network if they knew of any jobs available that might be a good fit.

After a few weeks of this, I could tell Bethany had turned a corner on the idea of finding a new job. She was excited about the prospect. The conceptual structure around her work life had expanded to include a potential new workplace. From there, the engines were revved. Amazingly, it only took about five weeks for her to interview for a new opportunity in an organization she found inspiring at an even higher salary and better benefits. She got a job offer and accepted it.

I then performed a shuttle mediation, going back and forth between Carl and Bethany, to discuss a reasonable severance package, in which Bethany would agree to leave peacefully and release any future claims against the organization. The monetary package was not as much as Bethany wanted, but she'd already found a great new job and so was okay with the compensation. The paperwork was signed, Bethany left with a new career trajectory she was excited about, and Carl could get back to work feeling safe from legal trouble.

When I followed up with each in the months following Bethany's departure, it was clear they were both in better places. Carl was refocused and reinvigorated on growing the organization and its mission. Bethany was loving her new role and company. And all it took was a little step outside the structure. No amazing feats of ambitious creation. Just a little motivation and courage.

Even simple examples of creative problem-solving warrant recognition and applause. And not just because of the innovative solutions we generate but also because of the astonishing processes happening in our brains and minds that drive creative ideation.

This Is Your Brain on Creativity

Creative thinking can be defined as the ability to perceive and approach problems and situations with a new perspective, leading to unique, novel, and effective solutions. Yet, as we well know by now, the brain is a predictive processing machine, using memories of past experiences to generate predictions about the world. This machine creates a predictive map or working model of the world, which often builds rigid conceptual structures of everything we perceive and experience and therefore counteracts our ability to generate new perspectives and novel solutions. In order to challenge or break free of these predictions and generate unique approaches and ideas, we must use particular neural networks that allow for imagination.

While both predictive coding and imagination rely on the brain's ability to simulate what isn't present, the scope, purpose, and network dynamics differ. Predictions are highly constrained, aiming for accuracy and efficiency as opposed to novelty. They are imaginative simulations of the near future tied tightly to survival and efficiency. Imagination, however, uses the same neural machinery of simulation but is less constrained, more exploratory, and often future-oriented in a broader, creative sense. To generate creative thought, we need both capacities and their underlying neural systems working together. Predictions still guide imagined possibilities, but in creative thinking they are less rigid, enabling broader associations and more flexible scenario building.

The default mode network (DMN) has been briefly mentioned through this book, but now we'll let it shine. The DMN is the major driver of imagination, employing various neural systems and regions, such as the medial prefrontal cortex, posterior cingulate cortex, and angular gyrus. It allows for a range of internal mental processes, including mind wandering, mental time travel and simulation, perspective shifting, theory of mind, connecting disparate ideas and knowledge domains, and self-referential thought. When you're dreaming in rapid eye movement sleep, the DMN is playing at full blast: you could be anyone and no one, everywhere and nowhere, in the past and the future, in the world and in a different dimension—all at the same time. In dreams, the boundaries of physical reality, including all predictions and constraints, essentially disappear. This is why dreams often feels so weird, incoherent, and different from waking life. This is also why we need to rein in the DMN imagination system if we hope to create useful and coherent solutions or products that actually make sense. Here's where the executive control network (ECN) steps in.

A major neural system involved in predictive coding, the ECN is also composed of several neural regions, including the dorsolateral prefrontal cortex and anterior cingulate cortex, typically associated with intense focus, working memory, and goal-directed thought. It acts as a reality-check system, evaluating, testing, and constraining imagination in order to identify ideas that are useful and worth pursuing. Too much DMN without ECN, and we've got strange, incoherent ideation; too much ECN without DMN, and we've got rigid, ultrastructured cognition based on predictive coding. So, we need the balance to produce creative thought. But these networks don't balance themselves; they need a third network to play mediator, as it were: the salience network (SN).

The SN is the regulatory network, including the anterior insula and dorsal anterior cingulate, that constantly monitors both internal and external information to determine what is most salient or important at any given moment. It acts as a sort of switchboard between the DMN and the ECN, allowing for the brain to employ both networks efficiently for productive, creative thinking.

This creative brain trifecta—switching between DMN and ECN with help from the SN—is facilitated by a range of neurochemicals. In the starring role is the dopaminergic system. As we've noted, dopamine plays a major role in motivation via reward seeking and in learning and memory, but this fascinating neuromodulator also plays a critical role in the creative system. Levels of dopamine determine how well the trifecta is working: balanced dopamine levels lead to a balanced switching between the DMN and ECN. For the DMN, dopamine from the ventral tegmental area to the hippocampus enhances novel associative linking, while dopamine in the medial prefrontal cortex supports the evaluation processes (i.e., how meaningful or relevant an imagined idea feels). The ECN also depends heavily on dopamine, specifically in the dorsolateral prefrontal cortex, where it regulates working memory and essentially tunes the ECN's ability to filter and structure the DMN's output. For the SN, dopamine-rich regions like the striatum and anterior cingulate cortex particularly support the salience detection function, deciding when to pivot between wild exploration and disciplined control.

Other important neurochemicals involved in the DMN-ECN-SN system include norepinephrine, which regulates arousal, alertness, and attentional shifting; serotonin, which helps the brain regulate mood, tolerate ambiguity, and inhibit impulsive reactions; acetylcholine, which enhances signal-to-noise ratio in cortical processing, supporting attention and plasticity to help us focus on key details of an idea without being distracted by irrelevant emotional noise; opioids such as endorphins, which help reduce hyperactivity of the ECN under stress, allowing the DMN imagination to flow; and oxytocin, which modulates DMN activity in social imagination, including perspective taking and empathic simulation. Recent research also suggests dopamine reduces the fear of judgment, which helps in the collaborative aspect of creativity, enabling people to share "wild" ideas without the social anxiety that usually triggers the ECN to shut them down.

Together, these neurochemicals facilitate adaptive functioning of the tripart creative thinking system, enabling useful, novel ideas and solutions to emerge. When they do, a number of interesting cognitive abilities become available to us, and these are especially useful in conflict resolution.

Creative Cognition in Conflict Resolution

When dopamine is in a balanced state, and the SN can mediate effectively between the ECN and DMN, some incredible cognitive capacities are at our disposal. One astonishing mechanism is *cognitive fluidity*. Coined in the 1990s by renowned archeologist and evolutionary psychologist Steven Mithen, cognitive fluidity refers to the brain's capacity to integrate and transition seamlessly between fundamentally different thought categories or knowledge domains and merge them into new, hybrid ideas. Unlike other animals, whose cognition is typically confined to narrow, specialized domains (e.g., food gathering, tool use, social behavior), humans can cross-pollinate ideas from art, science, technology, social reasoning, survival needs, and beyond. For example, a dog may recognize edible material as part of the category "food" and his bowl as part of the category "things that hold food." Due to a dog's inability to integrate cognitive categories, he would never conceive of combining the two. However, humans can and have merged the two, creating edible material that is also designed to contain food, such as ice cream bowls made of waffles or biodegradable camping plates made of edible wheat bran. This cognitive flexibility enables us to generate solutions that could not arise if knowledge domains were kept siloed.

Another cognitive function that is critical to creative problem-solving is called *divergent thinking*. As opposed to convergent thinking, which describes the devising of a single answer to a problem (e.g., the solution to a math problem), divergent thinking is employed when there are multiple possible solutions to a single problem and/or when the problem is not well-defined. Originally defined by psychologist J. P. Guilford in the mid-20th century, divergent thinking involves generating multiple possible answers, perspectives, or approaches. It's the mindset that asks "what if?" instead of "what is?" This is critical for ideating on novel solutions to complex conflicts.

Another important cognitive capacity for conflict resolution is *perspective shifting*. An active DMN enables us to imagine what it might be like to be in someone else's shoes, to feel what they feel and desire what they desire. This capacity is further facilitated by our theory of mind network, including the medial prefrontal cortex, temporoparietal junction, and posterior cingulate cortex, as well as mirror neurons, working in concert with the DMN. To the extent we can actually understand someone else's experience and perspective, this capacity significantly enhances the likelihood for peacebuilding.

With *mental time travel*, an additional psychological ability, we project ourselves backward in time to reexperience past events (i.e., episodic memory) and forward in time to pre-experience possible future events (i.e., episodic future thinking). This ability is also facilitated by our imagination system and helps us to envision various trajectories from current conflict processes. A critical question for those in conflict, for example, is what we believe will happen if the conflict does not get solved or gets worse. With optimism and opportunity in mind, we should also ask what we believe *could* happen should we solve the conflict and/or transform the relationship. Comparing these trajectories with past experiences and what we want for our lives, including the potential for different forms of the relationship and relational expectations, helps us test what may be ideal and achievable, what steps transformation might take, and over what period of time. The ability to mentally simulate what the future could look and feel like along either trajectory—stressful and conflicting versus healthy and productive—can be a significant motivational factor in propelling successful conflict resolution processes.

Finally, a creative mind helps to counteract the common mental heuristics that limit our creative potential. For example, *functional fixedness* is a cognitive bias that limits a person's ability to see alternative uses for an object beyond its traditional or intended function. It's when you get stuck thinking that something can only be used in the usual way you've always used it. In problem-solving experiments, such as those performed by Karl Duncker, who coined the term in the 1930s, people often failed to notice that a box holding tacks could itself be used as a platform, because they were focused only on the tacks inside the box. Another cognitive shortcut is called *mental set*, which describes the tendency to approach a new problem in a way that has worked in the past, even when it's not the most effective solution. In other words, it's the "if it worked before, I'll just do it again" bias. This is classically illustrated with the Luchins water jar experiments in the 1940s, where people learned a specific formula for measuring water volumes; even when later problems could be solved more easily, participants kept using the complex formula they had practiced earlier. These and related biases certainly show up in conflict processes, keeping people stuck in old patterns and historic approaches to their conflicts, unable to view new and potentially more effective solutions. An active creative network reduces these biases.

Altogether, these cognitive tools, fueled by our brains' creative system, enable us to move outside the traditional structures that contain and define our conflicts. Thinking outside the structure, however, doesn't mean *way* outside, as evidenced by the previous example with Bethany. New solutions can emerge from even a small step outside. But to get outside of a structure, we should understand what it is exactly and where its boundaries lie.

Stepping Outside the Structure

As we experience life, our brains create concepts out of everything we perceive: things, events, people, places, situations, and so on. In psychology, these concepts are called mental representations. Every object of thought is essentially a mental representation; that is, the thing as you experience or perceive it isn't the thing itself but rather simply represented in your mind as that thing. Even *you* are a mental representation—you exist for yourself as you are represented in your mind and for others as you are represented in theirs. And that mental representation of the thing, which we will call a *concept*, has a structure to it.

There are all sorts of concepts described in the psychology literature, such as conjunctive, disjunctive, relational, hierarchical, and so on. For example, conjunctive concepts require multiple features to be true at once (e.g., a bachelor must be both male and unmarried), while disjunctive concepts allow either/or features (e.g., a strike in baseball can result from a swing *or* a missed call). Relational concepts define relationships between items (e.g., taller than), and hierarchical concepts place items into layered structures (e.g., dogs are within the category of mammals).

For our purposes, however, we should just view a concept as an object of thought that the mind (i.e., working memory) is pulling from long-term memory and/or actively perceiving. The more often we interact with a concept, in the world or in our minds, the more layers its conceptual structure likely contains. When we experience or interact with the concept, our brains categorize it and create memories of it, which colors our perception of it and generates predictions about it, all layering onto the structure of the concept.

It works like this: We perceive something in the world or simply think of it (i.e., pull it from long-term memory); that perception or memory creates a mental representation in our working memory; that representation immediately calls on the concept of thing, which inherently contains a structure; the structure implicates top-down predictions about the concept, which are checked against any bottom-up perceptual signals as applicable.

While there are many ways to conceive of the various layers and dimensions of a conceptual structure, for purposes of problem-solving, we should focus on two main components: constraints and categories.

Loosening the Constraints   First, a conceptual structure, like any tangible structure, has boundaries to it. Otherwise, it would be hard to define or recognize the concept as a *thing* separate from other things. It needs boundaries to exist as a concept in our minds. Other people do not necessarily mentally represent the same concept with those same boundaries or constraints. No, these boundaries are yours. They constrain the concept in that they help keep it in a neat structure so your brain can perceive it in the world, pull it from long-term memory, mentally represent it, and create predictions about it.

For example, your concept of a motorcycle is likely composed, at its essence, of two wheels, an engine, and handlebars. These elements create the motorcycle's constraints; so, if an object of thought, presently perceived or pulled from memory, does not have all three of these elements, chances are you would not conceive of it as a motorcycle. Likewise, our conflicts, relationships, and "opponents" are all concepts, each of which is composed of specific elements, based on our past experiences with them, that constrain our conception of them.

To step outside their structures means to loosen, bend, or break through their conceptual restraints. Using our creative system, we'd have to mentally represent and approach the concept in even a slightly different way. If we wanted to come up with a new design for a motorcycle, we might ask, *What if the motorcycle didn't have handlebars? Could it still be a motorcycle? Would there be any other way I could steer it?* When it comes to conflict, we might ask, *What if I didn't have to be right this time? What would that look like? What if giving her this win opens a new path for us? What if there were a way for both of us to get our needs met, even if we can't yet see it?* This type of imaginative inquiry helps us loosen a concept's structural constraints.

Updating the Categories   As discussed previously in this book, the brain also organizes concepts into mental categories. For example, three large categories might be things that are bad (i.e., cause pain or create threats), things that are good (i.e., cause pleasure or create rewards), and things that are neutral. Within these categories are various subcategories, and there are other large categorical buckets potentially surrounding and connected to these. As of yet, neuroscientists and psychologists have not clearly identified a particular architecture or hierarchy of specific mental categories, only that categories exist and that we unconsciously place concepts into them.

These categories help to create the structure of a concept. Concepts are not typically only in one category but many, and particular categories are drawn on depending on the situation or context. For instance, the concept of ice cream might be placed in the following categories: food, dessert, cold, colorful, sweet, pleasure, fun, and a variety of others depending on your particular experiences and memories of ice cream. The concept is likely to exist more prominently (i.e., come to mind more readily) in certain categories; you may be more likely to pull the concept of ice cream from memory when interacting with an object that is cold and sweet than with an object that is colorful and fun.

When it comes to conflict, especially stressful, escalated conflict, you've likely categorized the concept of that conflict and the concept of your counterparts in categories such as the following: things that cause me stress, things that are threatening, things that are uncomfortable, and so forth. In creative solution building, instead of relying on the habitual categories of a conflict, we should challenge ourselves to categorize them differently. For example, you may consciously decide *I'm going to place this concept in a new category called "things that push me to grow for the better" or "things that make me wiser."*

This recategorization can be facilitated or enhanced by various elements discussed in this book, including reconditioning, opportunistic thinking, exposure with self-regulation, and caregiving, all of which create new experiences of the conflict and thus updated categorizations and predictions. However, engaging our creative brain networks is also a significant influence for updating a concept's categories. We can open our minds to the possibility that a particular conflict is not just bad, stressful, or uncomfortable, but with some creative ideating, it could also be the start of something fruitful.

A person, your relationship with that person, and any conflicts you have are each separate concepts with their own structures, constraints, and categories. If we find ourselves stuck in a problem and desire to create novel or innovative solutions, then we'll have to move outside the conflict structure, which means loosening its constraints and updating its categories. This is achievable with three particular mental states that are necessary for creative problem-solving.

The Three Pillars of Creative Problem-Solving

Our creative neural network produces a variety of useful cognitive mechanisms that help us solve complex or ill-defined problems in novel ways. These mechanisms run parallel with particular mental states that are often important if not requisite for creative problem-solving. The following three psychological states are indeed important fuel for creativity.

Inspiration   Inspiration drives us. Although not always necessary for creative problem-solving, it is a key motivator for getting creative in general. Many people who have solved complex problems, and likely all of those who have created great works of art or literature, have felt inspired to do so. Inspiration has been defined as a motivational state in which an external or internal stimulus evokes a sense of transcendent possibility and compels a person to translate that vision into action. It is closely tied to intrinsic motivation, a drive that is generated purely from inside oneself and not in response to external rewards or threats (i.e., extrinsic motivation). Yes, we might be motivated to solve a problem in order to mitigate the potential threats of conflict or reap the rewards of solving it. But extrinsic motivation, such as the fear of negative consequences or the desire for positive rewards, will only drive us so far. When we reach an impasse in conflict resolution and can't seem to find our way out, it's intrinsic motivation and inspiration that can motivate us to create new solutions to complex problems.

Inherent in inspiration is the belief that a new solution actually exists—that a problem is solvable—even if we can't yet see it. We might not find the right solution today, tomorrow, or next week. But if we're inspired to manifest a new vision for the relationship, inspiration helps remind us that we're likely still just stuck in the old structure and haven't found our way outside it yet. We haven't yet loosened the constraints or updated categories that keep the current conflict in place.

If you find yourself at an impasse and don't feel motivated to continue, you've lost the vision—the inspiration to chart a new path and build a new relationship. If you have even a glimpse that doing so would lead to a more harmonious, productive life, then it's time to get inspired. Keep thinking, keep believing, let your imagination explore, let your cognition run fluidly across categories and domains. Keep talking, brainstorming, ideating. A solution exists. You just haven't come to it yet.

Courage Another important cognitive state that can pull us over the hump of an impasse by stepping outside the structure is courage. It often takes courage to view and approach an old concept in a new way. As we know, updating our models of the world, which interrupts memories or conditioning and may thus update predictions, is typically not easy or quick. Doing so can create cognitive dissonance, instability, or incoherence.

Rearranging the constraints and categories of a conceptual structure can be jarring in general, but especially when parts of our identity or self-concept are wrapped up in layers of the structure. Suddenly, allowing oneself to step outside the structure of this particular concept may indicate stepping outside the structure of a *self*-concept. If being the one who is right and who is justified in clinging to resentment (i.e., the resentful one or the victimized one) has become part of one's identity, the idea of letting that go can be scary and cause a great deal of resistance. But when we're inspired to create a new, healthier relationship and/or life for ourselves, fostering the courage to do so helps push us past our suboptimal mental structures, leading us to new perspectives and ideas.

Fun A third motivational state worth mentioning when it comes to creativity is fun. The feeling of having fun is motivational in general; anything that feels fun to someone will typically drive them to re-create the experience.

Inherent in fun is the concept of play, which changes both the state of the nervous system and the frame of the mind, making imagination and divergent thinking much more accessible. Think back to when you would play as a child, specifically, imaginative play rather than competitive play. Think of the childlike wonder, curiosity, cognitive fluidity, and the willingness to step outside of structures. Conceptual structures were not hardened boundaries; they were soft, malleable contours that could be quickly traversed. Children more easily step outside of structures because the structures aren't fully formed. As we develop cognitively, the structures move and take shape, their constraints and categories shifting and tested along the way. The older we get, the more layers our structures develop and the harder and less flexible our structural constraints become. When we're brainstorming, the more childlike wonder and playfulness we can conjure up, the more easily we can step outside of structures.

The underlying neural mechanisms involved in play and fun illustrate their positive effects on conflict resolution. While conflict often activates the amygdala and stress hormones, narrowing thinking into fight-or-flight rigidity, play counteracts this stress response and increases parasympathetic activity. A relaxed brain is a flexible brain. Play also triggers dopamine release, which supports cognitive flexibility and exploration. And, of course, dopamine motivates us to keep playing. Play and fun further release endorphins, which not only create positive mood states but also increase social bonding. People who play together tend to trust one another more. Finally, play involves mimicry, rhythm, or joint attention when problem-solving together. These synchronic activities employ mirror neuron systems, promoting empathy and social attunement.

A solution-focused brainstorming session should be playful. Rather than playing on opposite teams, we and our problem-solving partners are playing on the same team, trying to solve a problem together using creativity. Even better if the playful brainstorming feels fun. We might think of our counterpart as our play partner. This context helps motivate imaginative exploration during solution-building processes.

Recap: The Imagination and Creativity Systems

Getting creative is an absolute cornerstone of building solutions to complex problems. If a conflict has persisted, especially when solutions and discussions have been attempted to no avail, we must start thinking outside the structure. That means understanding the constraints and categories we've placed on the conflict to identify how those might be loosened or updated. It also means finding the inspiration and courage to envision something new and work toward it with fresh approaches. And hey, if we can have fun developing and implementing those new approaches, even better.

There are lots of methods for creatively developing new solutions to old problems, and I highly recommend exploring various methods for yourself. Here are a few practical tools that might be useful for creative conflict resolution.

Tools to Move Outside the Structure

Have you found yourself at an impasse, unable to find solutions that seem to work for everyone? Try some of these exercises to get things moving in a productive direction.

Divergent Thinking

Recall that divergent thinking is how we come up with multiple potential solutions to a complex problem. If you've identified common goals or needs and potential ways of satisfying them (see "Tools to Do What We Were Built to Do: Collaborate" in Principle 6) but can't seem to agree on any of those ways, it's time to get creative.

First, it's helpful to acknowledge that there are almost always multiple paths to achieving a goal or satisfying a basic need. And that you may not have identified all of them yet. Here are a few ways to help uncover novel paths to reaching your goals and/or satisfying your mutual needs.

Collaborate with Artificial Intelligence   The most useful and advanced new tool of our era when it comes to building on accumulated human knowledge is artificial intelligence (AI). Let's use it to help get the creative momentum flowing. You can do this alone, of course, or while collaborating with your problem-solving partner (even better). Open up an AI chat and write a brief synopsis of the current situation, including what both of your common goals and needs are. End with this sentence or something similar: "We are looking to get creative in the way we get our goals and needs met. We need help thinking divergently about a new way to solve this issue and rebuild trust." Hit "enter" so you set the AI stage.

Next, we're going to play the "How can we _________ while also _________?" game. First try to fill in the blanks on your own; then ask the AI, and see what you all come up with.

Here are some examples:

- "How can we achieve A, while also achieving B?"
- "How can we achieve X, while also valuing Y?"
- "How can we build A, while also building B?"

When you're finished, here are a couple of additional questions you might ask yourself and the AI:

- "What are some ways other people satisfy their need for ___________?"
- "What are ways other people have achieved the goal of ___________?"

If after prompting the AI, you still haven't found a useful path forward, try another AI platform, as they may give different answers. Remember that your conflict is contained within a conceptual structure, so getting a fresh perspective from someone outside the conflict could help identify approaches that are outside the structure. If AI ultimately is not fruitful, you might try the old-fashioned way of getting a fresh perspective and ask the same questions of a trusted friend, colleague, coach, or mediator.

Loosen the Constraints To get creative with conflict resolution, you'll need to step outside your conceptual structures of the conflict, and that means loosening, bending, or bypassing the constraints. First thing's first, let's define and recognize the constraints. Take some time to fill out the following two columns about your conflict counterpart(s) or problem-solving partner(s). Write down your predictions, based on your experience, of your counterpart. Write freely, without a filter at first. You may find a lot of non-specific, abstract expectations. After you're done with free writing, try your best to also write any specific behavioral expectations as well.

I expect my counterpart to:	I expect my counterpart NOT to:
■ *(Abstract example)* Be rude to me.	■ *(Abstract example)* Consider my feelings when making decisions.
■ *(Specific example)* Interrupt me when I talk.	■ *(Specific example)* Say hello to me when I walk into the room.
■ _____________________	■ _____________________
■ _____________________	■ _____________________

Okay, these are the constraints placed upon the individual. Now, let's define some of the constraints placed on the conflict, again allowing for both abstract and then more specific examples. Free write first. Then get focused on specifics. Just one column here:

I expect this conflict/tension to:
- *(Abstract example)* Go on forever and never get resolved.
- *(Specific example)* Lead to me losing my job.
- ______________________________
- ______________________________

These are the constraints placed on the conflict and your counterpart(s). These constraining expectations, however true they may feel, create the conceptual structures of this conflict and the individuals involved, which is how those concepts are represented in your mind. If we want to get creative (i.e., step outside the structures), we'll have to start loosening the constraints. We'll need to question the expectations. This may feel uncomfortable, frustrating, or pointless at first. But remember that stepping outside structures can feel that way, and that it takes courage and belief to look at an old problem in a new way.

For each constraint you wrote down above, you'll ask the following question: "What would I need to see, hear, or know to stop expecting that?"

Get specific with your answers. Identify behaviors, events, or action steps. For some constraints, it might be obvious. (e.g., "He just needs to stop interrupting me.") That's okay, write it down anyway. When you're finished, you've got a list of specific actions that, if enacted, would presumably help you view the person and/or conflict in a new way.

Now, identify the top three change movers. What are the three most important action items that you feel would start moving the conflict in the right direction (i.e., toward more peace, care, and/or trust)? Use these as a starting place for a discussion or brainstorming session with your counterpart/problem-solving partner on what you'd like to see change. Here are some phrases you might use:

- "What do you think about trying [insert action item]?"
- "Would it be possible to . . . ."

- "I'd love to start . . . . Would you be open to that?"
- "Do you see a way for us to . . . ?"
- "I think we could collaborate better together if we could change a few things. Could you tell me the top three things you'd like to see change, and I can tell you mine?"

If you can start taking actions that help break down old constraints and structures, new approaches to solving the conflict and transforming the relationship should manifest as well.

Find Quiet Time to Explore When it comes to getting creative, one thing is certain: we need to get away from distractions. Both research and plenty of anecdotal experience tell us that giving ourselves space and time to simply mind wander, without interruption or distraction, is one of the most useful and important drivers of creative ideation. You could do this at home, in a quiet room. You could also do this somewhere in nature (highly recommended), such as the beach, a forest, a mountain path, and so on. What's important is you turn off all media, put away your phone, don't read a book—take away all items that require you to focus externally. Instead, this is all about letting your mind meander freely. You can write, think, build, create, or produce, but do not consume from outside your own mind.

You'll notice this is a different practice than mindfulness. Creative quiet time is not about being present in your body but rather about exploring in your head. In fact, you may be totally unaware of your body or your surroundings and simply lost in thought. That's what we want. Travel to distant places, explore creative peaks and valleys, let your mind bounce around. Question everything. Challenge everything. Test the boundaries, loosen the constraints, traverse the categories, let go of the rigid structures. Mind wander with a loose focus on solving the problem. Do it for long enough, and you're bound to devise new ways to approach old situations.

Implementing Playful Exercises

If you'd like to have a bit of fun and it's appropriate for the relationship and situation, you might try a playful exercise to get the creative ball rolling during conflict resolution. Here are a few games you could try.

Role-Swap Storytelling Game   Ask each party to *playfully* tell the story of the conflict as if they are the other person. The storyteller, in the role of their counterpart, will make themself the hero and argue their points and positions convincingly. The story should be playful but not condescending. This uses imagination and humor to foster perspective taking, often leading to new levels of empathy and insight about underlying needs.

Future Storytelling Game   Ask parties to imagine it's five years from now and tell a playful story of how they resolved their conflict and became allies. This playful narrative projection often surfaces underlying values and helps reorient the conversation toward shared goals.

Reverse Thinking Game   Together, ask, "How could we make this conflict worse?" List the ways. Be outlandish, even silly. All ideas are welcomed. Then flip each idea into a constructive opposite by asking, "What is the exact opposite of this path?" This can teach perspective-shifting and helps to highlight ideal outcomes.

Third-Party Report Game   Pretend you're an alien, historian, or journalist observing the conflict. Describe what's happening in their report. This exercise creates distance and inspires fresh perspectives on the situation.

What-If Game   Ask a whole bunch of what-ifs you've previously resisted or hadn't thought of. For instance:

> "What if this conflict turned into the best thing that ever happened to our team/relationship?"
> "What if we solved this whole thing tomorrow?"
> "What if I did your job for the week, and you did mine?"

Brainstorm wild, even unrealistic, scenarios. Answer with creative, specific, and elaborate scenarios, rather than something like: "That would be great." This game can shift our mindset from threat to opportunity, encouraging imaginative resolutions and paths to peace.

> **NOTE:** *As a final recommendation, when getting creative with a problem-solving partner, you may want to be in an environment that is not habitual to your relationship. If you want to step outside the internal structure, it helps to modify the external context. Instead of staying at the office, go grab coffee to brainstorm. Instead of talking at the kitchen table, take a walk around the neighborhood or along the beach. Whether you're divergently thinking, loosening constraints, or playing a game, changing your surroundings can support creative shifts toward productive solutions.*

Moving Forward

One method evolutionary biologists have used to determine the complexity of different species' brains is by observing the depth of each species' behavioral repertoire. They study how flexible and adaptive the creature's behaviors are, including how many different types of behaviors it tends to employ across various contexts. Presumably, the more behaviors an organism can display, especially if there is evidence of novel behavior, directly reflects its capacity for memory and imagination. With that said, it seems that humans have the most complex brains because we display the largest repertoire of behavior (at least, as far as we know). No other species can perform so many different types of tasks across distinct domains and contexts, including generating novel solutions to problems. This amazing ability to think creatively and solve problems in unique and unpredictable ways allows for an indefinite, we might say infinite, range of potential behaviors. We are indeed the creative powerhouse of the planet.

That said, creativity can also get us into trouble. It makes us not only fantastic problem-solvers but also highly imaginative conflict constructors. Our brains can get real creative with detecting, developing, and exacerbating conflict. In other words, creativity goes both ways: some of the most destructive forces and events have been created by the most imaginative thinkers. So, we need to be careful with creativity. When used with the right intention, creative thinking can make all the difference between transformational peace and enduring conflict. Use it wisely!

Conclusion

At the start of this strange journey through the brain and mind, I suggested that conflict was a moment of pure potential—that we could make a choice to be destructive or creative with the energy of friction. As we now see, this choice is a product of the way we hold conflict in our minds and nervous systems. I hope I have made the case that we indeed have the requisite wiring for peace.

We have self- and co-regulatory mechanisms for relaxing the mind and body during escalated conflict. We have the capacity to recondition our experiences and perceptions of conflict as opportunities for positive change. We can embrace a state of curiosity, recognizing that our perceptions are merely subjective representations of a multifaceted world. We can focus on interacting productively with every small movement and moment of communication. We can choose to be caring at any time with anyone and can take steps to build trust where it has been broken. We can use our built-in capacities for collaboration to partner with our counterparts rather than treat them as opponents. And we can engage our creative systems to imagine new solutions for habitual and complex conflicts.

In these ways, our brains and bodies comprise a robust platform for peace potential—the canvas on which we paint the colors and structures of conflict and paths to resolve it. Our nervous systems are not fixed and rigid. They are dynamic, complex, adaptive, astonishing networks that afford us so much potential to create or destroy. How you regulate, learn, perceive, communicate, care, collaborate, and create depends on your motivation to use the functions of your system constructively. Don't squander your amazing inner network. Don't pretend you have no control over your response to the situation. Instead, embrace your extraordinary nervous system, appreciate it, and use it deliberately for all it can do. For yourself, for others, for the world. When you do, you have the option of building peace. You can make the choice to create a new, more productive and collaborative path forward. So . . . will you?

Notes

Chapter 3

1. Nørretranders, T. (1998). *The user illusion: Cutting consciousness down to size.* Viking Press. Wilson, T. D. (2002). *Strangers to ourselves: Discovering the adaptive unconscious.* Harvard University Press. Zheng, J., & Meister, M. (2025). The unbearable slowness of being: Why do we live at 10 bits/s?. *Neuron, 113*(2), 192–204.

2. Huberman, A. (Host). (2023, October 16). *Dr. Lisa Feldman Barrett: How to understand emotions* [Audio podcast episode]. *Huberman Lab.* https://www.hubermanlab.com/episode/dr-lisa-feldman-barrett-how-to-understand-emotions

3. Kaczmarek, L. D., Kashdan, T. B., & Enko, J. (2024). How curiosity enhances performance: Mechanisms of physiological engagement, challenge and threat appraisal, and novelty deprivation. *Journal of Happiness Studies, 25*(7), 95.

Acknowledgments

In writing this book, I'd like to thank my amazing wife, Jenny, who has been consistently encouraging and insightful. We had our first child right smack in the middle of my writing, and I could not imagine being able to complete this work without her enduring flexibility and support. She is also a fantastic editor and brainstorming partner. I am indeed a lucky, lucky man.

I'm also incredibly grateful to my amazing team at Pollack Peacebuilding Systems, who stepped up to handle most day-to-day operations while I designated time to write this book (oh, and have a baby). I could never have created the time to focus, ideate, and write without their astonishing capacity to manage our clients and programs so effectively.

As with every piece of content I create, especially long forms such as books, I must acknowledge the long list of teachers and mentors throughout my life. I would not be the thinker, creator, or specialist I am without your patient and attentive guidance. You know who you are.

Finally, my parents and siblings deserve tremendous appreciation. They are and have always been so supportive of all my endeavors. They continue to inspire me to be a good man who brings peace into the world.

With love and gratitude,
Jeremy

About the Author

Jeremy Pollack is a social-organizational psychologist and a leader in the field of workplace conflict resolution and peacebuilding. He is the Founder of Pollack Peacebuilding Systems, a nationwide conflict resolution consulting firm. He is also cofounder and chairman of the Peaceful Leadership Institute, a 501(c)(3) nonprofit dedicated to promoting the model and theory of peaceful leadership.

Jeremy is a coach, trainer, mediator, and author. He coaches and trains executives and employees at a variety of levels and industries, from Fortune 100 companies to major nonprofits. Jeremy has mediated conflicts between business partners, co-executives, and coworkers at all levels of organizations, aiming as often as possible to transform relationships and create win–win resolutions for all parties involved.

Jeremy has been a regular contributor on the topics of leadership and organizational conflict management to publications such as Forbes.com, Fast Company, Industry Week, and many more. He is also the author of *The Conflict Resolution Playbook: Practical Communication Skills for Preventing, Managing, and Resolving Conflict* and the coauthor of *Peaceful Leadership: Tools and Techniques for Fostering Psychological Safety, Trust, and Inclusion in Your Organization.*

Jeremy holds a PhD in psychology from Grand Canyon University, a master's degree in negotiation, conflict resolution, and peacebuilding (NCRP) from California State University, Dominguez Hills, and a master's degree in evolutionary anthropology from California State University, Fullerton. He is also a Certified Organizational Development Coach (CODC™), a Certified Clinical Trauma Specialist—Individual (CCTS-I™), a Certified Workplace Mindfulness Facilitator (CWMF™), certified in pain reprocessing therapy (PRT), and an Associate Certified Coach (ACC) under the International Coaching Federation. He has formerly served as a research fellow at Stanford University's Center for International Conflict & Negotiation, where he led research projects in social psychology and conflict resolution, and prior to that as a research associate at UCLA's Center for Behavior, Evolution, and Culture. Currently, he is a faculty member in the psychology department at Arizona College of Nursing.

Learn more at:
www.JeremyPollack.com
www.PollackPeacebuilding.com

Index

R

rank choice matching
  elimination, 186
  highest matching solution, 187
  options cost analysis, 187
  prioritizing, 186–187
reality-check system, 194
reassociate contradiction, with
      curiosity, 106–107
reassociation, 54, 63, 70–72, 75
reassurance, 37–39, 133
rebuilding trust, 144, 161
receiver, 9, 82, 116–118, 136
  auditory sensory processing,
      118–119
  communication, 136
  language processing, 119
  reciprocation, 122–123
  role exchange between
      sender and, 131
  somatosensory processing,
      120–121
  valence and interpretation,
      121–122
  visual sensory processing, 119–120
reciprocal conditioning, 55
reciprocation, 122–123
reconditioning, 48, 54, 63–75, 77, 78,
      99, 136, 147, 173, 200
recondition uncertainty,
      100–101
reconsolidation, 63, 66–69, 71, 74
reflective listening, 158–159, 192
regulation function, xx–xxi
regulation-prediction machine, 90
relational concepts, 198
relational conflict resolution, 147
relational conflict transformation, 148
REM, 20
reperceiving wrongness, 101–103
respiratory sinus arrhythmia (RSA), 28
reverse thinking game, 208
Robbins, Tony, 15

robust platform, for peace, 211
Rock, Chris, 2–4, 19
role-based trust, 152
role-swap storytelling game, 208
Ryan, Richard, 15

S

safety
  acute interpersonal conflict, 32
  affirmations, 23
  interpersonal conflict, 35
  psychological need, 80, 91, 93
  reassurance, 38
  SAPIEN needs model, 15–17
  threat vs, 122
salience network (SN),
      194–195
SAPIEN needs model, 22–25
  affiliation, 17
  engaging activities, 18
  independence, 18
  noble pursuits, 18–19
  positive self-concept, 17
  safety, 15–17
second-order neurons, 121
selective attention, 86
self-awareness, 64–65, 73–74,
      132, 134, 142
self-care practices
  diet, 21
  exercise, 21–22
  life circumstances, 25–26
  sleep, 20–21
self-concept, 202
  incoherent self-concept, 19
  negative self-concept, 19
  positive self-concept, 15, 17, 18, 22,
      23, 32, 35, 38, 44, 78, 80,
      92–94, 98, 99
  from rightness, 103
self-esteem, 94, 97, 103
  aspect, 93
  positive self-concept, 17